Misplaced

New York City's Street Kids

Misplaced

New York City's Street Kids

Alexia Lewnes

XENIUM PRESS

NEW YORK

For information about permission to reproduce
selections from this book, write to Xenium Press,
532 La Guardia Place, Suite 287, New York, NY 10012
or Xeniumpress@cs.com.

Printed in the United States of America

Book design by Lesley Ehlers

Library of Congress Card Number: 00-111634

Publisher's Cataloging-in-Publication
(Provided by Quality Books, Inc.)

Lewnes, Alexia.
   Misplaced : New York City's street kids / Alexia
Lewnes. — 1st ed.
   p. cm.
   ISBN: 0-9702602-0-2

   1. Street youth—New York (State)—New York.
2. Homeless children—New York (State)—New York.
I. Title.

HV4506.N6L49 2001   362.7'08'6942
                                     QBI00-1076

First Edition

In loving memory of my father

Even in our sleep,
pain that cannot forget
falls
    drop
                by drop
upon the heart,
and in our own despair,
against our will,
comes wisdom . . .

—AESCHYLUS
(525-456 B.C.)

mis·place

1a: to put in a wrong or inappropriate place
1b: to set on a wrong object or eventuality

Contents

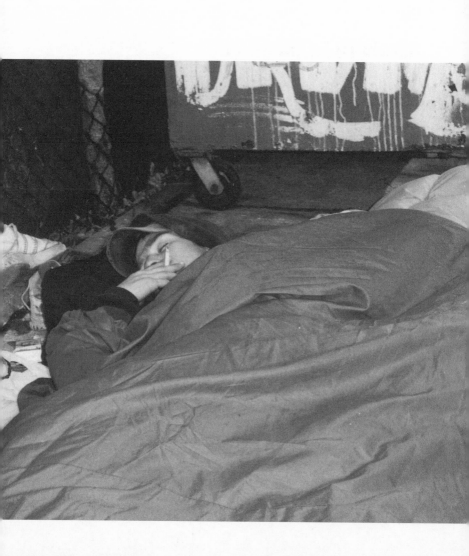

Preface

SOME SLEEP ON SIDEWALKS and beg on subways. Many more hide quietly on rooftops or in abandoned buildings. Still others couch-surf behind closed doors. They roam the streets day and night, yet if you aren't looking for them, they are easy to miss. With the exception of those who advocate on their behalf, they are, for the most part, dismissed and ignored. They are our invisible and forgotten children.

This is a book about New York City's homeless young people. It is an attempt to bring them out of the shadows and answer questions we all should be asking: How do kids end up living on our streets? What do they really think about their lives? Are they destined to become addicted to drugs, imprisoned, infected with HIV? What are we as a society doing for them?

This is also a book about race relations, adolescence, the criminal justice system, addiction, homophobia, the foster care system, child abuse and neglect, and parental responsibility.

Ultimately, it's a book about life and death.

No one knows how many kids live on the streets in the

United States. Some estimate that as many as 1.5 million youth are homeless or runaways; as many as 200,000 live as permanent residents of the street. Some are kids who have aged out of the foster care system; others are children of homeless parents; still others are "throwaways"—kids who have been tossed out of their homes by the very people who were supposed to support and protect them. In one study, more than half of the youth interviewed while staying in shelters reported that their parents either told them to leave or knew they were leaving and did not care. Many are kids fleeing neglect, alcohol and drug abuse, beatings and sexual assaults. In another study, 46 percent of runaway and homeless youth surveyed had been physically abused, and 17 percent had been forced into unwanted sexual activity by a family or household member.

In 1973, the *New York Times* reported that there were 20,000 teenage runaways in New York City at any given time. That figure is still cited today by journalists and experts in the field. No one really has any idea how many young people are on the streets fending for themselves. Some city officials believe the reported number is exaggerated; those who work with these kids feel it is a gross underestimate. Many do fear, though, that as families continue to be moved off the welfare rolls, the numbers of homeless youth will swell.

I started working on this book in the late spring of 1996. I began by spending afternoons and evenings in Tompkins Square Park. For at least four hours every day, I sat on a park bench, watching, waiting for kids to approach me. Two weeks passed before Zoe, about sixteen, came by to ask me if I would bring her books to read. The next day, another girl, Jewel, maybe seventeen, sat down next to me to talk. She wanted to know if I knew anything about diabetes. She had found out a week earlier that she was diabetic and hadn't been back to a doctor since learning the news. I offered to make her an appointment at a neighborhood clinic and to take her there the next day. She agreed, but when I went to meet her, Jewel was nowhere to be found. I saw her later that afternoon lying on a bench, high on heroin.

Other kids started to come by and talk. They showed me their tattoos, piercings and scars, and talked about the music they liked, the problems they had with their parents, the fights they had with their boyfriends and girlfriends, their adventures in other cities and their plans to leave New York. When they weren't drunk or high, they were often sick, still recovering from the alcohol and drugs they had done the night before. It was difficult to tell their ages, but as one boy told me, "That was the whole idea." Most looked to be in their late teens and early twenties.

I had been sitting in the park about six weeks when one teenager came by and yelled at me, calling me a cop. She told the others I was a narc, and they stayed far away. I continued to go to the park every day, sat on a bench, and read my newspaper. Almost two weeks passed before the kids began to talk to me again. Bass, a homeless man hooked on heroin, had spread the word: I was OK. He knew about the book I wanted to write and believed it was important. He said he would do whatever he could to help. I met many young people who answered my questions and would have allowed me to spend time with them, but more than three months passed before I met the young woman who seemed to be searching for someone who cared about what she had to say. I told her about the book within the first ten minutes of meeting her, and she invited me into her life without hesitation. It was a moment of complete trust that I will never forget. Later, her boyfriend also opened up to me with a courage that I will always respect.

Over the next few months, I spent countless hours hanging

out on street corners, subways and on the West Village piers to meet more kids. Some I spoke to once and never saw again; a few I met over and over, each time piecing together the bits of their fractured lives. Nearly all of these kids faded away: They stopped calling, and I stopped looking for them. But two young men in midtown Manhattan, not far from Times Square, called me regularly and often, and I knew that they would not disappear. More than a year later, I met a thirteen-year-old boy who had been spending time on the streets of the West Village, and I knew that he would also be in my life for a very long time. Each of these young people felt it was important that their stories be told.

The book follows these five kids: Stephanie and her boyfriend Fraggle, runaways from out of town who panhandled on the streets of the Lower East Side to support their heroin habits; Dakota (from the Bronx) and Cedric (from Brooklyn), who disguised their homelessness well, spending their days walking through the Port Authority bus terminal, their nights sleeping on subways or in city shelters; and Juan, a gay foster child, who, although not living out in the streets, struggled to find a foster home or group home where he could feel nurtured and safe.

For more than four years, I insinuated myself into the daily lives of these young people. I met them on street corners in the middle of the night, took sixteen-hour bus rides with them when they decided to leave town, sat with them in court, visited them in jail, interviewed their family members, and rode subways with them through the night. Wearing a beeper so they could reach me at anytime, I was on call twenty-four hours a day. I slept beside them on cardboard boxes, accompanied them to visit friends in prison, and watched as they slipped into abandoned buildings and lots to inject heroin or smoke crack. I saw producers lure them onto daytime talk shows. I was with them when adults offered them money and drugs for sex.

In the end, faced with the chilling details of their lives, I simply could not remain a detached journalist. Instead, I chose to participate in their lives, all the time striving to be accurate and fair. I grew to care deeply about them.

Over the years, I became part social worker, part therapist, part friend, part mother. I took them to the movies, celebrated their birthdays, gave them advice when they asked and sometimes when they didn't, consoled them when they cried, and worried about their safety. They shared with me their most personal thoughts, hopes, dreams, and fears. In return, I shared with them my own heartbreaks and disappointments. I often felt frustrated and disappointed when they got into trouble. I was awed by their determination and resilience. At times I felt I was doing too much for them; other times, far too little.

I tried to include them in the reporting process and asked repeatedly what they wanted others to know. Stephanie and Juan gave me their poetry to publish, believing it was the best way to convey their feelings. The street child fading into invisibility on one of the opening pages was drawn by Stephanie.

The individual kids I've written about do not represent anything in particular. Their stories are not extraordinary, nor are their lives especially exciting. But their isolation and extreme loneliness are dramatic nonetheless. Ultimately, I've written about these kids because they were willing to let me into their lives. They gave me their full cooperation and their trust. Their hope, as is mine, is that this book will enable you to look deeply into their hearts and listen carefully to what they have to say.

This is their book.

And I thank them.

A. J. L.

ONE

Heroin La La Land

Sometimes the no one . . . .
won't let me cry
She goes numb into
        the sugary
    heroin alcohol . . . .
the Fraggle flavored bruises
that put her into her
    misery . . . .

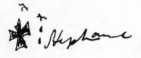 Stephanie

STEPHANIE wanted to get even.

A drug dealer she knew had used her as a guinea pig, giving her a bag cut with PCP to try, telling her it was just heroin. Stephanie, then a ten-bag-a-day heroin user, had injected it. Within minutes, she began shaking, her legs gave out, and she was unable to speak. Her boyfriend Fraggle grabbed her by the arms to try to get her walking, but Stephanie kept falling to her knees. Frightened, Fraggle tried to inject her with a speedball (a mixture of cocaine and heroin) to shock her system and keep her breathing, but Stephanie was shaking so much he couldn't find a vein. She yelled at Fraggle to leave her alone and pushed him away.

Eventually Stephanie passed out, and the drug wore off.

Weeks later, she was given thirty bags of heroin to sell by the same dealer, and Stephanie got even. She sold ten bags, bought some cocaine with the money, and went down to the East River to hide out and shoot up.

But on the fourth day, her twenty-second birthday, Stephanie ran out of dope. She walked to Seventh Street between Avenues C and D and stood there, scanning the block for customers while keeping an eye out for the dealer. It was early October 1996, and the remnants of Tropical Storm Josephine were pounding the New York area. Winds of up to sixty miles per hour knocked down trees and power lines, leaving more than sixteen thousand Long Island homes without electricity. The storm washed out the New York Yankees' American League Championship opener and forced Navy divers to halt their search for the wreckage of TWA Flight 800. Stephanie spent the afternoon on the street copping for customers. By the end of the day, the rain had soaked through the oversized navy blue parka she wore, and all she wanted was to get warm, to sleep in a dry bed, and to be with Fraggle.

Stephanie didn't know it at the time, but Fraggle was just two blocks away. At six that evening, I found him sitting at the counter in Leshko's, a twenty-four hour diner on Avenue A. The diner was warm, and the food was cheap and good.

"I really wanted to get Steph a gift for her birthday," Fraggle told me. He was soaked, his shirt and pants plastered to his skin. "But I don't have any money to get her something nice." Fraggle ordered a cup of coffee. Leaning his head on his hands as he stared into his thick white mug, he looked deep in thought. Slowly, his eyelids closed. He had just shot a bag of dope. Every few minutes he woke up startled, his eyes wide open. Finally, he stood up, told me he'd be back, and left.

Stephanie limped into Leshko's an hour later, a chilly wet wind blowing through the doorway with her. She was out of breath, and her hair was dripping wet, flattened on her head. Her bare feet, wrapped in newspaper, were stuffed into canvas sneakers. Over the sneakers were clear plastic bags, fastened around her ankles with rubber bands. Her toes ached, her teeth were chattering, and her eyes were swollen and puffy from crying.

Earlier in the day, Stephanie had called one of her aunts

in Ohio and asked her to pay for a night in a hotel as a birthday gift. Nearly a year earlier, the same aunt had sent her $75 for a hotel room when Stephanie called her from San Francisco, sick with the flu. This time, her aunt told Stephanie to call her back at three in the afternoon. When Stephanie tried her at three, the answering machine picked up. She'd called every hour since. It was now seven.

"Nobody cares about me," she said crying. "I have nobody." Nobody had given her a birthday present either, not even Fraggle.

Stephanie and Fraggle usually slept on the street, using a broken box as their makeshift mattress. When it rained, they set up temporary shelters, relying on umbrellas and plastic garbage bags to keep them dry. That night, though, the winds were too strong to stay outside. Stephanie was shivering. When she coughed, she seemed to be gasping for breath. Because I was worried she might have pneumonia and because it was her birthday, I offered to put her and Fraggle up in a cheap hotel for the night.

The walk to the St. Marks Hotel on Eighth Street, just five blocks away, took twenty-five minutes. Stephanie took slow baby steps, braced against the wind and wincing with pain. Her feet throbbed. Fraggle, in a hooded sweatshirt and olive green parka, was trembling. He walked about five yards ahead, his head down, his eyes squeezed half shut. As usual, they were fighting, Fraggle yelling, Stephanie crying.

At the hotel, Stephanie and Fraggle hobbled up the steep narrow stairs to their room. I followed behind to get them settled. The walls were a gray beige; the air smelled of insecticide. Stephanie lay flat out on a faded orange bedspread, staring at the ceiling. Fraggle sat on the edge of the bed, his back to her. "Baby, I'm going to make some money," he said, "I'll be right back."

"Please don't go," she asked. "Let's just go to sleep."

"I promise I'll be back."

Fraggle wanted to shoot cocaine, and Stephanie knew that if he left, she wouldn't see him for hours. Suddenly she sat straight up. "Fuck you," she yelled. "If you're going to stay, be here now, or don't bother. I won't let you stay here tonight if you leave now. I won't let you in again."

"I promise I'll be back soon," he said and shut the door behind him.

Stephanie collapsed back onto the bed.

In New York, Stephanie and Fraggle had nothing but each other. But they frequently left each other, if only for hours. When Stephanie threatened to leave, Fraggle begged her not to; when Fraggle left, Stephanie ran after him. The pursuit and abandonment was relentless and cruel—and it made them feel loved. But more than loved, they felt powerful.

Stephanie had already lost many people she loved. Her stepfather moved out when she was twelve. When she was fifteen, her mother died of cancer. When she was eighteen, her boyfriend Bruce died of a heroin overdose. She feared that Fraggle, too, would soon leave for good. Her most reasonable fear was that he'd end up in prison; her most terrifying was that he'd get killed. Either way, she'd again feel deserted by someone she loved.

This time, Stephanie decided she was not going to spend her birthday night worrying about Fraggle. Minutes after Fraggle left, Stephanie walked downstairs to the front desk. "Under no circumstances let him in again," she said to the desk clerk seated behind a thick pane of bulletproof glass. She wanted revenge. "This is my room. Do not give him the key."

Stephanie walked into the street crying. The wind was blowing the rain sideways and a terrific bolt of lightning lit the sky. She stepped into deep puddles to get to a nearby pay phone to make a collect call to her friend Jeanette in Ohio. Stephanie had known Jeanette for three years and considered her one of her closest friends. Jeanette had asked Stephanie many times to join her in Cleveland. But if Stephanie went to stay with her, Stephanie had to be off dope. Two months earlier, Stephanie had been shooting about four bags of heroin a day; now she was shooting more than ten. The last time she'd talked to Jeanette, she hadn't been ready to give up dope or Fraggle, but tonight she wanted to give up both.

"I want to come stay with you," said Stephanie. "I can't take this anymore." Once again, Jeanette told Stephanie that she could, and Stephanie hung up. Still weeping, Stephanie called Sharon, one of her customers who occasionally let her shower or leave her belongings in her apartment. Tonight, when she heard Stephanie crying, Sharon told her to come over. At Sharon's apartment, a drug dealer Stephanie knew gave her two bags of dope as a birthday present. Stephanie cooked down the dope and injected it. Within minutes, she passed out.

Stephanie woke up in the early morning, flat on her back on the hardwood floor and wearing only one shoe. The storm had ended. The sun was out, the sidewalks nearly dry. Broken tree branches and turned-out umbrellas littered the streets. At noon, when Stephanie and Fraggle saw each other again, she told him that she wanted to go to Cleveland— alone. They agreed that maybe if they separated for a while they could get themselves off drugs and then be together without always fighting.

Fraggle also wanted to get off the streets. He had left home and school at sixteen to "travel," and when he would grow tired of the streets, or was in trouble, or felt he was ready to be off drugs and go back to school, he would return home to Virginia. But never for long. Within weeks, he usually left again, often meeting up with friends he'd made in cities across the country. Over the years, he'd stolen a microwave from his stepsister, a ring from his mother, his father's car, and a portable CD player from his stepfather. When Fraggle heard that Stephanie was going to stay with Jeanette, he called his mother to see if he could come home. This time, though, she told him that she was tired of his promises to go back to school and to get off dope.

When Stephanie realized Fraggle had no place to go, her plan changed. She couldn't leave Fraggle. She called Jeanette back and left a message on her answering machine explaining that she wasn't ready to go back home. "I don't know what to do," she told me. "I can't just leave him here. I know that if he stays here, Fraggle's going to do something stupid that's going to get him killed. I couldn't live with that."

· · · ·

WHEN I ASKED other homeless kids where they hoped to be in five years, many couldn't respond; some told me they didn't expect to live that long. When I asked Stephanie, she told me, "I just want a roof over my head. Not a mansion, but a nice place to live, real friends, and an emotionally stable relationship. And support from people that are going to love me even if I disappoint them. And I want a dog."

I met Stephanie in August 1996, more than two months before her twenty-second birthday. A year and a half earlier, she'd met Fraggle in her hometown in Ohio from where they took off with friends to follow the Grateful Dead. They traveled to cities across the country, sleeping on the street, on couches and in motel rooms, finally landing in New York, where they had been living on the street for seven months.

When I met them, they were sleeping on the sidewalk and hooked on heroin.

The day I met her, Stephanie was eager to talk. A month earlier, she had appeared on Geraldo Rivera's daytime talk show on a program to reunite street kids with their families. "It's all a scam," Stephanie told me. "The people from the show tried to be our friends and made it seem like they were trying to help us. They said they'd buy us new clothes, but they didn't. They wanted us to look as pathetic as possible so that Geraldo could look like a hero coming to our rescue." After the taping, the show had sent Stephanie to a drug rehabilitation program in Georgia, but Stephanie left after twenty-two days. Back from rehab less than a week, Stephanie was still angry.

Sixteen-year-old Kim had felt even more betrayed. She had been homeless for two years when the producers had flown her to New York from New Orleans to be reunited with her family. Just before the cameras began to roll, a producer gently placed her hand on Kim's shoulder and told her that Geraldo had somehow "guessed" that she had been gang-raped twice while living on the streets—information she had asked be kept confidential. Kim threatened to leave but was persuaded to stay by a producer who insisted that this was an important part of her story that needed to be told.

Stephanie had agreed to allow me to report on her life because she wanted people to understand what it was really like to be homeless on the streets. More than anything, she wanted someone who would listen to what she had to say. "We're told 'go home' when we have no place to go and that we deserve this life," Stephanie said. "We're told we will never be anything more than this. Nobody cares that we're eating out of garbage cans, sleeping on the sidewalk, or sucking somebody's dick for $5 just to get straight. Nobody wants to hear who we really are or how we feel or what we have to say."

Months later, Stephanie told me she had another reason for wanting me to record her life on the streets. She said that when she was a teenager, she didn't believe she would live to be eighteen. When she did turn eighteen, she thought there was little chance she would make it to twenty-one. At twenty-one, when we met, she believed she had little time left; she could not see beyond her next bag of dope, and she'd already overdosed four times. Having me document her life was a way of, as she said, "making a mark before I died."

. . . .

NEARLY EVERYONE who spent any time in Tompkins Square Park knew Stephanie. She had smooth, clear skin, apple cheeks, and huge brown eyes. Her thick dark hair, a bouncy chin-length bob, always looked neat and clean, even when it hadn't been washed for weeks. The baggy purple jeans she wore hung inches below her navel and were held up with a thick black leather belt. At a local mall in a suburban town hanging out with other teens in loose low-slung pants and baseball caps turned backward, she would have gone unnoticed.

She was five feet three inches tall and thin, her arms and shoulders little more than bone. On her left shoulder was a tattoo in black of "the feathered serpent"—an Aztec god— about the size of a small saucer; on her right forearm, a black Chinese dragon, about three inches long. With a flat chest and straight hips, she looked like a girl of fourteen. Asleep, she looked even younger. Few people could guess she was twenty-one.

With her stuffed panda by her side, Stephanie was disarming. She knew how to play the innocent little girl, and people fell for it. The same people who walked by other pan-handling girls even younger than Stephanie often stopped for her, and seduced by her girlish smile and natural charm, gave her money, cigarettes, food, sympathy, and drugs. Even those who knew that she was older than she looked and addicted to heroin were drawn to Stephanie. Although she'd been on the streets of New York more than seven months, she still maintained a spirit and vitality, long lost by other homeless kids.

It was mid-August. We had an appointment to meet in Tompkins Square Park at 12:30. We had an appointment the day before, too, but she didn't show up, and the day before that, she was two hours late.

This time when I arrived, Stephanie was asleep on an iron bench under an old elm tree, hugging her panda. I sat beside her and waited for her to wake up. After about ten minutes, she coughed tentatively and jerked her right leg once, then again. Then she rolled over to face the back of the park bench and pulled her knees to her chest. Once again she was fast asleep.

It was not quite noon and it was hot. As Stephanie slept, a police officer on a motor scooter called out to a group of eight sleeping kids sprawled on a patch of brown grass to wake up. Hung over and weary, they stumbled to their feet and dragged their blankets and knapsacks across the dirt toward the cement. Some wandered out of the park to pan-handle; others quickly made their beds on the warm iron benches and fell back to sleep. A few staggered to the public fountain and splashed cold water on their faces; a couple slowly shuffled to the stinking public bathroom with its backed-up toilets and open stalls. One pot-bellied girl walked over to a tree, pulled her pants to her knees, squat-ted, and pissed. Nearby, shiny flies landed beside fat pigeons chasing after peanuts someone had spilled on the ground.

The scent of urine was strong.

An hour later, Stephanie jumped, as if waking from a nightmare.

"What time is it?" she asked.

"Three in the afternoon," I said.

"Shit. I was supposed to meet Fraggle at one o'clock at the A&P. He's going to kill me." She stood up and stuffed her comforter and panda into her red wire laundry cart. "Have you been here long?"

"A couple of hours."

"I'm so sorry. You could have woken me up. Watch my stuff? I'll be right back."

She didn't wait for my answer. She was always asking someone to watch her cart. More than a few times, she asked me to watch it, assuring me she would return in a few minutes; more than a few times, I waited over an hour. Other people walked away when they grew tired of waiting. I didn't have a choice.

When I went to search for Stephanie, I usually looked for her laundry cart and waited. It contained all her possessions and was easy to identify: Its left back wheel was held to the axle by a large safety pin. The cart was stuffed with a stained acrylic Navajo blanket, a weathered leather backpack, and a red-striped canvas duffel. The duffel itself was crammed with shirts, sweaters, jeans, and a few dresses, which had either been given to her or which she had found in Dumpsters or in garbage cans on the street. For Stephanie, trash cans were like treasure chests. In them, she'd found a box of brand-new Victoria's Secret underwear, a new package of Calvin Klein shirts, a pair of Dr. Martens boots, two new pairs of Adidas and Puma sneakers. A few things, like her navy blue hooded Yankee sweatshirt jacket, she kept for herself. Others she gave away or traded for cash. What she did keep, however, often got stolen or lost. She'd grown accustomed to losing things.

Stephanie also carted around a black folding umbrella, a red-and-green-striped canvas baseball cap, and notebooks neatly inscribed with more than fifty names, telephone and beeper numbers, and addresses of friends, acquaintances, drug customers, and strangers she'd met on the street. It was a list of people who genuinely cared, who seemed to care, and who didn't give a damn. Most of them lived in New York, but some were from places as far away as Oklahoma, Iowa, and Minnesota, all people she'd met while panhandling and copping on the Lower East Side. About two-thirds of them were men, aged eighteen to sixty, offering her a place to shower, sleep, or stay for a night or longer. One man in his forties who told her his pregnant wife had stopped having sex with him offered to set her up in an apartment as his mistress; another man who lived in the neighborhood let her use his studio to shower, leaving each time to give her privacy. Most of the women, in their twenties and thirties, were drug users themselves. Although Stephanie could rarely place the faces with the names, she guarded the list carefully and copied it neatly onto clean sheets of paper whenever the numbers began to smear.

In a plastic bag she kept color photos of herself and Fraggle that documented them shooting heroin step-by-step: cooking it down, drawing it into the needle, injecting it into their arms, and finally lying on the ground high. The photos were taken by a young woman who lived in the neighborhood. "I love her to death," Stephanie told me. "She helps me out a lot. She's a photographer and takes pictures of homeless people. I'm one of her projects." Stephanie also carried dozens of crossword puzzles, ripped from the pages of the *New York Times, Daily News,* and *New York Post,* which she would work on daily while panhandling. At the very top of the cart and precariously balanced sat her giant panda bear, given to her by a passerby on the street who'd seen her crying after one of her breakups with Fraggle.

When Stephanie returned fifteen minutes later, she was walking quickly, her steps small and hurried. She had done a shot of cocaine. "Come on. We have to go meet Fraggle."

We rushed to Union Square, just ten blocks away, Stephanie dragging her laundry cart behind her. As we raced through the streets, the cart broke down three times. Each time, Stephanie bent down, made a quick adjustment, and started off again. When we got to the supermarket, Fraggle was nowhere in sight.

By now, the effects of the coke had started to wear off, and like a toy winding down, Stephanie dragged herself down the block to look for Fraggle. When she didn't see him, she hauled herself back to the supermarket where they had planned to meet, collapsed on the ground next to the store's electronic doors, and went to work.

"Spare any change, ma'am?" She pulled an empty Styrofoam cup from her cart and set it on the ground. "Excuse me sir, can you spare any change?"

I stood a few feet away and we talked as people walked by, some dropping coins into her cup, but others mostly ignoring her. "I hate drama," she said. "My whole life out here is a soap opera. People get into everyone's business and get pissed off at everything."

Twenty minutes later, Fraggle arrived. He had started using "Fraggle," the name of a happy-go-lucky children's TV cartoon character, as an alias while selling drugs on a Grateful Dead tour. The first few times I'd met him, though, he seemed the opposite of his namesake: jittery, tense, and sad. He was twenty years old but looked like a thin, awkward pimply-faced teen, his eyes covered by the rim of his baseball cap. He would say hello and ask to speak to Stephanie privately. Within minutes, they would start bickering, and he would walk away angry. Today, he was angry that Stephanie was late.

Fraggle pulled out a new package of boxer shorts and white cotton tube socks from his backpack. He'd just ripped them off from a department store across the street. Normally, he would ask Stephanie to return them for cash, but this time he wanted her to exchange them for a different size. He needed clean underwear and socks.

Stephanie walked across the street with the packages. Fifteen minutes later, she returned empty-handed. "They took them from me when I went to the counter to exchange them and told me to leave," she said. "They must have known somehow they were stolen." She was lying. She'd returned the stolen goods and kept the cash for herself. Turning her back to Fraggle, she leaned over and rummaged through her cart.

Fraggle was angry. Half an hour earlier, he'd had underwear he couldn't wear but that he could trade for cash. Now, he had nothing. Fraggle started yelling at Stephanie, and she yelled back. Crying, she started to leave. "I have to go meet Lenny," she said.

Every day at four in the afternoon, Lenny met Stephanie at Tompkins Square Park and took her for pizza or to buy groceries. Every day, he gave her cigarettes and cash. People assumed Stephanie was having sex with him, but she wasn't. He was a lonely man, and she was homeless, hungry, and needed to get high. It was an arrangement that made sense.

She didn't want to leave Fraggle angry, but she needed Lenny's cash to buy her dope. "Can we meet later, Fraggle?"

"You know where I'll be," he said. "I'll be there for fifteen minutes. If you're not there on time, I'm not waiting."

Stephanie knew it would take her more than fifteen minutes just to get to Tompkins Square Park. She started crying. "Why are you being so mean to me?" She could barely pronounce the words.

Fraggle was already walking away. Stephanie chased after him, dragging her broken cart. More than once, he screamed back at her to leave him alone. She started crying even harder.

Several pedestrians stopped to watch. "She's just a baby," said one woman turning to the person beside her. A gray-haired woman, hunched over and leaning heavily on her cane, shifted to the right and to the left. "Should someone get the police?" she asked.

Fraggle walked back to Stephanie and put his face up close to her. "No, I'm not going to tell you I love you," he said calmly, staring directly into her eyes. "I am not happy." He stood for a moment looking at her, then walked away quickly.

Stephanie fell to the ground. Spasms seemed to shake her whole body. "He's all I have." Her nose was running, her eyes were swollen, and her face was cherry red. She continued to sob, choking occasionally on her tears. "I can't sleep out here alone. I have to put up with his shit so I don't get raped or molested."

Still crying, Stephanie walked over to her broken-down cart and started dragging it downtown. She had to meet Lenny, and she was late.

·····

LENNY was never late. Every weekday, Lenny was in the park at exactly four p.m. waiting for Stephanie. He worked as a mechanic and lived with his mother in Brooklyn. Lenny was in his late forties, balding, and wore cotton polo shirts with horizontal stripes that accentuated his broad belly. He spoke to Stephanie in abbreviated, stilted sentences, often repeating his final sentence, as if to reinforce the idea more for himself than for her. Every few phrases were punctuated with a "wow," which he repeated often, drawing the word into one long, whiny note. No one knew for sure why Lenny behaved the way he did. Many people called him "retarded."

Stephanie had met Lenny while panhandling. At the time, Lenny had been coming to the park daily to meet Dawn, a twenty-two-year-old heroin user from the Midwest. Dawn was rail thin and had a flat chest and stick legs. Her huge eyes, which earned her the nickname "Ladybug," were round and dark brown, accented with dark gray circles. She wore very short shorts, tight tank tops, white knee socks, and carried a clear plastic purse designed for ten-year-old girls to cart their play lipstick and blush in. When she wasn't nodding off, she sat on a bench reading children's books. After appearing on the same Geraldo Rivera program with Stephanie in June, Dawn had gone back home. After she left, Stephanie became Lenny's new friend.

Although Lenny would give Stephanie as much as $40 every day and buy her food and cigarettes, he would also tell her she was "no good" or "a waste of time" and that she should get rid of "Freckle." Most of the time, Stephanie just ignored his comments and often felt sorry for him. Sometimes, though, Lenny's comments bothered her, his words chipping away at her already low self-esteem.

When Stephanie arrived at Tompkins Square Park, Lenny was waiting in his usual spot, leaning against an iron fence near the center of the park, the jacket of his polyester sweat suit slung over his right shoulder.

"Hey, Lenny. Sorry I'm late." Stephanie bent over to

catch her breath, her heart still racing from rushing back from Union Square. "Come on, let's go." Lenny shrugged his shoulders, twitched his head, and followed.

I sat on a bench and waited for them. Ten minutes later, they returned with a plastic bag. Stephanie sat on the bench, and Lenny sat beside her. She opened the bag and pulled out pieces of baklava and blueberry pie that he'd bought her from the market. As she ate, she scanned the park, looking for one of her drug connections. Within minutes, a Puerto Rican teenage boy from the neighborhood came by and asked Stephanie if she had seen one of his friends. She chatted with him for a while before he walked away. Lenny sat quietly and watched Stephanie, jerking his head to the right every few minutes. Finally he said, "You've got a lot of friends. I don't have any friends."

"Yes, you do, you have me," she said. But her back was turned to Lenny as she said it. She continued to scan the park.

"Oh, yeah," he said. His words were flat, without expression. "Wooow."

When Stephanie saw the guy she was looking for, she took one more bite of baklava, closed the plastic container, and ran to the entrance of the park, where he was standing.

"She's too young for me, Stephanie is," Lenny said to me as we waited for her to return. He shifted nervously on the bench. "I had a girlfriend twenty-two years old, but she went back home. She was also young. But she didn't mind." He took long pauses between sentences. "They always need money, these girls." He leaned back and spread his arms out wide along the top of the bench. His neck jerked again to the right.

"Stephanie—she don't really know what she's doing. She could pick up a guy with an apartment and go live with him.

What's wrong with that? I live with my mother. I don't know what's going to happen when she dies. But Stephanie, she lives in the street. She doesn't know what she's doing. Wooow. I can't take her home anyways. I'd be on the street with her." He paused again, his head twitching. "Stephanie—she better go live with somebody. She could be on the street the rest of her life. I knew a girl who's in her thirties. She's been on the street since she was twenty-one. They don't always live on the street. They go on welfare. They eventually become hookers. That's what's going to happen to her. Eventually, your values drop." His eyes darted around the park looking at nothing in particular, the spasms becoming more extreme. "I don't know. She better go live with someone."

He looked at me for a moment and then turned away. Sometimes he scratched his head. "I had a girlfriend before Stephanie—she was twenty-two. She'd take her clothes off for me. I slept with her. I took her to a hotel, and I slept with her. You couldn't do that with Stephanie. No, you couldn't do that with her. She's too shy. You couldn't do that with her. She'd never let you. Wooow." He buttoned the top of his striped polo shirt and then undid it. He leaned forward and rested his arms on his knees. "She's a waste of time. She should have someone older who can take care of her. She's a waste of time. People should help themselves."

Stephanie returned ten minutes later. "Stephanie—she's a waste of time," Lenny said, this time to her face.

"Look, Lenny, I know you hate me," Stephanie said. Then she smiled and tilted her head to the side and sweetened her voice, "Lenny, can you give me $10?"

He put his hand in his pocket and pulled out a ten-dollar bill. Stephanie plucked it from his fingers and, while running away called out over her shoulder, "Thanks, Lenny, see you tomorrow."

Lenny stood up abruptly and, without saying goodbye to me, walked away.

．．．．

STEPHANIE AND FRAGGLE worked hard to support their drug habits. Both panhandled, yet to earn enough cash, they had to supplement their "spangeing" (from "spare any change"). On a good day, Stephanie made as much as $10 an hour panhandling. But she made much more money copping —purchasing drugs. By the summer, she had begun copping heroin regularly and cocaine occasionally for neighborhood and uptown junkies, clean-shaven professionals in Burberry coats, beefy young men wearing sweatshirts and gold jewelry and driving big cars with Jersey plates, scrawny college students hauling knapsacks packed with books, and strung-out artists, photographers, and musicians. She copped for an exterminator, an engineer, a chef of a five-star French restaurant, and a top model whose photo she had seen on the cover of a fashion magazine. Some knew where to buy the dope themselves and simply didn't want to risk getting arrested, but many didn't have a clue. For each $10 bag of dope, depending on the customer, Stephanie could make an extra $10, enough for a bag for herself.

She rarely "wasted" the money she made on food. Strangers or people she knew often would buy Stephanie her favorites: pizza, cereal with milk, noodles or mashed potatoes with gravy, oatmeal pies, Oreos, and chocolate soft ice cream cones. She also ate restaurant meals, leftovers people dropped on her blanket; soup and sandwiches from neighborhood churches and soup kitchens; and Chinese food dug out of garbage bins on the street.

Fraggle had less success panhandling than Stephanie did.

He was self-conscious, introverted, and male, and perhaps because he had been on the streets longer, much more cynical. Fraggle's main source of income was shoplifting. On the street, there was a market and fence for almost anything. Stephanie rarely shoplifted for fear of getting caught, but Fraggle lifted videocassettes, CDs, and the hottest titles from the major bookstore chains and sold them to street vendors who then sold them at a reduced price. He stole Colgate toothpaste, Café Bustello, Excedrin PM, Nyquil, Lysol spray, Black Flag roach killer, Endust, Ajax dishwashing liquid, cheese, and candy bars, which he sold to a bodega on the Lower East Side. He also stole clothes and backpacks and socks and underwear for himself. When he was dope sick and needed money, he gave hand jobs and received blow jobs.

It was a risky way to live, so Stephanie and Fraggle tried to meet daily at one p.m. to reassure themselves that neither was in jail or in trouble. They met again, late at night, and settled into a doorway or near a tree by the East River to sleep. In the morning, they separated and went to work.

Not every day, however, went as planned. One Tuesday in late August, it was ten o'clock at night before Stephanie saw Fraggle again. He'd left her sleeping in a doorway on Seventh Street early that morning and hadn't shown up at noon as planned. Stephanie had spent the afternoon worried. When Fraggle finally walked into Tompkins Square Park, she'd just shot a bag of dope and simply wanted to be alone with him.

But Fraggle was dope sick: His eyes were red, his nose was running, and his hands were trembling. If he didn't get a bag of heroin soon, his entire body would start to quake, his stomach cramp. The quickest way to make money was to shoplift. If he stole ten bags of coffee and sold the coffee for $1 per bag, he'd make enough cash for a bag of heroin. But there was a problem. At this hour, the supermarket would be empty. He'd have to go in with enough cash to buy something. When he told Stephanie his plan, she gave him $5 and reluctantly agreed to go with him. She hated it when Fraggle shoplifted because even though he seldom got caught, she knew it was just a matter of time before he was arrested, leaving her alone on the street.

Fraggle moved quickly and, dragging her laundry cart behind her, Stephanie struggled to keep up. When they reached Fourteenth Street, Stephanie parked her cart against an apartment building across the street from the supermarket. Grabbing her panda, she sat on the cement and leaned back against the bricks. Wearing an empty backpack, Fraggle crossed the avenue. He told me he was going to buy cereal. I sat beside Stephanie and waited.

Months later, Fraggle told me what happened. The first thing Fraggle did when he passed through the sliding doors was scan the room. He'd hit the supermarket many times before and knew the layout. There were no cameras or door alarms. That night, the store was nearly empty, and because it was late, only two store employees were working.

The bodega that Fraggle did business with wanted Café Bustello. His hands were shaking, but Fraggle walked confidently toward the coffee aisle. When he noticed one of the employees sweeping the floor nearby, Fraggle kept walking. He'd played this game of cat and mouse hundreds of times. Watching, waiting, and anticipating his opponent's next move, Fraggle felt the adrenaline surge through his body, his heart pounding. It felt good. Wandering through the store, Fraggle picked up cans of peas and boxes of detergent, inspecting the labels carefully, then putting them back on the shelves. By the time he grabbed a box of Honeycombs cereal, the coffee aisle was empty.

Quickly, he swung his backpack off his shoulder, unzipped it, and shoved in ten bags of coffee. Now all he had left to do was buy the cereal. Fraggle walked to the front of the store, his eyes focused on the checkout counter. He was just a few yards from the cash register, when the store manager grabbed him from behind. When Fraggle tried to pull away, a second man grabbed Fraggle and dragged him to a back room, where they dumped the ten bags of coffee out of his knapsack and onto a table.

The manager yelled at Fraggle, telling him he was tired of having kids like Fraggle rip him off. He dared Fraggle to run away and threatened to punch him. When Fraggle raised his hands to protect his face, the manager grew even more angry. When the police finally arrived forty-five minutes later, Fraggle was relieved to see them. His body was aching, his hands trembling, and in jail he knew he would get methadone.

Across the street, Stephanie sat slumped, clutching her bear, still high from the bag of dope she had done an hour earlier. Her head bobbed up and down as she drifted in and out of consciousness, saliva dribbling from the side of her mouth. People who walked by glanced at her, then quickly away: Some stared with sympathy; others with disgust. Some dropped coins and bills into her cup. A kid in his late teens, carrying a heavy backpack and wearing a silk-screened T-shirt of the Puerto Rican flag, bent over and dropped a ten-dollar bill in her lap.

Stephanie drifted awake for a second, bumping her head against the bricks behind her. She winced, rubbed the spot she hit, then sat up with her eyes still squeezed shut. She asked if Fraggle had returned. When the pain was gone, she relaxed her eyes, tilted her head back, and fell back to sleep. Four fire engines and two ambulances raced by, their sirens wailing. Stephanie continued to sleep.

Suddenly, two police cars with their lights on sped up to the curb in front of the store. Fifteen minutes later, nearly an hour and a half after he had entered the store, Fraggle came out handcuffed. "I love you, Stephanie," he yelled across the busy intersection, his hands locked together behind his back. Stephanie, out cold, heard nothing.

When Stephanie finally woke, she was angry that Fraggle had been arrested. Fraggle would be fine, she knew, and would probably be released in a day or two, but she was exhausted, hungry, and craving dope. And she needed to find a safe place to sleep. Stephanie slept soundly, making her an easy target. Once, she woke to find a man's hand down her pants; another time to a man rubbing his body against hers; still another time to a man rubbing her leg; a fourth time, a man had her shoes and socks off and was pressing her feet in his crotch.

Stephanie looked down and noticed the ten-dollar bill in her lap. She counted an additional $6 in the cup she had placed by her side. She had made $16 while passed out on the sidewalk. We went to buy a box of Honeycombs and a quart of milk before heading back toward Tompkins Square Park.

At two a.m., the streets were quiet and littered with broken beer bottles, cigarette butts, and men, some barely conscious, spread out flat on their stomachs or backs. As we walked, Stephanie scanned the pavement for broken boxes. She rummaged through piles of flattened stacks of cardboard as though flipping through a sales rack in a department store. Some were not thick enough to sleep on; others were stained with food or piss. Those that passed inspection, she collected for our makeshift mattress under her arm.

When Fraggle wasn't around and Stephanie was alone, she made her bed on Avenue A and Seventh Street. A late-night hangout for drug dealers and users, sex workers and their clients, and neighborhood prattlers, voyeurs, anarchists, and insomniacs, the corner was the busiest spot in the neighborhood and for Stephanie, the safest.

Snug against a metal grate, she slept between Leshko's and Ray's Candy Store, both brightly lit and open all night. Even in the still hours before dawn, there was always somebody ordering scrambled eggs or pirogis from one or buying a newspaper or egg cream from the other. Here, everyone knew Stephanie.

Tonight, because I was staying with her, she decided it would be safe to sleep on Ninth Street, against the brick wall of a walk-up. Stephanie spread out the cardboard and covered it with a colorful cotton fabric from India. On top, she laid out a blue-and-white-checked bed sheet. When she noticed water dripping from an air conditioner two flights up, she positioned an umbrella on her laundry cart like a canopy to shield us for the night. Once the double bed was made, Stephanie disappeared. She returned ten minutes later with a bag of heroin.

Stephanie sat on the sheet and poured the milk and cereal into a plastic salad bar container. She quickly shoved five spoonfuls into her mouth. Then, sitting cross-legged, the top sheet pulled over her legs to conceal what she was doing, Stephanie placed a small amount of water and heroin into a bottle cap and mixed the liquid using the plunger taken from her syringe. The dope she bought dissolved quickly and easily and didn't need to be heated. After replacing the plunger into the syringe, she placed a small piece of cotton, rolled up into a tiny ball, into the bottle cap, laid the needle flat on top of the cotton, and then drew the liquid up through the cotton and into the syringe. The cotton acted as a filter to catch dirt and other impurities. Making a fist with her left hand to make her vein pop, she injected the dope into her arm. Within minutes she was asleep. Two small rats, their fat tails dragging behind, darted from behind a nearby garbage can.

Stephanie was still sleeping when I woke a few hours later. Keys jingled as people locked their front doors. Car doors opened and slammed shut. The footsteps of people who had places to go were fast and steady. One lady in open-toed leather sandals, her toenails painted scarlet red, walked by my sneaker-clad feet, shaking her head. From somewhere overhead, I heard a man's voice: "This is revolting." I didn't dare look up. I tried to wake Stephanie, but couldn't, so I kept my head down when people got too near, pulling the sheet over my face. Finally, a police officer came by around nine and told us to leave. We folded the sheets, put them in her cart, threw away the cardboard, and went to the park. The stares and comments, she said, used to bother her when she had first started sleeping on the streets, but now she no longer cared. "Nobody has any idea who I am," she said. "They can think whatever they want, and they'll still be wrong."

....

AS A TEENAGER, Stephanie had never dreamed of visiting New York. "All my friends were hippies. And hippies don't like New York City," she said. "It was Fraggle and his friends who told me how much fun it was."

Fraggle had been on the road for three years, hitchhiking across the country, when he met Stephanie in Cleveland, Ohio, in March 1995. He was nineteen, Stephanie was twenty. Her boyfriend Bruce had just died days earlier from a heroin overdose, and her friends were leaving Ohio to follow the Grateful Dead on tour. Fraggle was part of the group.

When Stephanie first met Fraggle, she didn't like him.

"He was arrogant and cocky," she said. But in Philadelphia, their first stop, everything changed. Fraggle was selling mushrooms when he told Stephanie, who was holding his money in case he got arrested, that he'd been busted thirteen times. Stephanie, thought that was cool. Among their friends, it was cool to be on tour following the Grateful Dead; it was cool to be into the club scene and to be into drugs. These kids got excited by shoplifting, running from the cops, cutting school—by breaking rules and getting away with it. It was their way of saying "I won't be who you want me to be." For the first time in weeks, Stephanie was no longer crying. Fraggle was funny, charming, and attentive; he made Stephanie laugh.

Stephanie and Fraggle talked about being junkies, waking up with painful stomach cramps and aching joints, the pain of seeing their friends die; about wanting to get an apartment and a job and giving up the traveler's lifestyle without giving up the dope; about being scared and feeling hopeless. She saw that Fraggle was not only listening but shared her feelings. "I thought I'd found my soul mate," Stephanie told me.

For the next seven months, Stephanie and Fraggle hitch-hiked—from Philadelphia to Charlotte to Atlanta following the Grateful Dead; then to Knoxville, back to Cleveland, and finally to San Francisco, where they stayed for five months and made nearly $100 a day selling marijuana. Both had been heroin users for more than a year, but in San Francisco their habit got increasingly expensive. Strung out and spending most of their pot profit on heroin, they decided, after a particularly expensive week, to join friends who had gone to Seattle to kick their habits.

Within a week of arriving in Seattle, Stephanie and Fraggle broke up. Stephanie returned to San Francisco; one week later, Fraggle followed. It was a pattern that they would repeat many times over the next year. They both wanted to stay off dope and knew that they could not stay clean in San Francisco. After two weeks, with Stephanie strung out and Fraggle using, they again decided to separate. Stephanie went back to Ohio to stay with her sister, and Fraggle went back to Virginia to stay with his family. "We were both depressed, both sick from kicking, both missing each other," Stephanie said. "We felt like we couldn't live without each other." Four days later, Fraggle bought Stephanie a bus ticket to Virginia, and they moved into Fraggle's stepsister's trailer.

About one month later, Stephanie and Fraggle took their first trip to New York. Fraggle and his friends, who'd been there before, said it was a fun place to visit and a great place to get good dope cheap. Stephanie and Fraggle and four other kids drove there in a car belonging to one girl's mother, taking the company credit card belonging to another kid's father. "We stayed in a huge room in some crack hotel in Jersey City for $28 a night," said Stephanie.

They had arrived in New York on Stephanie's twenty-first birthday. "We were doing dope in Tompkins Square Park, and I just went out," she said. Fraggle also passed out but woke up one hour later. "When he couldn't wake me up, he started freaking out." It was not uncommon to see people overdose on drugs in Tompkins Square Park. Bystanders urged Fraggle to get her to a hospital. But instead, he shot her with cocaine. Stephanie instantly woke up.

That afternoon, Stephanie and Fraggle went back to the hotel and continued to shoot heroin. "I started to feel really sick, and my whole arm blew up and turned blotchy with red-and-white patches," said Stephanie. "That's all I remember." Fraggle called 911.

In the hospital emergency room, Stephanie overdosed—

the fourth time since she had started using heroin at the age of eighteen. Doctors gave Stephanie an intravenous drip of naloxone to reverse the heroin high. Chemically, naloxone strips the drug from overloaded receptors in the body; the medical effect is "like pulling a plug from a socket."

"It was like someone shot me up with coke," said Stephanie. "Everything was black, and you could see a little hole of light getting bigger and bigger, and boom—the whole room came back. I was hot, wide awake, and scared. They were going to strap me down because I was freaking out and I was freaking out because they wouldn't let me leave. I was crying, 'It's my birthday, I don't want to be by myself.' They wouldn't let me smoke or see Fraggle or use the phone, and finally I passed out." A nurse woke her up four hours later at 5:45 in the morning and told her she could leave. Stephanie and Fraggle spent the rest of the day together, lying in bed and shooting dope.

The group stayed in New York less than a week and spent nearly $2,000 before returning to Virginia. Stephanie and Fraggle eventually went to Cleveland, where they stayed with Stephanie's older sister, Laura. Stephanie worked in a bakery, and Fraggle got a job as a host in a sports bar. Stephanie and Fraggle fought constantly, breaking up one day and then getting back together the next. They fought about sharing drugs and about real and imagined flirtations they each had with other people.

About a month after they had arrived in Cleveland, Stephanie, feeling lonely and rejected by Fraggle after one of their breakups, decided to go to New York with Gambit. Gambit was twenty-three and in town visiting one of Stephanie's friends. Stephanie and Gambit had instantly hit it off the night they met. He lived in a small town in Pennsylvania with his mother and had just enough money for a bus ticket home, but Stephanie had convinced Gambit to spend his bus money on dope. They hitchhiked to New York City, where Gambit eventually caught a bus back home.

"It took us three days to get to New York, but a whole day and a half just to get out of Ohio," said Stephanie, who had spent the first night with Gambit sitting in a truck stop on Interstate 80. "As soon as the sun came up the next day, we started walking and singing Grateful Dead songs. We walked along the highway in thirty below temperatures for more than three hours that day before we were picked up."

Stephanie stayed in New York for three days before returning back home to Cleveland. Although memories of her first trip to New York were hazy, when she stayed in New York by herself, she fell in love with the city. "I loved the people, the subways, the architecture, the drugs, the kids," she said. "It's big. It's dirty. It's everything a city should be— grubby and grungy. There are bums and graffiti everywhere. People are fucked up. It makes you feel normal."

She hadn't expected to love New York, and she also hadn't expected to fall in love with Gambit. Stephanie returned to Cleveland only because Fraggle had apologized to her just before she left, and she had promised him that she would be back. But back in Ohio, Stephanie missed Gambit. They spoke on the phone every day and for hours at a time. Gambit finally asked her to come stay with him. The day after Christmas, Stephanie left Cleveland to meet Gambit in New York, in Greenwich Village. She and Gambit agreed to stop shooting heroin, and in a symbolic gesture, they broke their needles. They then took the bus to his mother's house in Pennsylvania.

Fraggle was miserable without Stephanie and followed her as far as New York. "He called Gambit's house every single day collect, telling me how much he loved me and that he was going to die if he couldn't be with me," said Stephanie. "He was totally fucked up on drugs and was getting thrown out onto the street."

Stephanie agreed to meet Fraggle in New York for a couple of days. When she started talking about returning to Gambit, Fraggle broke down. "He said, 'I'm going to die if you leave me,'" Stephanie recalled. "'I love you. I need you. You're the only person in the world who ever loved me. Baby, I'm so sorry. I'm just so fucked up. I have nobody else.'"

Stephanie feared that if she left Fraggle, he would die. She couldn't leave. She still had nightmares about Bruce, who died of an overdose after he and Stephanie had an argument. Said Stephanie, "I ate it up—everything Fraggle said to me."

Besides, New York was a great place to get high.

． ． ． ．

HEROIN—also known as dope, chiva, horse, brown sugar, junk, smack—has long been alluring. In *Junky*, William Burroughs in 1953 described a shot of junk as "a spreading wave of relaxation slackening the muscles away from the bones so that you seem to float without outlines, like lying in warm salt water." In the 1960s, Lou Reed in the song "Heroin" refers to the drug as being an addict's wife and life. Jazz legends Billie Holiday, Charlie "Bird" Parker, Chet Baker, and John Coltrane were all hooked on dope. In his autobiography, Miles Davis explained, "The idea was going around that to use heroin might make you play as great as Bird. A lot of musicians did it for that. I guess I might have been waiting for his genius to hit me."

In the 1990s, heroin was again in vogue, discussed in the media as a new, widespread phenomenon. On August 26, 1996, a *Newsweek* story, "Heroin Alert: Rockers, Models and the New Allure of Heroin," reported a dramatic rise in the presence of heroin in popular culture. Newspaper headlines recorded the deaths of teen icons and rock musicians such as Kurt Cobain and Jonathan Melvoin of the Smashing Pumpkins who had either overdosed on heroin or were battling their addictions at the time of their deaths. (After Melvoin died, according to New York City police, demand for the brand that killed him, Red Rum—"murder" spelled backwards—rose in Manhattan's Lower East Side.)

Fashion magazines like *Allure* and *Marie Claire* reported on the industry's worst-kept secret: young models on smack. A "junkie chic" look capitalized on the trend and, some argued, fueled it. "Instead of the brazen strut of yesterday, catwalkers regularly adopt a slightly dazed, strung-out demeanor on the runway," wrote Robin Givhan, fashion reporter for *The Washington Post* (July 1996). "More and more models are being photographed slouched in dingy bathrooms or cheap motels with their makeup smeared and their hair tousled. And while they're decked out in the latest pricey designer fashions, the implication is that a hypodermic needle is somewhere just outside of the frame . . . Designers copied this from the street from the addicts themselves. They cleaned it up. Validated it. And now they're selling it."

Heroin was back in style at the movies as well. In *Pulp Fiction* (1994), John Travolta shot up and Uma Thurman overdosed after snorting too much heroin. In *The Basketball Diaries* (1995), Leonardo DiCaprio played a promising young writer and basketball player who ended up on the streets a junkie. *Trainspotting* (1996), though raw in its portrayal of junkie life, had a counterculture following that viewed heroin addicts as rebel heroes. Says Renton, the movie's narrator, about getting high: "People think it's all about misery and desperation and death and all that shit, which is not to be ignored, but what they forget is the pleasure of it. Otherwise we wouldn't do it . . . Take the best orgasm you ever had, multiply it by a thousand, and you're still nowhere near it."

Part of the resurgence had to do with simple economics. Since the mid-1980s, the amount of heroin being imported to the United States had doubled to ten to fifteen metric tons per year, according to rough government estimates. In the 1980s, average $10 bags were about 2 percent to 8 percent pure; by 1996, average purity for bags in New York hit 72 percent, which allowed new users to snort it rather than inject it. Heroin was also cheap. In 1994, the street price of heroin in New York fell to just 37 cents a milligram, down from $1.81 in 1988.

From 1991 to 1995 in New York City alone, city emergency room incidents involving heroin rose from six thousand to over eleven thousand. Fatal heroin overdoses rose from 478 in 1994 to 869 in 1995, an 81 percent increase. Although most hard-core heroin users were still older, poor, and black or Hispanic, more teenagers of all races were snorting and shooting up. A 1997 national illegal-drug survey found that overall drug use among teenagers had leveled off for the first time since 1992, but the use of heroin as well as synthetic drugs like LSD, MDMA (Ecstasy), and ketamine hydrochloride (Special K)—used by veterinarians to anesthetize animals and snorted by kids—was on the rise. In 1996, 2.4 percent of eighth graders said they had tried heroin, double the rate from 1991. Although these figures were extremely low and statistically not significant, social policymakers were starting to take notice.

The Lower East Side, where Stephanie and Fraggle made their home, had for decades been known for its thriving drug trade. In the 1980s, people brazenly lined up to buy heroin and cocaine from drug stalls that opened up daily in abandoned buildings along Avenues C and D. Hawkers in front of drug houses they represented called out brand names and delivered their goods using buckets dropped from windows to buyers on the street below. Dealers used pregnant women to transport drugs from one area to another and hired grade school children for $100 a day to act as lookouts or couriers, hiding heroin in their lunch boxes.

Since the early 1970s, the New York City Police Department had made arresting street-level drug dealers and buyers a low priority. But in January 1984, the city's new police commissioner, Benjamin Ward, launched Operation Pressure Point, which targeted small-time dealers. More than two hundred police officers, some working undercover but most in uniform, invaded a seven block by fifteen block area on the Lower East Side. Four mounted officers patrolled Tompkins Square Park, and a helicopter surveyed the rooftops. Dogs were brought in to sniff for heroin. Although nearly twelve thousand arrests were made during the eight-month siege, most of the drug dealers were back on the streets in weeks, and some were arrested a half a dozen times in less than a month. Instead of leaving the area, though, some drug sellers moved into poorer parts of the neighborhood, which received less attention; many more moved indoors, selling out of bodegas, small shops, and fake record stores. By the late 1980s, the Lower East Side was still a thriving drug marketplace.

In 1996, when Stephanie and Fraggle were in New York, scoring drugs on the Lower East Side was again a risky business. New York Mayor Rudolph Giuliani's war against crime was well under way, and part of his strategy was to launch an aggressive campaign against the drug trade, with the Lower East Side one of his prime targets. New York City's assault on so-called quality-of-life crimes enabled police to use nuisance laws to attack drug activity. Arrests for drinking in public, jumping subway turnstiles, playing loud music, and other minor offenses, which had been ignored for years, became routine. Misdemeanor arrests soared by more than 50 percent from 133,446 cases in 1993, the year before Giuliani took office, to 205,277 cases in 1996.

Plainclothes police officers from the city's Tactical Narcotics Team, Street Crime Unit, Warrant Squad, and the Ninth Precinct's Anti-Crime Unit, disguised as middle-aged tourists or pretending to be drug users, traveled in pairs through Tompkins Square Park. These undercover "buy and bust" sweeps of the park were frequent, and small-time drug runners, dealers, and buyers were arrested daily. The drug trade was forced to move underground, and increasingly, drug gangs recruited young kids to make deliveries on bicycles to customers in neutral locations and began to use beepers to contact customers.

In this climate, Stephanie flourished. She knew who was selling and where to buy. She was known and trusted by the local drug dealers and gangs who stamped brand names like Kiss of Mint, DOA (Dead on Arrival), Pink Lady, Sudden Death, Flatliner, Pleasure, Paradise, Poison, NYNEX, and Life onto their bags to develop customer loyalty. Because she was a user herself, she knew which products were good. She also wasn't afraid to go alone into the projects or cross over to Avenues C and D at all hours of the night to make a pickup. If the area was "hot" and the cops were around, the dealers would motion to her to keep walking. If they had the drugs, they would give her a signal to wait. Returning with the goods, they would hand them off quickly, discreetly.

When Stephanie raced back and forth between the park and the blocks farther east, she greeted dozens of people along the way, often hugging them or giving them a peck on the cheek. The conversations were short, limited to who had good dope or who had been busted, and she would often walk off with a casual "I love you."

Stephanie excelled on the streets in New York. As a young teenager in Ohio, Stephanie never felt accepted by her family or by her peers. She had been suspended from school for truancy in the eighth grade, eventually dropped out of high school her junior year, and had disgraced her family on numerous occasions with her drug use. For most of her young life, she felt she was disappointing others, never meeting their expectations. In New York on the Lower East Side, though, Stephanie didn't feel judged. Her behavior was acceptable, and she felt at home.

She also worked hard. Fraggle, who'd been on the streets longer, had schooled her in the basics: where to sleep, how to panhandle (don't sit where store owners can see you and only ask for money when customers leave the store), how to hitchhike (always make the female stand closer to the road), what to do if arrested (carry no identification, use fake names, and never give away your Social Security number). In New York, she studied people tirelessly, observing who was cool, who was bad news, who ripped people off. She watched how people talked to one another and how they earned respect.

In less than six months she developed a solid reputation with customers and drug dealers. She also knew where to get all the food and clothes she needed, where she would be safe when she slept alone, and how to make money. She was no longer afraid to fight back verbally when she was ripped off, threatened, or attacked. For Stephanie, surviving on the street was an accomplishment. She was respected for what she did well. And her self-esteem grew.

....

STEPHANIE first shot heroin when she was eighteen. Her boyfriend at the time, Bruce, had traded some acid for morphine. For months, she'd been getting drunk daily, blacking out on beer, Carlo Rossi jugs of blush wine, Jagermeister, whiskey, and rum. She was also eating acid and taking pills. The alcohol relaxed her but clouded her thinking, making her do things she would regret the next day; the microblot acid intensified her emotions, often heightening her fears and inciting panic. When Stephanie drank a bottle of liquid morphine, she felt clarity and "total peace." She was told that she could get even higher if she shot the morphine, but Stephanie resisted. Once she saw how euphoric her friends seemed after they had injected, Stephanie agreed to let her friend shoot it into her arm. "The rush was incredible," she said.

The next day, her friend shot her again, but this time with heroin. More than alcohol, marijuana, acid, cocaine, or pills, heroin hit her hard. "I loved it," she said. "I was laying in bed with Bruce, and both of us were so in love. You can feel it going all the way up your neck and all the way down your body. It's warm, and it feels like someone is hugging you. You're in heroin la la land, and then you puke a lot."

Heroin took her far away, and in a hurry. Stephanie slipped into a dreamy wakefulness. All pain, thoughts, and confusion melted under its lazy spell. She felt pleasantly listless, calm, and content. That first week, afraid of getting hooked, she shot it only a couple of times. But when her supplier told her it took years to develop a physical addiction, Stephanie and Bruce quickly began shooting every other day and then every day. Then, just three weeks after the first time she'd injected, Stephanie knew she was in trouble. Her dope connection hadn't shown up one day, and her body reacted.

Stephanie felt like she was coming down with the flu. She was scared.

When the dealer finally called later that evening, she told him she didn't want to see him again. That night she got sicker; her stomach hurt, she was nauseous, she felt anxious and empty, her craving intensified. She prayed for the emptiness and anxiety to go away, but it only got worse. In the morning, Stephanie called her dealer. Within an hour he delivered her dope.

After awhile, she was shooting heroin not to get high but to get straight—to feel normal. When she was dope sick, her eyes watered, her nose ran, her stomach cramped. She felt nauseated and had diarrhea. Her pupils dilated, her arms broke out in goose bumps, and her heart beat faster. Eventually, her whole body hurt, especially her joints and muscles. Even the simple motion of blinking became painful. She lived in fear that her connection would go to jail. Her entire life centered around shooting dope—getting it, cooking it, injecting it. Said Stephanie, "On heroin, I felt less alone—a part of something."

Stephanie also loved that on heroin she was thin. In grade school, she'd been chubby and extremely self-conscious about it. And although her weight had fluctuated in adolescence, the alcohol she started drinking in her late teens plumped her up to a chunky 140 pounds. On heroin, she shed about twenty-five pounds, and for the first time, she was skinny. With her new body, she felt she had also shed that insecure fat little girl who had been teased by her classmates. Now thin, she felt desirable and self-confident.

By the time I met Stephanie three years later, she was shooting an average of four bags a day, and every decision she made revolved around getting her next bag. She had kicked heroin more than a dozen times, but at this point she was addicted to being a junkie. Heroin gave her an identity. There was no Stephanie without dope. She had to have it. She had to have it all the time. And she had to have it now. "I'm a junkie," she would repeat, proud she had something to call herself. And she loved the way heroin made her feel, like curling up in a feather bed under a down comforter on a cold day.

But with pleasure came pain. A six-inch pink scar spread like a grotesque spiderweb from the crook of Stephanie's arm. The disfigurement was so ugly that bystanders believed her when she would tell them she had been caught in a fire or been mangled by a boat propeller.

The real story was just as grisly. Stephanie had been in San Francisco with Fraggle just two weeks. They were in a bathroom stall together shooting up and using spit to cook down the dope. Stephanie was having trouble finding her veins. Fraggle had just injected himself with a speedball and offered to help. "He kept jabbing me and jabbing me and I was crying and there's blood just pouring down my arm and I was pleading with him to let me hit myself," Stephanie said. "Then he slapped me across the face and told me to shut the fuck up. I finally just told him to shoot it all." Fraggle shot the heroin into Stephanie's arm but had missed the vein. The heroin pooled in her tissue under the skin. Within days, she developed a large abscess, the resulting cellulitis—a bacterial infection—spreading through the skin's connective tissue in the crook of her arm. Her skin got red, hot, and sore to the touch.

One week later, Stephanie went to San Francisco General Hospital, where doctors told her if she had waited one more day, she would have lost her arm. It took three surgeries to cut out the infected lump and intravenous antibiotics to get the infections under control. "They didn't care what I looked like," said Stephanie. "They hacked my ass up because I'm homeless and I don't have insurance."

As a heroin and cocaine user living on the street, Stephanie

had been lucky. Still, by the age of twenty-one, she'd contracted cellulitis in her feet that caused them to swell and blister, a
severe case of strep throat, and lice. She'd had seizures from
shooting cocaine and had overdosed four times. Surviving
what she had experienced made her feel strong.

When I asked Stephanie if she took precautions against
contracting HIV, she assured me she did. A 1997 report prepared by the Mayor's Office of AIDS Policy Coordination
estimated that between 30 percent and 40 percent of New
York City's 250,000 injection drug users were infected with
HIV. That same year, the federal Centers for Disease Control
and Prevention estimated that intravenous drug users and
their sex partners and children accounted for more than one-
third of new HIV infections. Stephanie went to the Lower
East Side Needle Exchange, a storefront operation on Avenue
C near East Fourth Street, three to four times each week to
exchange her used needles for clean syringes. She also got
tested every few months for HIV, paying $5 each time.
"Needle exchange saved my life," she told me. Needle
exchanges cut in half new HIV cases among New York City's
intravenous drug users, according to the Chemical
Dependency Institute at Beth Israel Medical Center.

But Stephanie didn't use condoms when she had sex with
Fraggle, and she shared needles with him. "I guess part of me
is afraid of getting HIV," she conceded. "But if I get it, I get
it. I mean I'm already dying out here, it doesn't really matter."

. . . .

IN AUGUST 1996, bankers, lawyers, and accountants in
jackets and button-down shirts flew to New York from their
investment firm in Boston and descended on Tompkins
Square Park to hand out hundreds of photocopied fliers

bearing a young girl's photo. Fourteen-year-old Melissa Gay had disappeared a few days earlier from her parents' home after telling them she was going to the country club to play tennis. Later, they learned she had caught a ride with two friends heading for a rave party in New York City. The only other time Melissa had been to New York was to see the Rockefeller Center Christmas tree.

Popularized in basements and warehouses in the late 1980s in the United Kingdom, raves were now being held in communities across the United States. These all-night dance parties, where teenagers danced until dawn to loud trance-like house and techno music, often featured an abundance of designer drugs like Ecstasy, LSD, or Special K. Although some raves were illegal, many were fully licensed events in warehouses, clubs, stadiums, and outdoor parks and fields.

Melissa was found in New Jersey a week after her disappearance. After going to rave parties, one at Randall's Island, the other under the Whitestone Bridge in the Bronx, she'd met a group of New Jersey teenagers who offered her a place to stay. Melissa told them that she had left home because her parents were worried that she smoked cigarettes, occasionally used marijuana, and had started dating.

Teenagers often ran away to the East Village. Sharing the streets with the homeless, squatters, undocumented immigrants, and others who simply liked the feel of the neighborhood, runaway teenagers were almost invisible. Hell's Angels, Guardian Angels, Hare Krishnas, and Rastafarians lived beside punk rockers, hippies, priests and nuns, drug dealers and users, financial traders, and lawyers. Restaurants served Tibetan and Afghani food and featured drag-queen waitresses. Shops sold feather boas, bright pink vinyl microminis, Tarot cards. Tattoo and piercing parlors stood beside trendy art galleries and Spanish-language book shops. Self-proclaimed anarchists protested alongside street peddlers who sold leather underwear, stringless guitars, flesh-toned mannequin limbs, moth-eaten sweaters, bleached animal bones, Spider-Man comic books, copies of *Junky* and the *I Ching*, and old LPs by the Bay City Rollers, the Ramones, and the Sex Pistols. In the neighborhood, entertainment included Spanish flamenco dancing, rhyme and verse at poetry slams, amateur film screenings, and modernized Greek tragedies staged amid the neighborhood's tenements.

Descendants of Italians running from poverty and Eastern European Jews escaping anti-Semitism who had poured into the area's tenements in the late 1800s still lived mostly on the west side of Tompkins Square Park. Puerto Ricans seeking economic opportunity in the 1950s, joined in later years by other Spanish speakers, mostly Dominicans, remained on the east side and in pockets on side streets. Hippies had flocked to the area in the 1960s, and pioneering artists and students settled throughout the neighborhood in the 1970s and 1980s.

By the mid-1990s, professionals and semiprofessionals able to afford the newly refurbished lofts moved in. Hundreds of squatters, including several families with children, who had illegally moved into vacant buildings in the 1980s, were displaced. Cold-water flats that once rented for $300 a month went co-op and sold for $100,000. Construction crews built high rises on vacant lots. Suddenly, one-bedroom apartments were renting for more than $1,500 a month, and the mom-and-pop stores that had sold homemade pastries and fresh bread for decades were crowded out by chain stores like the Gap, upscale cafes that offered lattes, designer cookie shops, and restaurants that served Cosmopolitans and frozen daiquiris.

At the heart of the changing East Village was Tompkins

Square Park, and the new neighbors were eager to clean it up. Drug runners who paced back and forth, looking for their customers and whispering "sens" or "*sin semilla*" under their breath, shared the ten-acre park with elderly Poles and Ukrainians, who camped out on benches to feed the pigeons; skateboarders and rollerbladers; new mothers who pushed strollers; and restless, sometimes violent, homeless men and women. People with jobs sat in the sun, eating lunch alongside unemployed drug users, who sometimes overdosed, turning blue or convulsing in the shade of trees or on iron benches.

In the summer, scores of young people, mostly in their late teens and early twenties, descended on Tompkins Square Park. They had pierced tongues, cheeks, eyebrows, nipples, noses, lips. They wore cartilage studs, nose rings, lip plugs. Their hair was spiked, chopped, matted. Their clothing was often lice-infested and their footgear designed for combat. Many of them spent their mornings, as Stephanie did, passed out on park benches; their afternoons in doorways begging for spare change; and their nights, when the park was off limits, on neighborhood streets getting drunk, shooting dope, snorting coke, and struggling to stay awake until six a.m. when park gates opened again and they could return to get some sleep.

Most of these kids were not from New York. Some labeled themselves as "homeless," others called themselves punks, grunges, skinheads, straight-edges, Dead Heads, burnouts or Gothics; many said they were "travelers," on a journey of some sort, straddling a thin line between self-discovery and self-destruction. They hitchhiked, hopped freight trains, and took Greyhound buses from one city to another. Some followed the music and club scene; others, seasonally mobile, migrated like birds to warm weather, moving from Pioneer

Square in Seattle to Polk Street in San Francisco to Decatur Street in New Orleans to Tompkins Square Park in New York, often making prolonged stops along the way.

Often called "crusties" and "gutter punks" for their unwashed and squalid appearance, many of these kids "dumpster-dived," excavating pizza crusts, half-eaten sandwiches, flat soda, and torn clothes from trash bins. They went "ground-scoring," trolling the city's streets and sidewalks for treasure—absolutely anything they could use, wear, or sell. They slept on broken boxes on the sidewalk, begged for money and food, urinated behind parked cars and trash bins, washed their hair, teeth, and even bodies in open-air water fountains. These were in-your-face homeless kids who didn't know what to do with themselves, and who were often inconsiderate, rude, and, a few, shamelessly offensive. They were difficult to like.

Some were from poor backgrounds, but many came from higher-paid blue-collar, pink-collar, and middle-class families. Some of these teens simply didn't want to live at home, but many had run away from sexual or physical abuse, extreme discipline, neglect, or discrimination. They often felt abandoned and powerless. On the streets, they attempted to conquer people, things, spaces—anything to make them feel loved and powerful again. Friendships rapidly turned into intense rivalries, the kids copying their dysfunctional families.

This generation had grown up with drugs and guns in schools, had seen repeated violence and crime on television, and had heard about much publicized political duplicity and corruption. In their world, people got shot for a wrong look and died from having sex. Their parents, who often worked long hours in tedious jobs they despised, seldom had time for them. Finding it difficult to imagine that things were going to get better, many of these kids didn't care about much of anything. Living on the streets consumed them. They got drunk and high, not to have visions but to black out. On the streets, they sometimes incited panic among adults because they seemed so alienated.

On their own, the runaways learned quickly how to meet their needs. They went to the needle exchange for clean needles, to churches and food pantries for hot meals, to drop-in clinics or outreach vans for delousing or scabies treatments. Most were literate, and all were mobile and feverish networkers.

The longer they were on the streets, the more difficult it was to get them off. They witnessed or were victims of violence, rape, and sexual abuse. They used drugs to stave off hunger and fear and to anesthetize emotional pain. Out of necessity, they stole, hustled, and begged to support their drug habits. They ended up addicted, incarcerated, infected with HIV. Some ended up dead. One Seattle study that tracked 364 homeless youth, aged thirteen to twenty-one, for an eighteen-month period during the years 1992 through 1995 found that 68 percent met the criteria for at least one mental or emotional disorder, including depression, schizophrenia, post-traumatic stress disorder, conduct disorder, mania, attention deficit or hyperactivity. Forty-five percent of these youth had attempted suicide, with almost half reporting more than two suicide attempts. Thirty-one percent said they had been treated in an emergency room for assault, trauma, rape, or illness in the three months prior to their first interview.

During the eight months I spent in the park, I got to know dozens of young runaways. Although the details of their lives differed, the theme of abandonment was strong. One girl, fifteen-year-old Annie, told me that she had left her home in Illinois because her stepfather was sexually abusing her. When Annie told her mother, she was called a liar. When

I first met Annie, a drug dealer who learned that her uncle had wired her money was offering her free heroin samples, trying to get her hooked.

Sixteen-year-old Heather, pretty and blond, told me she'd been raped in the eighth grade by six high school seniors who lived in her neighborhood in Virginia. For years, they continued to harass her. Eventually she felt she had no choice but to run away. The first day I met her, two days after her arrival in New York City, Heather was hungry and homesick for her boyfriend. Three days later, she was "dating" a man in his thirties, who spent his days in the park drinking forty-ounce bottles of beer and his evenings with Heather in his car. He had told her that he had fallen in love with her. A week later, she was getting drunk and smoking pot.

Kelly was fourteen when she ran away from her home in Georgia because her mother had blamed her for her father's departure and their resulting divorce. By the time I met Kelly, she was seventeen and hooked on heroin. All day long, she sat in the park reading Stephen King and science fiction, trading the five or six books she always had with her for new ones. She panhandled and copped to make money.

In the park, teens who lived at home easily slummed with homeless peers. These kids were looking for a break from their own lives or simply had found that they shared the same taste in fashion and music, desire to get wasted, or disgust for those who played by the rules. Lying flat on the patches of brown grass and listening to music blasting from their boomboxes, these kids with homes to return to mingled comfortably with the homeless kids and adults who slept on benches, washed up in the public toilets, and injected drugs in nearby doorways. They shared a camaraderie that was both intense and tenuous.

People who spent their days in the park had names like

Charlie Bananas, Purple, Hot Dog, Slug, Star, and Split. They asked each other "How ya doin'?" or "Man, did you hear that Bass was busted again?" or "Did you hear what Reggie did?" They gossiped about one another—who'd been arrested, who was the latest to get infected with HIV, whose T-cell count went up or down, who'd been seen getting ripped off, busted, or beaten up. They did what came naturally, just carrying on, adjusting, surviving, and creating the drama that came from living on the street or knowing those who did.

One summer morning, before I had met Stephanie, a boy about fifteen walked into the park. He'd started coming to the park a month earlier, after the semester had ended at an uptown prep school he attended. His hair was freshly washed and cut into a neat wedge. His brown leather jacket was stiff and new. By the entrance of the park, a group of kids sat on a bench blasting music by a local punk rock band. As the new kid approached the group, he smiled. From under his leather jacket, he pulled a roasted chicken he said he had stolen from Grand Union. Presenting his prize to the others as if part of an initiation process, he placed the chicken on a bench. Kids lunged for the chicken and, quickly, one at a time, tore off a piece of the bird, sat down, and gnawed away at the meat.

Five minutes later, the kids walked away. On the ground lay nothing but bones.

. . . .

A WEEK AFTER Fraggle had been arrested, Stephanie and I met on her corner to go to Rikers Island jail to see him. Normally, for shoplifting, he would have been released after a few days with a summons to return to court at a later date, but he had had an outstanding warrant from 1993 for a drug charge and was being held.

When I arrived shortly before eight, Stephanie was nowhere in sight, and her cart was gone. About an hour later, she showed up looking disheveled and exhausted. Her hair was uncharacteristically greasy, falling in mats across her face. Her shoelaces were untied.

Stephanie walked into Leshko's and down the aisle to the bathroom in the back. The waitress reluctantly buzzed her in, the system in place to keep restrooms free for paying customers. With the door locked behind her, Stephanie injected herself with cocaine. A few minutes later, she came out.

We walked to the subway station to catch the N train to Queens. Stephanie had a large black vinyl bag over one arm and her panda in the other. The coke had given her a boost, widening her eyes, stiffening her arms and legs, but she still looked messy and confused. At the station, I handed her a token. She took it, stashing it in her pocket. She then tossed her panda and bag over the turnstile and crawled under it. At Queensboro Plaza, twenty minutes later, we walked upstairs to the street. She needed to use a bathroom and walked into the doughnut shop on the corner. The sign said "For Customers Only," but the manager didn't seem to care.

Across the street at the bus stop stood a long line of mostly black and Hispanic women and children waiting for the bus to take them to Rikers Island—home to more than fifteen thousand inmates, of whom more than 55 percent were black, about 35 percent Hispanic, and fewer than 10 percent white. The jail housed males and females, sixteen and older, who, after being arraigned on criminal charges, had been unable to post bail or had been remanded without bail, pending trial. It also housed those sentenced in the city to terms of up to one year, parole violators awaiting parole revocation hearings, and people charged with civil crimes. Prisoners sentenced for more than one year were held at Rikers until they could be transferred to the State Department of Correctional Services.

Nearly 90 percent of the visitors to the island's ten jails were women. Waiting for the bus that took them to visit boyfriends, husbands, fathers, brothers, and uncles, the women carried paper bags from McDonald's or brown bag lunches. They knew the routine: Many of them took the trip three times each week, the maximum number of visits allowed for each detainee. For much of the day, they would wait in lines to go through metal detectors and pass physical inspections with shoes and socks removed—all so that they could sit for an hour in plastic chairs and talk, fight, or quietly hold hands with their men.

We stood in our first line to board the bus. People stared at Stephanie. She didn't seem to notice. Forty minutes later, after a ride through the commercial district in Queens and through Astoria, a neighborhood of neat row houses with small front lawns and driveways, we finally crossed over a narrow bridge to the island.

"I know the first thing he's going to ask me is, 'Are you selling your ass?'" Stephanie said. She was excited, a wide smile spread across her face. "Every time we're separated for a while he asks that."

The bus stopped and we got off to wait on a twisting line that led into the reception area. A guard paced up and down the queue. "No beepers, tape recorders, cameras, cellular phones permitted inside," he repeated. "No firearms, ammunition, knives, drugs, alcoholic beverages, recording devices. Anyone with a Walkman or radio, goodbye."

Stephanie pulled a phony birth certificate from her pocket, its edges torn. Stephanie carried no identification and used a false name if she was arrested. For emergencies, she used her friend's birth certificate, which she kept at another friend's house. But this time, when she got to the window, she was told that anyone eighteen or over had to have photo identification. Although she could have passed for a girl of fifteen, her phony document was that of a twenty-one-year-old girl. Stephanie was relieved. She didn't want to spend the day standing in lines.

If she couldn't see him, she could at least put some money on Fraggle's books—his account. We walked through a corridor to wait in a much shorter line to leave a care package for him. Dropping her panda on the floor, she rummaged through her black shoulder bag and found two one-dollar bills. She then picked out nickels and dimes, separating them from the gum wrappers, Oreo cookie crumbs, pieces of dirty cotton, and lint that collected at the bottom. When she was told that she couldn't leave coins, she walked up and down the line of people, her palms filled with all the change she had. And although she wasn't asking for money this time, with her hands outstretched and her quiet pleas, she looked for the first time like a beggar. Eventually Stephanie converted the silver and copper to three dollar bills. At the window, she handed the man a note for Fraggle and the five singles. When he told her they didn't take notes or letters, she rummaged around in her bag for anything else he might be able to use. She pulled out a pair of dirty cotton girls' socks and an X-Men comic book and slid the pile through the hole in the window. Then, she picked her panda up off the floor, dragged herself outside, and sat on the curb, waiting for the bus to take us back to Queens.

. . . .

THAT NIGHT, a bit before ten, I went out to see Stephanie. At her corner, she was sitting on a blanket spread out on the sidewalk, her knees pulled up close to her chest.

She wore a powder blue halter top so stretched out she used safety pins to keep it snug around her chest. Over it, she wore the blue Yankees sweatshirt jacket, unzipped and hanging off one shoulder.

A guy who knew Stephanie walked over to say hello. "Hey, bag lady, where's Fraggle?" he asked.

"Don't call me that," she snapped back. She pulled a small black comb from her pocket, smoothed her hair back into a ponytail, and fastened it with an elastic band she kept around her wrist. Then she adjusted her halter top, tightening it around her ribs. The man started to walk away. "He got caught boosting at a grocery store. He had an outstanding warrant, so they're keeping him."

As we sat there, an older Polish man who spent time in the park and had seen her on the Geraldo Rivera show came by and offered to pay her $2 if she would show him her scar. She rolled up the sleeve of her sweatshirt, extended her arm, and showed the mutilation, turning her head away. Then she asked for the money. He gave it to her, and she put it in her pants pocket.

A few minutes later, Stephanie's friend Heidi knelt down in front of us. Dressed in a short, pleated miniskirt, her long blond hair pulled up high on her head in a ponytail, and wearing yellow high-top sneakers, she looked like she'd come from cheerleading practice. "I'm homeless again," she said. "My boyfriend's parents think that I'm a bad influence, so I had to move out."

Heidi was twenty, shot dope, and worked for an escort service. The service covered Brooklyn, Queens, Manhattan, Long Island, and New Jersey. Every night at nine, a driver in a black sedan picked up Heidi in front of Tompkins Square Park. She worked until six in the morning, pocketing $55 for calls that usually cost the client $125. She said she averaged about $250 a night, plus tips. Heidi often bought Stephanie heroin and sometimes invited Stephanie to stay with her when she got a hotel room for the night. "We were breaking up, anyways," said Heidi.

A black car pulled up to the curb, and the driver honked the horn. Heidi walked to the car and got in.

A minute later, a slight but tall man, his hair shiny black and slickly parted on the side, stepped over to Stephanie's blanket.

"Hey, you're too pretty to be out here," he said, dropping a dollar bill into her cup. "Would I deserve it if I was fat or ugly?" snapped Stephanie.

Startled, the man stepped back, then walked away.

When Stephanie wasn't copping, she was panhandling on the corner of Avenue A and Seventh Street, where she spread her blanket and sat, her cup just in front of her bent knees. Here, she was both a social outcast and a neighborhood landmark to the police, mail carriers, restaurant owners, and residents, who frequently gave her change, food, advice, or just a quick hello. Although these people really didn't watch over her, they helped to sustain her existence and, in the same way that buying the morning paper becomes a habit, had incorporated her into their lives.

The most generous were people who seemed to have little to give. Some, once homeless themselves, gave because they empathized with Stephanie or wanted to return the kindness that they had themselves received. Still others gave fearing that a fight with a partner, a loss of a job, or a drug or alcohol binge at the wrong time of the month could set them along a similar path. Many gave because Stephanie served as a reminder of how fortunate they were. A few dropped coins in her cup hoping to feel good about themselves.

There were also people, both homeless and housed, who

had little sympathy for Stephanie, believing it was her choice to be on the street. They told her to get a job, get a life, or go home. One day a man, about twenty-five, in khaki pants and Topsiders, walked by her and yelled past his shoulder at her, "Give me a fuckin' break and go back to Connecticut." Another day, a young man in a sports jacket and black jeans spit in her face. She had spit on the ground near him a day earlier, and he returned to retaliate.

Stephanie hadn't become a homeless junkie overnight. Getting off dope and off the streets would not happen quickly or easily. When Stephanie was sent to the drug rehabilitation program in Georgia by the Geraldo Rivera show, she found out that her problems didn't go away when the drugs were taken away. Off heroin, she felt more alone, depressed, and panicked than ever before. Her pain, which she had successfully kept buried, became unbearable. Staying off drugs meant that she had to commit to facing a past that included her father's abandonment, and her mother's emotional instability and death. It meant that she would have to drop her junkie identity to figure out who she really was and what she wanted to do with her life. And she would have to drop Fraggle. It was like someone telling her to jump out of an airplane without a parachute. It required trust and faith, and Stephanie had neither, especially in herself. "I've disappointed others my whole life," she said. "Why should things be different now?" So Stephanie left rehab after twenty-two days and went back to New York to meet Fraggle. Within hours of arriving in the city, she got high. The anxiety, fear, and loneliness melted away. She no longer felt empty and unloved. She was back to feeling just numb.

In New York, many people wanted to help Stephanie. Both men and women offered to let her sleep over, use their showers, or keep her cart in their apartments for safekeeping.

Most of these people had struggled with or continued to struggle with their own addictions. Some people even offered her a place to stay. The offers, however, were always for her and did not include Fraggle. And Stephanie wouldn't leave Fraggle. "These people think, I'll help her, give her a place to stay, and feel good about myself," she said. "But they don't help me. Maybe for a few weeks, while it's convenient, and then when I don't act the way they want me to, or do what they want me to do, or it takes me longer than they expected, and I disappoint them, they toss me out. I'm on the street and have nothing again."

To Stephanie, help came with expectations, conditions, and responsibility. Most people who wanted to help her get off the street wanted her to get off drugs. "I'm not ready yet," she told me. At twenty-one, she was legally an adult, but she just wanted to be a kid. And she wanted to be a junkie.

• • • •

IT WAS EASIER to spend time with Stephanie after Fraggle was arrested. She missed him and was lonely. I had asked her to call me on my beeper whenever she wanted to see me, but she never did. Instead I went to the park to see her every few days. If I arrived too early and she was asleep, I waited for her to wake up. If I arrived after four in the afternoon, she was either with Lenny or had started networking for the night. After eight at night, it was nearly impossible to spend time with Stephanie alone. Every few minutes, customers came by her corner and asked which brands of dope were good and asked her to go get them some. She walked a block with them and then disappeared, calling over her shoulder, "I'll be right back." When she returned, anywhere from ten minutes to more than an hour later, another "custie" strolled by and she was gone again.

"Where were you yesterday?" she asked me one day. She seemed upset. I had told her I'd drop by but hadn't. I had assumed she wouldn't even notice. But I was wrong. From then on, I always showed up when I said I would, even if just for fifteen minutes.

One Saturday night, several weeks later, I was sitting with Stephanie on her blanket for nearly an hour when a man in his early forties, fit, his hair graying, came over. He wore jeans, a pressed denim shirt, and white sneakers, bright and new. He squatted down beside me, positioned himself on one knee and smiled. I was wearing a pair of baggy jeans and an oversized crumpled white T-shirt.

"Are you working tonight?" he asked me.

"I'm just visiting Stephanie," I said, turning my head away.

"How about some freelance work?"

"What do you have in mind?"

"I'll give you a tenner for a hand job." When I said no, he raised it to $15.

"Get away, pervert," Stephanie yelled.

He stood up, still smiling, and leaned back on the wall beside me for a few minutes, perhaps expecting me to change my mind. He then walked away and stood on the corner across the street, watching, waiting. About fifteen minutes later, he walked over to another young woman, perhaps nineteen, who was begging with her dog. Stub-tailed, skinny, and limping, the dog was not so much a pet but a tool used to generate cash. The man knelt beside her, his head only inches above the dog's. He talked to the girl. She listened, smiled, and then after a few minutes, she picked up her cup, stood up, and handed her dog's leash to a friend nearby. As she walked down the street, the man followed a few steps behind.

There was a relentless line of people who roamed the streets at all hours, willing to pay to have their sexual fantasies become reality. Leg Rub Steve paid more than $100 just to have his upper thigh rubbed; a Polish man on Sixth Street who preferred young boys paid $5 for blow jobs; a middle-aged married man from Brooklyn paid kids to squeeze his nipples while he jerked off. One man regularly offered Stephanie $100 to sit naked in the back seat of his car while he jerked off. She'd declined because she sensed that he wanted more.

Stephanie was offered money for sex all the time because she looked young and clean. When I first asked her if she had accepted any of the offers, she told me she hadn't because they disgusted her. About two months later, though, when I asked her again, she told me she had gone to a hotel with a man once, but because she had been so nervous, the man had left before anything happened. It wasn't until many months later that Stephanie admitted she'd had sex with him. She'd been too ashamed and embarrassed to tell me sooner. According to Stephanie, the man was in his thirties, handsome, and freshly shaved. He'd spotted Stephanie panhandling and had offered her $50 to give him a blow job. When Stephanie had refused, the man raised his price. At $200, Stephanie agreed.

They checked into the St. Marks hotel, about five blocks away. The hotel's sixty-six rooms went from $30 for transients who stayed for just a couple of hours to $80 a night for a double room with a bath. Only cash or personal checks were accepted. Stephanie and the man walked past a desk clerk who sat behind bulletproof glass on the second floor, then up a steep flight of narrow stairs to the room. Less than six months earlier, James Jones, a video technician, had walked up the same stairs with thirty-eight-year-old Sandra Lasure, a prostitute. Her nude body was found a few hours later lying face down on a bed in Room 19. She had been sodomized and strangled.

Once inside the room, with the door locked, the man offered Stephanie an extra $100 if she would have intercourse. Stephanie had never tricked before. She saw what happened to young girls who had prostituted themselves. "They look old and used," she told me. "I have too much self-respect for that."

This time, Stephanie hesitated. Finally, she convinced herself that "just one time" wouldn't do much harm. But when she insisted that he use a condom, the man protested. Stephanie threatened to leave. Eventually he agreed and left the room to buy condoms. Stephanie took off her clothes and showered. A few minutes later, the man returned.

Stephanie lay down naked on the polyester bedspread, her eyes fixed on a bare bulb screwed into the ceiling. After pulling down his pants, the man climbed on top of her, his shirt and socks still on. "You've got to chill out," he said. Stephanie's body was stiff, her muscles contracting. As he groped at her body, she lay motionless, holding her breath and turning her head to the side to avoid his mouth on her lips. She was nauseous and hoped she wouldn't throw up. The man put the condom on; seconds later, he was inside her. Stephanie said she squeezed her eyes closed, repeating to herself silently, "Please, God, hurry up."

Almost immediately, the man climbed off her, frustrated that Stephanie had been unresponsive. He thought if he got her some dope, she would relax. When he left, Stephanie got dressed. The man returned just minutes later. He'd seen police in front of the hotel. Abruptly, he told Stephanie she would have to leave.

"Give me my money," said Stephanie, standing by the door.

"You didn't do anything," he said.

"I'm not leaving without my fucking money." The man tossed a ten-dollar bill at her and pushed her out the door, slamming it shut.

Stephanie continued to protest, but the man wouldn't come out. Eventually, she picked up the bill, turned around, and walked down the stairs and onto the street. Angry she had been ripped off, Stephanie waited for the man outside the hotel. When she saw him about half an hour later picking up someone else, Stephanie yelled to the girl, "Hey, he fuckin' owes me money."

"That's your problem," the girl replied. "He's with me now." The two walked away.

When she was really dope sick, Stephanie occasionally agreed to "turn on" a man for money, always making it clear that he could not touch her. Usually she just stood there partially clothed as the man jerked off. The few times she let a man touch her, she remained fully clothed.

At times, she left with Louie, who paid girls to allow him to rub himself against their bodies. "The agreement is that the first time you go down a stairwell fully clothed, you smoke a cigarette while he's doing it," said Stephanie. "It's nothing. He rubs up against your side and touches you over your pants, and it takes about three seconds, and literally in three minutes he's done, and you get twenty-five bucks." Stephanie had done it a couple of times, but one time he'd started "talking dirty" to her and pulling up her shirt. "He was saying these nauseating, really disgusting things and trying to kiss me and taking his dick out and rubbing against me," she said. "Trying to get me to touch it and trying to kiss me and really pawing all over me, and I kept telling him to stop, and he kept doing it. At first, I thought, This is the easiest fuckin' money I've ever made. But he's disgusting. I won't see him again."

When she was dope sick, feverish and sweating, she was an easy target. One night, just a couple of weeks after I'd met her, a man in his fifties with waist-length gray hair told her he would pay her to dress up while he jerked off in the back of his van. Nauseous, her skin milk white and clammy, she finally agreed for $30. When he countered with $15, sensing the desperation in her voice, she said she wouldn't do it for less than $20. He agreed.

When Stephanie stood up, the man eyed her as if she were a prized cow. "You got any muscles? I like girls who have a little meat on their bones," he said. "Take off your jacket and let me see your arms."

Stephanie unzipped her sweatshirt and pulled it away from her body. She was nervous and self-conscious. "You're a little on the skinny side," he said, inspecting her arms.

Stephanie was humiliated. "Look, forget it. I don't fuckin' do this anyway. I don't need to be sized up by you. The only reason I was going to do this was because I was sick, and I'm not willing to do it anymore." She walked away.

The guy came looking for her later, which upset her even more. "It's bad enough that I'm seen walking around with Lenny," she told me.

After hours of panhandling, Stephanie's cup was filled with only about $4 in change. It was nearly midnight, yet there was a crowd on the corner where we sat. Stephanie was pleading, practically in tears for people to move away. Nobody seemed to listen. Finally, she got up. "I can't take this anymore," she said. "I've got to get out of here."

Stephanie lived in almost complete isolation on the street yet had no personal space. Tonight, she was desperate to be alone. We walked, Stephanie dragging her cart behind her, about three blocks to a dark, quiet street. Stephanie picked up a piece of cardboard from the ground, placed it on the sidewalk near a building, sat cross-legged on it, and put her cup in front of her.

A drunk man on an old three-speed bicycle pulled up to the curb. "Hey, I'd really like to get off tonight."

She said nothing. He rode away laughing.

"It never stops out here," she said. "They know I have a boyfriend, but they don't care. Sometimes I wish I weighed four hundred pounds, but that wouldn't even stop them." She put a cigarette to her lips and dropped her face over her hands to light the match, her hair falling dangerously close to the flame. She leaned her head back against the wall and started to cry. "Sometimes I just start crying," she said. "Do you blame me? You have to always be calm and patient and put up with so much shit because you never know when someone is going to just go off."

Just a few months earlier, sixty-four-year-old Ray Alvarez, owner of Ray's Candy Store, was hit on the head with a sidewalk grate by Hotdog, a skinny homeless woman who for years begged for change and cigarettes from passers-by. Although Hotdog sometimes heckled customers, Ray occasionally fed her and let her sleep in his basement. But one night while she was drunk, she slammed the grate on his head as he was leaving the basement of his store. Ray collapsed in a heap on the stairs. Hotdog was convicted of attempted assault in the second degree.

Staying on the streets with Stephanie, I'd seen a woman smash a beer bottle over her partner's head, a man punch his bench-mate square in the nose, and another man pull a meat cleaver from his long wool coat, the wide shiny blade cutting through the air.

Stephanie had been spit on, pushed to the ground, punched hard in the face, and chased by a homeless man throwing cans of food at her. She had learned to expect the worst. "I'd like to trust people, but I've been screwed too many times," she told me. "You can only take so many times trusting people and being let down and being robbed and beaten up and touched and taken advantage of." And although she loved Fraggle, the longer she was with him, the less she trusted him. "I trust him for certain things, but I don't trust Fraggle to take care of my money. I don't trust him to be straight with me when I ask him where he's been when he disappears for a long time, because I know that he lies to me so that he won't get bitched at."

Stephanie had already made $10, enough for a bag of dope. Now at one a.m., she was panhandling for money for a second bag for the morning, so when she woke up sick, she wouldn't have to worry about getting her fix. "Fuck it," she said finally and stood up. She threw the plastic cup she was using in the trash.

She was tired. It looked like it was going to rain, and she rummaged through her cart for her umbrella and a large garbage bag she used as a slicker. When she found them, she placed them on top of the pile. We sat quietly for a while.

"All Fraggle and I want is an apartment and jobs like normal people," said Stephanie. "We used to dream of having an apartment where we could eat Cap'n Crunch cereal and watch cartoons."

She stopped, not wanting to say more, perhaps attempting to hang on to the dream. But she couldn't hold on. "I'm scared. I'm afraid that me and Fraggle are going to get better and that either he's going to die or some great big disaster is going to happen, and everything is going to be taken away from me." She then leaned back, took off her sneakers, and closed her eyes. "I really miss Fraggle."

As she rested, a thick short man of forty, his head balding, staggered over to where we were sitting. He stopped in front of Stephanie, bent over, and with a wide grin said, "Hey, I'd really like to come in your face tonight."

. . . .

A THICK STACK of the *New York Times* crashed to the ground inches from her head, but Stephanie didn't flinch. She lay sleeping in front of a storefront on Avenue A, swaddled in a stained acrylic blanket, her childlike feet bare and blistered.

A police car pulled up to the curb, and an officer got out and walked toward her. With one hand resting on his hip, the other on his nightstick, he stood silently above her, the tips of his shoes on the flattened cardboard box she used as her mattress.

Without warning, he smacked his nightstick, as if swatting a fly, against the metal store gate beside where she lay. "Hey, wake up and go to the park," he said. Stephanie's head had been too close to the metal gate; she was shaking, her ears ringing. Drawing the blanket over her head, she pulled her knees to her chest. It was August, yet she was shivering, her skin dotted with goosebumps. She had been awake for more than forty-eight hours before collapsing from exhaustion at four that morning.

While Fraggle was in jail, Stephanie was awakened regularly by the police. She told me she'd been woken up twice by a police officer kicking her in the head and in the back. One morning, a cop had smacked her on the soles of her blistered feet with his nightstick, yelling, "Get up, you piece of street trash."

But the police were not always the bad guys. Stephanie was often left alone by police officers who knew she was on heroin, and if they wanted to, they could have found a reason to arrest her. The one time she had been arrested, she was treated well. Just one week after returning to New York from rehab in Georgia, Stephanie had gone, with $70 and a single bag of dope in her pocket, to cop at a local drug spot, but when she arrived, no one answered the door. Police stopped her as she was leaving the building, and they found the one bag of dope she had stashed in her pocket. Stephanie was taken to the Ninth Precinct, where she stayed for four hours, and then to Central Booking at 100 Center Street. She appeared before a judge the next day, who released her, sentencing her only to a four-hour drug education class and a tour of a drug rehabilitation center.

"Get up now or I'll take you downtown," the officer said. "You're wearing out your welcome here." She recognized the voice. Some police officers would let her sleep, but this one, patrolling the neighborhood for just a few weeks, didn't like her and let her know it. "Working people shouldn't have to start their day walking by you passed out on the sidewalk," he said.

The officer struck the gate a second time, and Stephanie staggered to her feet. Still groggy, she piled her bedding into her cart. "It's not even six a.m.," she complained. "I'm not bothering anyone."

"You kids are like animals," he said. "Look at the mess you've made. Go home."

"I have no home," she shouted back. "My mother is dead." When she turned, she was crying.

Stephanie rolled her cart across the street to the park. She sat on a bench and stared quietly ahead. "They took down Merlin's memorial yesterday," she told me. Just a week earlier, forty-one-year-old Paul Hogan, a homeless man who went by the name of Merlin and who was a popular fixture on Avenue A and Sixth Street, had died of internal bleeding from liver failure and chronic ulcers. To neighborhood residents, homeless and not, Merlin was a raconteur and philosopher, both witty and generous. To Stephanie, he was a friend. He'd watch Stephanie's cart and deliver messages between her and Fraggle. When Stephanie was upset and crying, she'd often sit by Merlin, who, with a half-pint of Wild Irish Rose in his hand, would recite poetry and talk in rhyme. But more than that, when Stephanie was upset, Merlin would listen. "I loved Merlin and felt safe with him," said Stephanie. "Everything he said was from his heart. He really cared about me."

Merlin had survived eight winters on the street, losing three toes to frostbite. At a memorial service, more than 100 people paid tribute to him with songs, poems, and anecdotes. Then, for more than a week after his death, friends kept a twenty-four-hour vigil at the patch of sidewalk where he slept, which was crowded with candles, flowers, photographs, and children's drawings. When the police dismantled the makeshift shrine, Stephanie cried. "We can't have that," she said sarcastically. "We can't have anybody caring about homeless people."

The police officer had reminded Stephanie that she was little more than a sidewalk obstruction. She felt unwanted and alone. She missed Merlin. She also missed her panda bear. A few days earlier, she gave a group of squatters some change to watch her cart; when she returned fifteen minutes later, it was gone. She got her stuff back, but not her bear. She heard that the kids had gotten drunk and strung it up high on a fence somewhere.

Stephanie pulled a pair of thick jeans out of one of her duffel bags and rolled them tightly to use as a pillow on the bench. "I'm just going to sleep an hour," she said. "Are you going to still be here when I wake up?"

I told her I would.

"Will you wake me if you leave?" she asked.

"I'm not leaving."

"But will you wake me if you do?"

I nodded. Then she slept until noon.

. . . .

I SAW STEPHANIE again five days later.

"I was fuckin' robbed last night," she told me. She'd gone to sleep with $6, but in the morning, her blue vinyl coin purse, which she kept pinned to the waistband of her pants, was empty. When she checked her cart, she saw that two pairs of a brand-new three-pack of white sweat socks, dropped off for her the night before by a friend, were also missing. She had planned to give them to Fraggle when he got out of jail.

She bent down, grabbed her blanket, and stuffed it in her cart. She scanned the block for someone she knew to borrow money from for her first bag. Then she saw Ricardo.

Ricardo was in his late forties or early fifties, and looked as though he had been handsome at one time. I was told that he had been active in the Young Lords, a group of radical Puerto Rican youth formed in the late 1960s. The Young Lords had had its headquarters on East Third Street and advocated both political revolution and self-help programs for the Puerto Rican poor. I was also told that over the past decade, Ricardo had been periodically homeless and in and out of alcohol treatment programs.

Most of the time, Ricardo was lucid, yet once in awhile, he would just scream for no apparent reason. He'd been hauled away by ambulance more than a few times during one of these episodes. Others called him an operator, suggesting

that his fits were a performance, an attempt to get hospitalized and off the streets for a few days. Today, Ricardo was
wearing what he generally wore—black jeans, a black leather
vest over a bare chest and fat belly—and, as usual, he was
drunk.

Stephanie was staring at the beaming white socks he had
on his otherwise bare feet. The day before, Ricardo had left
his cowboy boots on the curb while he slept. When he woke
up, they were gone, along with the garbage he'd been sleeping near.

She started yelling at him, but Ricardo kept walking.
"Fuck you, I don't take your money or your socks," he said.
Stephanie started following him up the block, shouting at
him. Even when she spit at him, he kept walking, yelling
"Fuck you" back at her. After about a block, Stephanie gave
up. She was tired and her joints ached.

At nine that evening, Ricardo returned. Stephanie was
sitting on her blanket, her knees pulled up close to her chest.
The sweat socks, still on his feet had turned a dirty brown.
Still drunk, and standing a few feet, away, he said, "Hey, if
you spit at me again, I'm going to smack the shit out of you."

Stephanie was about half the size of Ricardo, but she
stood up, pulling up her pants, which were hanging below
her navel. "You're such a big man—you rob a little girl."

"Fuck that shit. You spit at me. I'm going to smack the
shit out of you." He stood about three feet away from
Stephanie. "You can fuck your friends out here, 'cause I'm
going to rock your shit. You better respect me."

Stephanie and Ricardo continued screaming at each
other. One threw a false punch to the face, the other attempted a kick, inching toward each other and then rebounding
back at the slightest movement. For more than five minutes,
the two continued, advancing and retreating as they hollered,

their movements fluid but cautious. "Let a real maniac kill you," said Ricardo, his spit splashing Stephanie's cheek and eye. She wiped it from her face with the sleeve of her hooded sweatshirt. "Let a real maniac do all kinds of things to you, kid."

"They all do, motherfucker," she screamed. Her face was tomato red.

People stopped and gathered on each side to watch. Everyone wanted something to see, something to report. They listened as Ricardo threatened Stephanie; some laughed as Stephanie stood her ground. Such fights on the street were common: entertaining to the spectators, often forgotten within hours by the participants.

"She wakes up every morning sweating and shit," said Ricardo addressing his new audience. More spit flew from his mouth with each sentence, forcing Stephanie to repeatedly wipe her face.

Stephanie started to back away. Ricardo was getting too close. I screamed at him to leave her alone. He heard nothing. "Shut your fuckin' teeth. You spit on me again, and you try to kick me again," he said inching even closer.

"Get the fuck away from me," Stephanie interrupted. She was scared. Ricardo had backed her up against a metal gate. Without warning, he smashed his right hand, just above her head.

Stephanie darted away from the wall and bolted down the street. She ran to a police car parked up the block. "He stole all my money while I was sleeping, and I spit on him," Stephanie told the officer sitting in the passenger seat. "That was ten hours ago, and he's gone crazy." The officer opened his door, got out of the car, and walked back to the corner with Stephanie.

Meanwhile, Ricardo had walked steadily, quietly down

the street in the opposite direction. By the time the officer had arrived, Ricardo was gone.

Stephanie dropped to the ground. "I've got to fuckin' deal with this shit," she cried. "They're fuckin' proud of it—to be old school here. That fucker would have hit me."

It started raining. Stephanie pulled a shiny new trash bag out of her cart, ripped a hole in it, and then put it over her head. Then she ran down the street, promising me she would be back soon. I waited for her inside Leshko's.

When she returned an hour and a half later, she was mellow, relaxed from the shot of dope she had just done. It had stopped raining, so we went outside to her cart, which she'd left under an awning to keep dry. She dug her hand into the pile and fished out a plastic bag.

In it were comic books she had gotten for Fraggle—X-Force and Excalibur. "Fraggle loves X-Factor and Wolverine," she told me. "We used to collect Animaniacs [cartoon character toys distributed in children's meals] from McDonald's."

She had also made him a card. She'd gotten a piece of white paper, found some wallpaper and sparkles in the garbage, and borrowed glue, scissors, and magic markers from Ray's Candy Store. On the outside of the card she had written a big "21" and inside, with neat childlike block letters, "Happy Birthday Fraggle." She had added a note: "I love you, baby, more than you'll ever know. I promise you that we will be able to spend your birthday together. Hang in there kid, I'll always love you." She'd drawn a big red heart on it. She addressed the envelope carefully for Rikers Island, making sure to include his inmate number and cell block, handed it to me, and asked me to mail it.

· · · ·

WHEN I SAW Stephanie the next day, she was sitting on the sidewalk tossing in the air a four-inch bronze statue of a cheerleader. It had been presented to her as a gift, along with a garbage bag full of mini-trophies embossed with "Second Place Borough Champion Girls Volleyball League, NYC Housing Authority 1967."

"I hate cheerleaders and what they represent—stupid prostituting women, sluts," said Stephanie. Her face hardened, her voice angry. "They give women a very bad name." Stephanie walked over to a trash can and pulled out a plastic bag. With her teeth, she ripped off the handle, then tied the plastic, like a noose, around the trophy's neck. With a lit match, she melted the plastic to keep it from slipping. Once she was finished, Stephanie walked over to the corner, climbed up onto the base of the "Don't Walk" sign and, with great effort, hung the statue from it. Only when the cheerleader was dangling above Stephanie's head did she seem satisfied.

Later, when I asked Stephanie why she hated cheerleaders so much, she told me: "Throughout my childhood I was rejected and harassed by people like them—the most popular girls—because I didn't have the clothes or the money to be like them. They made my life miserable. They still make me sick today."

. . . .

SIX-YEAR-OLD STEPHANIE often played by herself in the basement of her mother's house in Bay Village, Ohio, a suburb of Cleveland. Like most girls her age, Stephanie's favorite companions were her Barbie and Ken dolls. Yet while other girls imagined Barbie and Ken falling in love, getting married, and living happily ever after, Stephanie's Ken always left Barbie. The scenario was a familiar one to Stephanie. When Stephanie was just two years old, her father moved out, leaving her mother, Susan, alone to raise Stephanie and her six-year-old sister Laura.

Bay Village is on a five-mile rectangular piece of land on Lake Erie. The smaller houses, two- and three-bedroom bungalows and ranch houses averaging almost $100,000 in the late 1990s, were located in the far east end of the village. The larger homes and properties, starting at $300,000 and exceeding $1 million, were located in the far west end and along the northern lakefront. Stephanie lived in central Bay, closer to the east end, in a small three-bedroom ranch house on a quiet tree-lined street.

Susan had eloped when she was eighteen. She was a high school graduate and worked as a data processor at a hospital and as a clerk for an accountant. Susan was extremely emotional and at times grew extremely depressed. After her husband left, Susan had to be hospitalized for a few months. Stephanie was told years later that her mother had had a nervous breakdown. One day, when Stephanie was still in grade school, she returned home to find her mother on the floor in the family room, a half-empty bottle of pills on the carpet beside her. Stephanie never knew if her mother had ever been diagnosed with clinical depression, but she was told when she got older that her maternal grandfather was mentally ill, although she was given few details.

On her own, Susan struggled to raise two children and pay the mortgage on the new house. In her spare time, she took classes at the local university, trying to get her bachelor's degree. She relied heavily on her mother and babysitters to watch Stephanie and Laura.

When we talked of her mother, Stephanie's eyes often welled with tears, her voice quiet, hesitant. Stephanie vividly remembered the hurt her mother had caused her, but she also remembered her love. "She used to tell me all the time that she loved me and hug me," Stephanie told me. "I used to try to give her a little hug, and she would say, 'A hug isn't a hug unless it lasts fifteen seconds.' You just don't want it when you're a kid, but now I'd give anything to have it."

Stephanie and her mother fought regularly, and Stephanie lived in fear of her mother's emotional outbursts. Once, when Stephanie was three, she threw the clothes from the hamper into the bathtub and hid in the basket until her mother calmed down. Often, when angry, Susan blamed her children for her problems, saying, "I can't have anything because you kids are in my life," or "I can't have a man because of you." What Stephanie remembers most, though, was her mother reminding her of her dad's desertion, yelling, sometimes in her face, "You're the reason your dad left me."

Stephanie, at times, would rub the skin around the corners of her eyes until it bled. "It was my way of getting attention," she told me. "I remember wanting other people to see that I was abused, but my mom would drop me off with the babysitter and tell her I'd done it myself and that would be the end of it."

In grade school, Stephanie dreaded returning home on summer evenings. While other girls were greeted at home by mothers who offered them home-baked cookies or asked concerned questions about their day, Stephanie often returned to a dark house and a mother who sat alone weeping by candle-light. On these nights, Stephanie sat outside on the lawn, the grass wrinkling beneath her, staring up at the stars.

When Stephanie was seven, her mother remarried. When Susan and Ron told the girls they were getting married, Stephanie ran across the room, dived face down onto the couch, and cried. "I'm not sure why I was so upset," said

Stephanie. "Maybe I just knew that he would end up leaving, too."

Five years later, Ron did leave. Initially Stephanie had felt he was an intruder. When he tried to be a father, Stephanie resisted and fought back. Ron and Susan fought frequently, but Stephanie gradually grew closer to Ron and eventually loved him. When Ron and Susan divorced, Susan again blamed Stephanie.

Growing up, Stephanie and her sister never wanted for the basics of life. Yet a decade later, what Stephanie remembered most about her childhood was feeling deprived. Susan worried constantly about money and not being able to pay the bills. At one point, when the girls were in grade school, Susan had to withdraw the girls' small savings they had collected from birthdays and holidays to pay the bills. "I lived around a lot of rich kids who got everything they wanted," said Stephanie. "I never had anything they had and they were always mean about it."

Status was important in Bay Village. "It was all about spending money and having expensive things," said Connie Prok, whose son attended school with Stephanie. "A lot of the kids from the east end could not afford what the kids from the west end had, so half the community was going into debt to get their kids what they needed just to belong. If you had parents who couldn't afford to buy what the other kids had, you were out. You were ridiculed and ostracized. Stephanie felt like she never fit in."

In fourth grade, the girls *had* to have Forenza V-neck sweaters. Nobody knew that Stephanie's hot pink V-neck sweater was not a Forenza until one day a classmate, Trudi, grabbed the back of the sweater to check the label. When Trudi made her discovery, she shrieked and spread the news throughout the school. Stephanie was humiliated. By sixth grade Forenza sweaters were out, and Coca-Cola shirts were in. "I got one for Christmas, but by then something else was in style," said Stephanie. One day, when the girls noticed she had worn the same pair of jeans two days in a row, they called her "gutter trash." At the time, Stephanie only owned two pairs of jeans.

Although Stephanie still has vivid memories of the harassment she endured, she admitted she was not always the victim. As in most schools, roles reversed frequently as new friendships and cliques formed. In fifth grade, Stephanie and her best friend became the aggressors, harassing one girl to the point that she was afraid to go to lunch and to walk to and from school.

While Stephanie dreaded going to school, Laura was a flag girl in high school and made friends easily. Unlike Stephanie, Laura preferred to blend in with the crowd. She was an achiever: She did what she was told, and she did well. "We fought all the time, but we were close," said Laura. "We were fist-fighters. She was a real fighter."

At twelve and entering adolescence, Stephanie was typical of many girls her age: She was emotional, self-absorbed, preoccupied with peer approval, and forming her own identity. She was often depressed, restless, and awkward. Mostly, though, she was angry. Toward her mother, Stephanie felt obligated and resentful, loving and angry, close and distant, all at the same time.

A wrong look could send either Susan or Stephanie into a screaming rage. They frequently destroyed each other's things and hurled breakable objects at each other. Susan ripped posters off the wall in Stephanie's room, took Stephanie's bedroom door off its hinges, and tore up her daughter's favorite clothes. When Stephanie was twelve, Susan grabbed a pair of scissors and cut Stephanie's new $80

Benetton sweater, which Stephanie had paid for with her Christmas money. Sometimes Susan ordered her to leave the house, and Stephanie would, slamming the door behind her. She would return, often hours later, but when she didn't return or left without permission, her mother called the police, who usually found her and brought her back. Susan often told Stephanie she was a bad child and a constant disappointment. During one of their fights, Stephanie screamed at her mother in retaliation, "I wish you could get cancer or something so you could have something really serious to bitch about." Years after her mother died from cancer, Stephanie still felt guilty.

Stephanie always felt she was a disappointment to her family, even though throughout most of grade school she was always in the top third of her class. So when her mother and aunts praised her artistic abilities and even enrolled her in art classes at a community program, Stephanie felt only pressure to meet her family's high expectations. "I was just average, and I was fine with that," she said. "But everyone wanted me to become a great artist, even though it wasn't what I wanted. I wanted to be something, not because somebody else wanted it for me, but for myself. And I didn't want to disappoint anyone when I couldn't meet their expectations."

When Stephanie started seventh grade, she began to hang out with the skateboarders. Unlike most of the kids at school who proudly wore Benetton sweaters and Liz Claiborne clothes, these kids wore baggy T-shirts and plaid polyester pants that they'd cut off at the knees. Instead of listening to pop artists like Madonna, Whitney Houston, and Bon Jovi, the skateboarders listened to punk rock groups such as the Misfits, the Ramones, and Bad Brains who celebrated the outrageous and the obnoxious. Stephanie loved that these teens did not conform to the standards set by the school and community she lived in. With these kids, she could be herself without being judged. Whereas others in school were starting to smoke marijuana and drink alcohol, these kids were "straight edge"—they didn't drink or do drugs. Neither did Stephanie, and she became "straight edge" like them.

Stephanie enjoyed hanging out with these kids, yet grew curious about those who experimented with drugs. She started smoking cigarettes, and although she got drunk a few times, she stayed away from other drugs.

When Stephanie met Ronda, the summer before eighth grade, her behavior changed dramatically. "Ronda was bad, and I loved it," said Stephanie. Stephanie cut school regularly with Ronda and started stealing makeup and clothes from the local Drugmart. At a time when Stephanie felt inferior to others around her, Ronda was the one person who made her feel good about herself. Ronda told Stephanie, "Just because you don't have money, it doesn't mean you're a bad person. You don't have to be like them."

Stephanie had broken up with John, her first serious boyfriend, around the time she met Ronda. John was four years older than thirteen-year-old Stephanie and was straight edge. Their relationship had lasted almost a year—until John found out that Stephanie had betrayed him: She'd kissed another boy. John confronted Stephanie at the beach. "John tried to karate kick me and beat my ass in front of all his friends, and all they did was just laugh," said Stephanie. "I was heartbroken. I was humiliated in front of all those people who just kept laughing at me. I sat there crying, and nobody gave a shit. They thought it was fuckin' hilarious."

In eighth grade, Stephanie cut classes regularly to hang out with Ronda. When she was given twenty days of in-school suspension at the high school where John was a student, Stephanie began to cut those days as well, this time because she was scared. At the high school, John's friends followed her through the hallways, calling her "whore," "bitch," and "white trash." They started rumors about her and threatened to beat her up. One day, she found a porcelain doll with its head broken off lying on her front porch. About the same time, she also learned that her mother was dying.

.....

SUSAN had no health insurance, so when she felt pain in her left armpit, she decided not to see a doctor. Months later, when she was no longer able to bear the pain, Susan finally went to the emergency room. Doctors discovered a cancerous tumor above her right lung; the pain was caused by the tumor hitting a nerve. Stephanie was starting eighth grade.

Susan immediately began radiation treatment, yet less than a month later, she learned that the cancer had spread to her brain. Susan continued with radiation treatments and chemotherapy. Her skin turned yellow and then brownish-green. She lost all her hair, her face ballooned, and she developed scabs on her scalp, neck, chest, and back.

When Susan was first diagnosed, Stephanie cried for days. In the following months, she was depressed, had frequent thoughts of suicide, and broke into tears regularly. She was also angry and resentful. More than anything, even though she knew it wasn't possible, she felt responsible.

Up to this point, Stephanie had never used drugs. But she had grown increasingly isolated. The only students who seemed to want to spend time with her when she was depressed were the ones who smoked pot. In the beginning, she hung out with them without smoking, but one day when she was feeling miserable, she saw one of her friends giggling and laughing after he'd gotten stoned. Stephanie, wanting desperately to feel good again, joined him. The first time she smoked marijuana, she loved it. It was getting dark, and a walk through the woods turned into an adventure, with shadows and trees coming alive with each step. Stephanie was laughing again and her depression instantly lifted. "I had so much fun," she said. "For a few hours, I was able to escape from my life."

As her mother got sicker, Stephanie got progressively more depressed. She stopped sleeping at night, skipped school, and began to smoke pot regularly. Smoking pot not only helped her to relax and feel good but also gave her an identity. As a "pothead," a "burnout," Stephanie knew how to behave and what was expected of her. Her fifteen-year-old boyfriend Michael, her only friend at the time, was a social introvert who smoked pot every day. With Michael, Stephanie could get high, have adventures in the woods, at the creek, or in the sewer tunnels, or just sit in the basement and listen to music, watch cartoons, and talk about life. With Michael, she could also talk about her mother.

Susan and Stephanie now fought more bitterly than ever before. One minute Susan would ground Stephanie; the next, she'd throw her out of the house. Once, Susan purposely let Stephanie's six-month-old puppy out the door. Other times, she would yell at Stephanie, "You made this happen to me. You prayed for this." Stephanie, in retaliation, responded with words that she'd later regret. She called her mother "a bitch" and a "stupid fucking cancer patient." When Stephanie apologized, Susan told her she didn't believe her, which hurt and infuriated Stephanie even more. At one point, Stephanie even tape-recorded her mother to show her how irrational she had become. When she played it for her during another fight, her mother just screamed. "I felt so not heard," said Stephanie. "No matter how loud I yelled." The police and Ron came to the house regularly, acting as mediators between mother and daughter.

One day when Michael looked up in the *Physicians Desk Reference* the medications Susan was taking, Stephanie realized the pills could also help make her own pain go away. She started with codeine and then one night took eight Adavans, which made her laugh one minute and cry hysterically the next; eventually she threw up all over the basement. She began taking her mother's Dilaudid pills daily. She grew increasingly withdrawn and began to watch television constantly. "*The Donna Reed Show*, *Mr. Ed*, and *Patty Duke* were my favorites," said Stephanie. "I loved the fact that people pretended to see life that way."

During this time, Stephanie's aunts and grandmother began coming to the house in shifts to watch Susan and hired a nurse when they were unable to be there. When Stephanie's aunts noticed that sixty-six out of one hundred Dilaudid pills had disappeared in one week, they put Susan's medication in a locked box and bolted it to the floor in the bedroom closet. Her aunts never confronted Stephanie about the pills. "When I got caught and had no more pills, I felt twice as lost, twice as angry and more scared," said Stephanie. "Then I felt guilty. How could I take my mother's medicine when she was dying? My family obviously knew what was going on. I was so ashamed." Stephanie's grandmother, her aunts, at times even Laura yelled at Stephanie for behaving so badly toward her mother. "Everybody kept telling Stephanie how awful she was," said Connie Prok. "Stephanie had nobody to go to except Michael." When she spoke about her mother, Stephanie showed no emotion. Alone with Michael, she cried all the time.

Susan stopped trying to get Stephanie to go to school or

even to wake up in the morning. Eventually, the school filed truancy charges, and Stephanie was put on probation. But she continued to miss classes. With two months left in the academic school year, Stephanie was expelled.

The following year, she attended a small Lutheran school, from which she was also expelled after a few months, again for truancy. During this time, she was also arrested for public intoxication. She was sent back to the original school she had been thrown out of and placed on probation. Stephanie kept skipping classes but continued to see her assigned social worker. "They were supposed to send me away for violating probation, but they didn't do anything," said Stephanie. "They felt sorry for me because my mom was dying."

Susan's health deteriorated rapidly. Laura was away at college, and although she often came home on weekends, Stephanie was alone with her mother much of the time. Eventually, Susan didn't have the strength even to walk. In the weeks before she died, Stephanie and Susan stopped fighting, and Stephanie spent much of her time in the basement or in her room by herself, coming out only when her mother needed her to carry her to the bathroom and hold her up on the toilet. Her mother's skin turned pea green and brown. Stephanie couldn't bear to look at her. When Susan died a year and a half after she was diagnosed with cancer, Stephanie was relieved. She was fifteen.

The day after her mother died, Stephanie sat quietly, alone in her bedroom. She was scared and wondered how she was going to manage on her own. Lying on her bed, staring at the ceiling, she heard a knock on her door. Stephanie looked at the tall man standing in the doorway and knew immediately who it was. All her life she had heard from her mother how her father had abandoned the family and left them to struggle on their own. Now, thirteen years later, Stephanie felt little more than resentment for the man who stood before her.

At the funeral she sat with Michael, apart from the rest of her family. She was heartbroken, but more than anything else, she felt alone and unsupported by her family. "I know they lost a sister, but I was hurting," she told me. "All they could see was that I was just a bad kid."

Stephanie still needed someplace to live. A couple of days after the funeral, her father asked her to come live with him, but Stephanie immediately said no. Instead, she moved into her aunt Mary Ann's house, the only aunt who had offered to take her in. But Mary Ann was a devout Christian and missionary, and after a couple of days, Stephanie left. "She was all about rules and God, and I wasn't hearing it," said Stephanie. She decided she could live only with her stepfather, Ron.

"It was a decision I'd made partially with my wife, but it was more mine," said Ron. "I took her in because she was my daughter. Nancy, my wife, agreed mostly for me. They got along for about five minutes. Nancy told her, 'OK, you're here and you'll be treated no differently than anybody else in issuing commands and chores.' But at one point, Stephanie told her that she wasn't her mother and she wasn't going to listen. They're both hard people. They both hit a wall, and they never meshed."

Nancy had four kids of her own, and Stephanie from the start felt that Nancy didn't want her living with them. But according to Connie Prok, who told me that Nancy was "just horrible" to Stephanie, "Stephanie also found Nancy's buttons very quickly and learned how to use them." Often angry, Stephanie admitted that she would blast loud music in the room she shared with one of Nancy's daughters, called

Nancy a bitch to her face, and regularly told her that she hated her.

But Stephanie, when talking about her time with Ron and Nancy, focused on the threat she said she regularly received from Nancy—that she would be sent to live with her father if she didn't toe the line. She knew that Ron loved her, but she always felt unwanted.

When Stephanie moved in with Ron and Nancy, she hadn't been to school in months, so she was immediately enrolled in a new school in Lakewood, again in the eighth grade. But Stephanie went to school only three days each week and only to see Michael. All she wanted to do was to get high. She stayed out late almost every night and rummaged through the medicine cabinets looking for drugs.

Ron and Nancy tried to gain control over the situation by imposing strict house rules. Stephanie could not watch television during the week and could not go out on weeknights. If Stephanie got caught skipping study hall, she'd have to stay home on weekends as well. Stephanie wasn't used to living in a house with rules.

Eventually, though, during her sophomore year in high school, Stephanie started going to school every day. "I only went to get out of the house," said Stephanie. At her new school, Stephanie wasn't harassed, and she did well academically, getting A's and B's. When she came home in the afternoon, she would run to her room, lock the door, draw, and cry. She started eating obsessively and gained fifteen pounds.

Stephanie continued to feel like a visitor in her new home. "Nancy sat me down one night and said, 'You offend everyone in this house—your hygiene, your morality, your friends, your music,'" said Stephanie. "Then she asked me if I had plans for when I turned eighteen. When I said no, she said, 'Well I suggest you start making them. We don't want you to live here.'" When Stephanie asked Ron if he felt the same way, she said that Ron admitted that, at times, he did.

Laura, who was a student at Kent State University, knew that her sister was miserable and agreed to let Stephanie live with her over the summer. Laura's intention was to move back to Cleveland after she graduated in the fall and have Stephanie live with her until she finished high school. But although Stephanie was turning eighteen in October, Ron would not let her live with her sister. "I feared Stephanie would never finish high school if she left," said Ron.

Laura went to a referee in juvenile court and was given custody of her sister. Stephanie moved in with Laura in a house near campus that summer. After Laura graduated, they moved back to Lakewood, just in time for Stephanie's junior year.

Back home, Stephanie grew increasingly isolated. "I would sit at home all day, drink beer, watch *Columbo* marathons on television, and play with my cats," she said. Her boyfriend at the time was an alcoholic and the two fought constantly. Stephanie gained thirty pounds. When she looked at herself in the mirror, she was disgusted. She started throwing up her food and taking laxatives to try to lose weight.

At Christmas of her junior year, Ron's fear came true: Stephanie decided to drop out of school. On her eighteenth birthday two months earlier, Stephanie had inherited some money. Her mother's house had been sold for $80,000, and after medical bills were paid, Stephanie and her sister each received $25,000. "I had all this money in the bank. I thought, I don't have to go to school," said Stephanie. "I was getting drunk every night until five o'clock in the morning and then having to wake up at seven for school. I just couldn't do it anymore, and I decided not to. I still regret it today."

Stephanie moved in with her new boyfriend, Bruce, paying rent at both her sister's and Bruce's apartment. Bruce had hazel eyes, thick black eyelashes, multiple tattoos, and Stephanie adored him. Stephanie first tried heroin with Bruce, and within three months they had developed between the two of them a $600-a-day habit, all with Stephanie's money. She had never learned to manage money, and she was rapidly spending it, withdrawing hundreds of dollars each day from her cash machine for alcohol, her rent, her friend's rent, CDs, video games, new clothes, drugs, and a pair of wedding bands: She and Bruce had decided to get married in Las Vegas. But the trip would cost more than she had expected. Just before they left, Stephanie discovered that her friend had stolen her bank card. It was a holiday weekend, and without the bank card she wouldn't be able to access her account for days, so she hocked their wedding bands, all her CDs, and her video games to pay for their trip. In Vegas, she and Bruce shot dope, ate acid, and got robbed of $800 at gunpoint.

In four months, Stephanie went through $20,000. Not until she was told at the bank that she would have to wait six months to cash the last of her money, a $2,500 bond, did she realize she had nothing left. She started screaming and then crying, falling to the floor in front of the teller. She owed her dealer $140, had no money left, and was nauseous and shaking, her body craving heroin.

Over the next two weeks, Stephanie and Bruce kicked their dope habit. Six weeks later, they started shooting cocaine. They were selling acid to pay for it. The adrenaline rush hooked them immediately, and their lives rapidly spiraled once again out of control. Stephanie's arms were now constantly swollen and bruised, and the needles they used were so dull that the plungers often got stuck. Stephanie stopped bathing and eating, and she rarely slept. On cocaine, she and Bruce were constantly paranoid and delusional. They stopped paying their rent and eventually were evicted from their apartment. Stephanie was broke again, and she had sold nearly everything she owned, including her stereo, microwave, television, and an opal ring that had belonged to her mother. She and Bruce even traded in a broken-down Volkswagen Rabbit they owned for one and a half grams of coke, worth about $100.

When their dealer told them they could live with him rent-free as long as they sold his cocaine, Bruce agreed. Stephanie at first thought it was a bad idea, but when she later agreed, Bruce refused to let her live with them. He also told her she'd have to start paying him for her drugs. After supporting his habit and keeping a roof over his head for months, Stephanie was deeply hurt. She went to live with her sister.

In the two years they spent together, Stephanie and Bruce fought constantly, often humiliating one another in the process. Their arguments were mostly about drugs and Stephanie's jealousy of Bruce being with other women. Bruce regularly threatened to leave Stephanie, a pattern Stephanie would repeat on the streets of New York with Fraggle.

One night at Bruce's house, she decided she'd had enough. Bruce had been speedballing all day, and Stephanie wanted to do dope again—she hadn't done any for six weeks. But Bruce wouldn't give her any. As Stephanie yelled, Bruce kept nodding out, his head bobbing back and forth. All she wanted was to be heard, and he wouldn't listen to her—the same way she'd felt as a child with her mother. Stephanie decided then that she wanted to kill herself.

When she told Bruce that she just wanted to die, he stood up, walked over to the table, picked up a razor blade, and handed it to Stephanie before passing out again.

The blade was very dull, but Stephanie started sawing

back and forth, first her left wrist, then her right. When she started bleeding, she squeezed the blood out, but after a few minutes, the bleeding stopped. She tried again and again, digging deeper each time. The pain was excruciating, and she was crying hysterically. Finally after two hours, she lay down on the floor, prayed to God to let her die, and passed out.

The next day she woke up to see her wrists crusted with blood. Bruce and his friends started laughing at her. "I felt shame and self-pity," she said. "I thought, I can't even kill myself right."

Eventually Bruce followed his mother to Florida. When she finally was able to cash her $2,500 bond, Stephanie joined him a few months later. She and Bruce rented a small efficiency near Tampa, where they lived for ten months. In Florida, Bruce worked from noon to nine p.m. in a telemarketing firm, raising money to set up drug education programs in North Carolina schools. He and Stephanie sold pot and acid to supplement their income. "I was a little housewife," said Stephanie. "I made lunch and dinner and kept the house clean. I played with my cats and watched cartoons."

Stephanie weighed herself constantly. She took laxatives and threw up regularly. When she didn't lose weight, she started starving herself and eventually dropped down to ninety pounds. Taking drugs helped keep her thin. Stephanie and Bruce smoked pot and ate acid. Stephanie also started taking pills every night: Hydrocodone, an opiate and pain killer, and Xanax, a tranquilizer. She developed seizures when she didn't take the pills. She was addicted. Eventually, Bruce lost his job, and they moved back to Ohio.

Back home, Stephanie worked in a bakery, Bruce in telemarketing. Stephanie was doing Ecstasy and smoking pot, and Bruce began to shoot Adavans. They hadn't shot heroin for a year and a half, but one day after being back in Ohio almost four months, Bruce told Stephanie he had gotten a dope connection through some of their old friends. A week later, Stephanie was spending the night at her sister's house when she was awakened by her friends. "Stephanie, you have to wake up," said one girl, nudging her shoulder. Stephanie opened her eyes. "Bruce died in his sleep."

Stephanie had left Bruce just hours earlier at a friend's house. They had been shooting dope all evening, but after awhile, Stephanie stopped. She begged Bruce to leave with her, but Bruce gave her a kiss and told her he would see her in the morning. Since moving back to Ohio, Bruce went to parties without Stephanie, broke plans at the last minute; he had even kissed another girl in front of her. Tired of chasing after him, she left and went to her sister's. The next morning, a friend found Bruce in bed, purple and cold.

Stephanie started screaming and pounding her fists against the walls. She fell to the floor, curled up into a fetal position, and cried. She had loved Bruce. At the same time, she was ashamed she could love somebody who, she had begun to believe, didn't love her.

Although we talked about Bruce, it was many months before I knew the complete story. Each time we talked about him, we reached a point where Stephanie would start to cry. But one thing she told me every time: "The day Bruce died, he told my friend, 'Stephanie drives me crazy more than anyone else. I could never love anyone the way I love that girl.' That made me feel so much better. It made me feel loved." Years later, she was looking to Fraggle to give her that same feeling.

· · · ·

I FOUND FRAGGLE sleeping on a bench in Tompkins Square Park the day after he had been released from Rikers

Island. He was wearing a baby blue T-shirt and jeans so baggy the crotch hung almost to his knees. His eyes were hidden by the brim of his baseball cap, and scraggly hair grew from his chin. Fraggle had spent three weeks in jail. The judge had given him five years' probation for selling LSD at a Grateful Dead concert in 1993. He was due back in court in six weeks to set the terms of his probation.

Fraggle had just turned twenty-one, but he had been arrested thirteen times before he was taken to jail that August for shoplifting. The first time he was arrested, he was sixteen. He was in Virginia, and the charge was simple assault. The boy he hit needed stitches for a cut in the back of his head. Fraggle spent a night in jail and was told he had to pay the boy's hospital bill or face forty-five days in a juvenile facility. He did neither. The next year, at seventeen, Fraggle was arrested again for simple assault in San Jose, California, where he had threatened to hit a man in a grocery store parking lot with his skateboard. The man eventually dropped the charges, and Fraggle spent two days in a juvenile facility. He was released on his eighteenth birthday.

Over the next two years, Fraggle was arrested ten times in cities across the country. When he was arrested for selling LSD to undercover police officers at a Grateful Dead concert in New York City—his first felony—he spent the night in jail and had been told to return at a later date for sentencing. When he didn't appear in court, a warrant was issued for his arrest. A month later, in Breckenridge, Colorado, Fraggle was caught during a routine traffic stop and held until he could be picked up by New York authorities. They never came and he was released thirty days later.

In San Francisco, Fraggle was arrested four more times. Stopped while skateboarding on the sidewalk, he tried to get away from the officer. According to Fraggle, the officer hit him and spit on him. Fraggle was charged with resisting arrest and battery of a police officer. After spending a couple of hours in jail under a false name, Fraggle was released with a summons to return to court at a later date. He never did, and eventually the charges were dropped. Two weeks later, Fraggle was arrested for selling marijuana. Fraggle said he had been carrying it for personal use, and there was no evidence to prove otherwise. He spent a night in jail, and the charges were dropped. Two days later, he was arrested for selling two grams of Ecstasy. Again, because of lack of evidence—he had not been seen selling it and had no money in his possession—the charges were dropped to possession. He was released after a night in jail and was again issued a summons to appear in court, which he did not do. Two months after that, Fraggle was charged with a second felony: sale of marijuana. He was sentenced to forty-five days in jail followed by three years' probation, but he never saw his probation officer.

Before he returned to New York in December 1995, Fraggle had been arrested for inciting a riot at a Grateful Dead show in Indiana; consuming alcohol as a minor on his way to Georgia; driving without a license in Ohio; shoplifting in South Carolina; and committing simple assault in North Carolina. Except for the assault charge, for which he served fifteen days in jail, Fraggle spent only a couple of nights in jail and was issued summonses to return. All his arrests were under false names, and he never honored the summonses.

When Fraggle did spend time in jail, he talked with the other inmates about drugs and exchanged information on scams. Each time he was arrested, he learned new ways to work the system. From other inmates, he learned to use aliases and not to carry identification and how to smuggle cigarettes, drugs, magazines, and books into jail. "You can't just sit around in jail and keep to yourself," he told me. "You have to fight, stand up for yourself, develop an attitude of being a badass. Otherwise people will mess with you. When you come out, it takes time to get rid of that attitude."

When Fraggle woke up and saw me sitting at the foot of the bench, he sat up and rubbed his eyes. "I want to do it different this time," he told me.

At Rikers, Fraggle was locked up in building C-95, which were called the "Juice Dorms," where he received and was eventually weaned off methadone. This had been his first time at Rikers, and Fraggle was the youngest in his sixty-five-bed dorm. Because most of the other inmates had been arrested on drug charges and were themselves detoxing, he said he was left alone much of the time. He was also the only white kid, until a teenager he had shot coke with in Tompkins Square Park arrived a week later. The television was on all the time, and the men crowded around the set daily to watch *Jerry Springer* and a nightly video. But Fraggle, bored by television, spent most of his time reading newspapers, doing crossword puzzles, and playing cards. He told me he fought only once: He punched a guy who had threatened him.

Fraggle stretched his arms over his head and yawned. "I'm trying to get things going," he told me. "I already called a guy about a job with a moving company I'd lined up before I went to jail. I'm waiting for them to call me back at a friend's house."

It wasn't easy to get or hold a job without a place to live, and getting a place to live was much tougher without steady income. Doing all this while shooting heroin was nearly impossible. And although Fraggle had been able to get a job as an usher at the Angelika movie theater on Houston Street, he was only able to keep it because he stepped outside to get high during his breaks. He was fired three weeks later, after another employee had seen him shooting up.

Now just days out of Rikers, Fraggle was already doing dope again. He felt the only way he could keep a job and live on the street was to be on methadone. And the only way Fraggle could get on methadone was to be on Medicaid. To get on Medicaid, he needed identification, and he had none. That day, Fraggle asked me if he made $10, would I mail it to the Tennessee Department of Records for a copy of his birth certificate. "I don't trust myself to do it," he told me. "If I don't give you the money right after I get it, I'm just going to use it for drugs."

I said I would. Fraggle laid back down, adjusting his knapsack under his head, and closed his eyes. He never again mentioned getting his ID.

· · · ·

WHEN STEPHANIE SPOTTED Fraggle sprawled on a bench, she stuffed her bare feet into her canvas sneakers and stumbled to her feet. She had been sleeping on the grass nearby. With her shoes untied, she walked toward us, scratching red bug bites on her calves. The shiny black flies that fed off the park's garbage also fed off the people who slept there.

"Fraggle, can I have some money?" she asked. Fraggle told her he only had a few dollars and needed it to get straight himself. When Stephanie asked again, Fraggle got angry. He jumped up and said he was leaving to find more money. Stephanie walked away tearful.

"One person's always going to get mad at the other person if they get high and they're sick," said Carrie, sitting on the bench facing me. With chipmunk cheeks and a short pixie haircut, Carrie looked no older than twelve, but she was eighteen and showed me her driver's license to prove it. She told me that she came to New York to see Liza, a seventeen-year-old girl she had met in a drug rehabilitation program in New Hampshire four months earlier. Both Carrie and Liza had been detoxing from heroin. Carrie lived in Massachusetts, and when her stepfather accused her of doing dope again, she called Liza on Long Island. A few weeks earlier, Liza had stolen her mother's Jeep Cherokee and sold her mom's cellular phone for dope. Her father wanted her out of the house.

In New York just a few weeks and homeless, Carrie was already doing up to five bags of heroin a day. Although she had snorted heroin in Massachusetts, in New York she began injecting it for a more intense rush.

When Fraggle returned half an hour later, he sat next to Carrie. They talked for a few minutes and then got up and left the park to go to Western Union to pick up $100 that Carrie's grandmother had wired her.

Liza came by looking for Carrie a few minutes later. When she heard that Carrie and Fraggle had left the park, she sat down, placed a large black vinyl bag on her lap, and waited for them to return. Liza was tall and bald, the shape of her head like a lopsided egg. Her face was covered with pimples that she picked till they bled. Sitting on the bench, Liza pulled out from her bag a small compact and alcohol swabs. With her eyes closed, and her head swaying unevenly, she held the mirror to her face. Then she opened the swabs and methodically wiped her face, inspecting the dirt on the cotton for minutes after each swipe. When she was finished, she patted her cheeks and chin with chalky pressed powder, compulsively rubbing the tiny scabs as if trying to erase them.

It was getting dark. Stephanie suddenly appeared. "How do you think I feel when I hear from Fraggle, 'Not only will

Liza be shooting me up with coke, but she'll be sucking my dick on the flight on the way to San Francisco?'" For a few months, Liza had been one of Stephanie's closest friends. Liza regularly received money from her parents and shared the dope she bought with Stephanie. But when Liza and Fraggle began spending time together without Stephanie, she was hurt and convinced that they had slept together. Fraggle denied it to her and to me.

"You know, Stephanie, he always says shit like that. Why can't we just be friends?" Liza stood up and stepped closer to Stephanie.

"Bullshit, I'm not going to be your friend now. You used me. All you do is fuckin' use me. That same day I was so fuckin' sick. And you bought Fraggle a fuckin' speedball." Stephanie stepped back, turned around and started to walk away.

"I did not buy him a speedball." Liza chased after Stephanie.

Stephanie stopped and turned around to face her. "And I was begging you to split a bag with me because I was sick. And now you've promised him a fuckin' plane ticket to San Francisco, and he's throwing it in my face." Stephanie was standing right in front of Liza and yelling.

"I didn't offer him a plane ticket."

"Well, I don't give a fuck. I don't love Fraggle."

"Stephanie, I don't want him."

"Well, you got him, whether you want him or not." Stephanie walked away laughing.

Suddenly Stephanie noticed that her duffel bag, with all her clothes, had disappeared. While she was fighting with Liza, the police had cleared the grassy knoll: Everything was gone. Stephanie ran to a police officer nearby. "Excuse me," she said. "All my stuff was laying there, and now it's gone.

Do you know what happened?"

"Beats me," he said and walked away.

Stephanie's blanket and two bags of clothes were missing. But as upset as she was, she cared more about finishing with Liza. She walked back. "Look, I am not jealous of you. I'm fuckin' hurt, all right?" she said. "I don't need to have you thrown in my fuckin' face. Every minute, I hear 'Liza's going to be sucking my dick,' 'Liza's flying me to Frisco,' 'Liza's getting me high.'"

"He says that to make you mad," said Liza calmly. She stood up and stepped closer to Stephanie, who was standing nearly three yards away. A young man on roller blades flew through the narrow corridor between them, but neither moved from their positions.

"It's just a coincidence that every time we get into a fight, you're right around the corner waiting for Fraggle."

"Stephanie, don't say those things. I'm not like that at all." Liza was speaking slowly, her words slurred.

"I told you a thousand times, I'm not worried about you guys fucking. But I was hurt because you and me used to be best friends. Any other girl I've ever been friends with is always 'friendship before guys.'" Stephanie was lying. She cared very much if Fraggle and Liza had slept together.

"Fraggle and I are also friends."

"The last time when I was hysterical and I said, 'I really need a friend right now,' you told me, 'I'm not going to be your friend right now.'"

"You had called me a whore!"

Stephanie and Liza walked away talking.

Two hours later, Carrie returned alone. Fraggle, she told me, was avoiding people he owed money to. Carrie and Fraggle had already spent $60 of the money Carrie had picked up on heroin and coke.

"We're not going to go to Oregon," Carrie said. She seemed disappointed. "I know Liza's mom will buy her a ticket, and she swears to God her mother's going to buy me a ticket, but now I hear that she offered Fraggle a ticket. Her mom is going to pay for everybody? Yeah, right."

Carrie had realized that she couldn't rely on Liza. "I'm just finding out that the girl is a compulsive liar. She told Fraggle one thing and me another." Carrie sat down and put her face in her hands. Then she sat up and took a deep breath to stop herself from crying. "I'm going to try to get the fuck away from here as soon as I can. I already spent most of the money I was sent. My natural dad, for the first time ever, said I can come and live with him. Maybe I could try that."

The night before, Carrie had slept on a roof in the neighborhood and the night before that in a park in New Jersey near a bus station. It was about nine now, and she had no idea where she was going to sleep that night.

Two hours passed before Fraggle returned, and there was still no sign of Stephanie.

....

THE FIRST FEW TIMES I saw Fraggle, he and Stephanie were arguing, and he always stormed off before we were introduced. When we finally met, he was sullen and didn't look me in the eye. He told me later, "Everybody blames me for keeping Stephanie on the street." He assumed I'd be no different.

When I told Fraggle what I was doing, he was eager to talk to me. "Maybe it will help open up people's eyes," he said. "It's a lot worse out here than the things they show on after-school specials on television."

Fraggle had left home when he was sixteen to travel. By

the time I met him, he had been on his own for almost five years. "You start just traveling, but you do this too long, and then you get caught up in it," he told me. "The switch came a couple of years ago when the heroin started bad—when I started getting really strung out and everyone started giving up on me. The switch doesn't happen in one day. As time goes on, it just happens. Traveling is just a year or two, then you're homeless."

Not long after he left home, Fraggle began touring with the Grateful Dead. With a crew of kids, Fraggle worked as a "security guard" for the hippies who followed the band, securing the parking lot where they camped out. When a drug dealer he met asked him if he wanted to make some real money selling marijuana and acid, Fraggle agreed. Fraggle was well liked and trusted. He proved a good salesman. Within a few months, he was making hundreds of dollars a day.

At fifteen, Fraggle had started smoking pot and, for about a month, crack; at sixteen he had started using Ecstasy and drinking heavily, mostly beer. On tour, at seventeen, Fraggle tried heroin. At first, he snorted it, but just forty-five minutes later, he let his friend inject him. "The very first time shooting, I didn't really get that high," Fraggle told me. "But I took more and then got really sick. The best time on heroin is when you've been really sick for hours and then you get it." After his first time shooting heroin, Fraggle didn't stop. One month passed before he could inject himself. He didn't know anyone addicted to the drug and hadn't realized the damage it could do. Within weeks, he was strung out, doing about half a bag a day. Over time, he began shooting more and staying strung out for longer periods of time. When I met him, he was shooting four to five bags of heroin a day.

"You should have seen me before New York," Fraggle often said to me. "I used to be so styled out." Stephanie had told me that Fraggle had always been concerned about his appearance, and that he never wore the same clothes two days in a row. "Your hands get so dirty here," Fraggle said to me, almost apologetic. "You scrub and you scrub and you scrub and you can't get them clean. The dirt is ingrained in the cracks."

But the changes in Fraggle since he had arrived in New York were not just superficial. "In San Francisco, everybody really loved me," said Fraggle. "I was trustworthy and had a lot of friends. In New York, everybody hates me. It's the cocaine. I started doing so much cocaine that I just started ripping people off." Fraggle had started to shoot cocaine in San Francisco, about one to two shots a day, but in New York, his habit had grown to ten to fifteen shots a day. On cocaine, Fraggle was erratic and impulsive. When he copped on cocaine, he regularly disappeared with people's money. "I don't even trust myself anymore." To support himself, Fraggle had to rely increasingly on shoplifting. When shoplifting didn't earn him enough money or was too risky, he turned tricks.

Fraggle was seventeen the first time he exchanged a sexual favor for cash. He had just gotten out of jail in Colorado and was hitchhiking to San Francisco. The night before, he'd been dropped off in a small town in Nevada and had fallen asleep at the side of the road. Just after sunrise the next morning, he was sitting on the pavement cold and barely awake, when a skinny man, about fifty, pulled his truck to the side of the road. The man rolled down the window and leaned out. "I'm not going anywhere, but I figure you'd like to get warm," he said.

Fraggle stood up but didn't get into the truck.

"It's really cold out there," he said. Fraggle still didn't move. "Would you like to make some money?" Fraggle knew what he wanted. "Let me give you head. And I'll give you $30."

"No." Fraggle didn't move.

"Are you sure? It's $30."

Fraggle stood by the truck. Thirty dollars would get him a Greyhound ticket to San Francisco. Eventually, he got into the truck. "All I could think about was getting out of town," said Fraggle. The man gave him porn magazines to look at, and then bent his head down and unzipped Fraggle's pants. For the next few minutes, Fraggle held the magazine over the man's head and pretended that a girl was giving him a blow job. Afterward, the man dropped Fraggle off at the bus station. "I had this knot in my stomach the whole next day," said Fraggle. "I told myself, You're not attracted to men. I guess this is what a girl feels like when she does this shit."

Three years later in New York, Fraggle did it again. He was dope sick and desperate. Leg Rub Steve was looking to spend money. Steve, about forty, was tall, skinny, and wore glasses. Kids on the street who knew Steve said he had a wife and kids on Long Island.

Steve approached Fraggle while Fraggle was panhandling, and Fraggle agreed to go with him. Steve bought Fraggle a beer and some cigarettes and headed out to a spare apartment he kept in Brooklyn. In Steve's apartment, they sat together on the couch and talked. Fraggle made $130 rubbing Steve's leg while Steve jerked off. "The first time, I did it for forty-five minutes but he didn't come," said Fraggle. "I guess I didn't do it well enough." Steve rarely saw the same kid more than once, but if a kid introduced him to someone he liked, the kid would get $40 as a finders' fee. Fraggle saw Steve twice, then introduced him to other kids. After introducing him to someone who Steve didn't like, Fraggle didn't work for him again.

Now, released from Rikers for shoplifting, Fraggle was

fearful of getting arrested again and relied increasingly on turning tricks to make money. Eventually, Fraggle found Howard. Howard was fat, about forty, and unmarried. He'd told Fraggle he was a former New York City councilman. When Fraggle visited Howard, they would go into the bathroom, and Howard would masturbate. Fraggle would twist and squeeze Howard's nipples and slap him in the face. "He gets mad at me because I can't really slap him hard because I'm just not into it," said Fraggle. "But then he switches into this little-boy mode, and he tells me that he doesn't deserve me—like Chris Farley in *Tommy Boy*. His whole face changes. He talks like a little boy, and he has this little puppy-dog face. He tells me he knows he's been bad. And then he'll switch back to normal mode. One time he freaked out at me and started yelling. I guess I fucked up a couple of times."

Howard usually finished in ten minutes, and Fraggle would make $20. Sometimes, Howard would feed Fraggle, let him take a shower, and occasionally let him wash his clothes. For about five months, Fraggle saw Howard two to three times a week. Fraggle also had three other regular customers, who paid $20 or $30 to give Fraggle blow jobs. All the men knew each other, and all lived in the neighborhood.

"I hated it in the beginning and freaked out a little," said Fraggle about turning tricks. "But I needed the money. And then it got easier and easier and easier." The more he tricked, though, the more depressed Fraggle seemed. One day, he admitted to me that he was deeply ashamed about the way he was making money. He also wanted me to know that he would never give blow jobs and that he would never "go all the way."

· · · ·

WHEN FRAGGLE and I talked about his family, he always spoke about his father, Frank. "He's a sick man," Fraggle told me the first time we sat down to talk. "He molested my sister, Pauline, and my sister's three-year-old daughter." Pauline, four years older than Fraggle, was his stepsister. She was two when Fraggle's mother, Alice, married Frank. Alice was seventeen when they married; Frank was twenty. Said Fraggle of his father: "He was a very abused child. His dad used to beat him. He would hit him in the face, and all his mom would do was take his glasses off. He's told me some sick stories. It don't make it right, and that's no excuse for what he did, but I see where it comes from."

Fraggle's father was in the military, and while growing up, Fraggle and his family moved frequently from one base to another. Fraggle, who was named Eric, was born in Tennessee, but by the time he turned thirteen, Fraggle had moved nine times to cities both in and out of the United States.

Fraggle learned to fight when he was a small boy. "My son's not going to grow up to be a pussy," Fraggle said he often heard as a child. If Frank found out Fraggle had had an argument with another boy at school or that someone had teased his son, he made Fraggle go back to fight the boy who had picked on him.

During his nearly twenty-year military career, Frank won a number of medals and awards, including a humanitarian service medal and three good-conduct awards. But at home, Frank expected his children to abide by his rules, and when they didn't, he could be brutal and cruel. Fraggle frequently rebelled. If he and his stepsister were told to be home by five, Fraggle returned at six and received a beating. Pauline often helped Fraggle with his homework and with chores around the house so he wouldn't get into trouble. "But I could never keep him safe enough to keep him from being beat on by Frank," she said.

When I asked Fraggle to tell me about the beatings, he couldn't recall many details. "When I was young, he would punch me or knee me in the stomach," said Fraggle. "It wouldn't really damage me or anything. I guess that was so I wouldn't go to school with big marks. But the look on his face was fuckin' scary. As I got older, it happened more often. He punched me in the face only a couple of times. He knocked me out once. But when he punched me, he'd cry and pick me up and feel badly about it. The good thing about him was when I really needed him, he was around. He made sure I had what I needed, like clothes and money for things if I was going out."

Pauline's memories of specific incidents, however, were still vivid. "I can remember back when Eric was four years old," she said. "We had this big, huge mango tree in the backyard, which we weren't supposed to climb because Eric and I were both allergic. Eric climbed the mango tree, comes in the house, and said, 'No, I didn't climb the mango tree.' But his face had already broken out. We had this long hallway, and Frank literally kicked him in the stomach. Eric just slid down the hallway." Later in first and second grade, Fraggle's teacher called home to complain about Fraggle giving other school children a hard time. Pauline said that instead of talking to his son, Frank knocked Fraggle from his chair and kept knocking him down each time he stood up. "Frank's favorite thing was to tell you to get back up after he'd hit you," she said.

Fraggle was extremely bright and did well academically, but from an early age he often got into trouble at school. In grade school, when he would finish his work before the other students and the teacher would tell him to read, Fraggle would draw or play. He played the games he wanted to play, read the books he wanted to read, and did his work in the order that he wanted. In sixth grade, Fraggle's teachers suggested placing him in an academically gifted class, but his mother refused, arguing that he was too socially immature. In high school, Fraggle was the top student in his biology class, and even though he did no homework, he aced his exams.

At home, Frank's moods were erratic and his behavior unpredictable. When he was angry, Frank would go into his children's rooms and empty all their clothes out of the closet onto the floor, dump all the books out of the bookcases, and strip their beds, and then he would tell them to clean up the mess. The children never knew when he would explode.

"Eric got into trouble with Frank every day," said Pauline. "If we got up on a Saturday morning and Frank told us to get dressed and eat breakfast, Eric went outside to play, and Frank would give him a beating. If we had to be home by five, Eric would be home by six. I'd tell him, 'Just do what you're supposed to do. Just try,' but he wouldn't. Eric did these things because he didn't care enough to be afraid of Frank. It didn't matter what punishment Frank gave Eric, he still was going to do what he wanted to do. Frank would make us do push-ups and kick us in the stomach while doing them. And with Frank you're not allowed to fall."

One night when the kids were too loud, Frank made them stand in the living room with their arms stretched out straight ahead, holding a heavy book in each hand. They were told to hold that position without dropping their arms until dinner was made.

Fraggle's mother, Alice, was usually at work when the beatings occurred. When she was home, Frank hit her as well. "One time Eric asked for a sip of a drink, and Frank said no," remembered Pauline. "Mom gave him a sip anyway, and the next thing I know she's on the ground because Frank punched her, and then he smacked Eric for asking. He beat her up real bad. I remember being in the bedroom with Eric and trying to hold him back because he wanted to go out there. It was terrifying."

Later that year, Fraggle, about eight, lunged for his father after Frank had smashed a bowl of ice cream into Alice's face. Frank grabbed him and punched him hard in the chest and stomach, warning Fraggle never to lay a hand on him again. The abuse continued: One day Pauline came home from school to find a trail of blood from the front door to the patio. Later that evening, her parents returned from the emergency room. "My mom had stitches all over her face," she said. "Her nose was all swollen. Her eyes, her jaw, her nose were all bruised."

The beating that frightened Pauline the most, and ultimately changed the course of her family's history, occurred in December 1986, when Fraggle was just eleven. They were living in Pennsylvania. Frank had just finished smacking Pauline for not bringing home a good report card. When Fraggle returned home from school and Frank saw that he wasn't wearing socks, he got furious.

"Where the hell are your socks?" asked Frank.

Fraggle didn't answer. Frank looked at Fraggle and punched him in the stomach, sending Fraggle to the ground.

"Now get back up."

Fraggle staggered to his feet. Frank punched him again. Fraggle stood up. Frank knocked him down. In tears, Fraggle pulled himself up again. Frank knocked him to the ground four more times, before Fraggle, no longer able to stand, lay limp on the floor. When Fraggle didn't get up, Frank, wearing boots, repeatedly kicked him in the groin. After a few minutes, Frank stopped. "Now get up and turn the water off," he said, motioning to the tap in the kitchen sink.

Fraggle stood up, and Frank kicked him back down.

"I can't turn that water off while you're kicking me," said Fraggle, with tears in his eyes.

Frank then picked Fraggle up, held him high off the ground and dropped him. "You're worthless," he said. He then dragged Fraggle into the bathroom, where he threw his son up against the tile, bouncing him off the walls. Fraggle was crying, and Pauline begged him to stop. When she grabbed Frank's arm, he hit her, giving her a black eye. Frank eventually stopped, warning Pauline and Fraggle, "If you all tell your mother about this, I promise you life will be worse for you."

After Frank left, Fraggle told Pauline, "I really hurt." She pulled up Fraggle's shirt and saw the purple and black bruises that had formed around his neck, chest, and abdomen. "I just looked at him and I hugged him," said Pauline. "I promised him this would never happen again and that I would take care of it."

That evening, Pauline tried to poison Frank. "My mom wasn't getting home until midnight that night, and it was my job to fix the drinks," she told me. "I took those [silicon] packets that you get in packages that say 'Do not eat.' I put like three of them in his tea. But it didn't work. He never said a word. He drank the tea. I was lying in my bed praying that something would happen to him, but nothing ever happened. I never said anything to Eric. Nobody knew."

The next day, Pauline did keep her promise to Eric to make the beatings stop. After Frank dropped her off at school, she went to her guidance counselor. She was planning to tell him only about the beatings. Eventually, she told him that Frank had been molesting her. She was fifteen.

The counselor left the room and returned with three policemen. "I know he did the right thing, but I hated him for telling," said Pauline. "He should have let me make that choice to report it. I could have done it later."

Pauline's guidance counselor was not the only person she told. When she was ten, Pauline said she had told her mother. "Frank, her, and I sat down and talked about it," said Pauline. "My mom had asked him to stop. Then we went to my grandmother's for the weekend. It stopped for a while, and a couple of weeks later, it started happening again. I wasn't going to tell my mom again." Pauline said her mother didn't know the extent of the sexual abuse. "The only thing I ever told my mom was that he was touching me. I never told her anything else."

．．．．

FRANK had begun sexually abusing Pauline when Pauline was in preschool. "He would get up early in the morning, when it was still dark outside, and come in my room, pretending he was going to the bathroom," said Pauline. "Before he went back to bed with my mom, he would be in my bedroom doing that other stuff. When it started, he was just fondling me.

"One day he got mad because the pin I was wearing in my kindergarten picture was crooked and he started slapping me. Then he took me to the bedroom. He tried to put himself inside me. I remember lying on my bed. I thought I heard my mom and leaned up to look out the window, and he just punched me. I blacked out, and when I woke up, I was in the bathtub with ice cubes because I was so bruised up and swollen."

When the family lived at her grandmother's for brief

periods of time, Pauline was safe. But in Puerto Rico, Frank sexually abused her at least two or three times a week after school. Pauline said he also sexually abused one of her friends.

When she got older and her mother started working nights, Pauline said Frank forced her to sleep in the same bed and have sex with him. "My mom would work five nights a week," she said. "I had to sleep in bed with him every night my mom was at work. For two years, he would come in my room and get me at midnight. I was terrified. He would threaten me, saying that things would get worse for my mother or that they would take me away if I told anyone. Sometimes it was used as a punishment. Sometimes it was because he wanted to." When Pauline started cheerleading, things got even worse. "A couple of times he would do it in the car, and then a couple of times he used utensils, like a turkey baster. He would tie up my hands, blindfold me. He hurt me a lot."

Fraggle found out that Frank was molesting Pauline the day she told her counselor. "Eric was mad at me," Pauline said. "The family broke up after that, so he felt I had taken his father away from him. He got in trouble with the law. It seemed that he was angry all the time."

Frank was charged with custodial sexual battery. Nearly four months later, Frank pleaded guilty to one count of a lewd, lascivious act in the presence of a child. Frank never went to jail; instead, he was given ten years' probation on the condition that he pay $252.50 in court costs, participate in psycho-sexual therapy, and have no contact with minor children without supervision. He left the military one year later.

The family entered court-ordered therapy. For about a year, each family member had individual counseling in addition to group therapy. Frank and Alice eventually divorced.

"At the end, we had to have an apology meeting, and he still never owned up to what he did," Pauline said.

Alice moved out of state with the children, but after about a year, she decided to try a reconciliation with Frank, who had moved to Virginia. Pauline was now seventeen, married, and had given birth six months earlier to a girl, Celia. Her husband accompanied them to Virginia, but unable to find a job, he returned home to work for his father's company. Alice, Frank, Eric, Pauline, and her daughter lived together in a three-bedroom house.

One night, only after a few months together, Pauline woke to a strange smell. A man was in her room. She screamed and the man ran out, but she knew it was Frank. "I told Eric that Frank had tried to do something to me that night, but I didn't want to tell my mom because things were going so well for her at that time. He started crying and hugged me."

The next day, Fraggle found a broken bottle of pure ethanol in the trash and a stinking rag in the laundry room. Pauline assumed that Frank had planned to knock her unconscious and rape her. "I called my mom at work and said I did not want Frank to come home," Pauline said. "I wanted to call the police, but my mom wouldn't let me." A few days later, Alice moved out of the house with Eric and into an apartment down the road. Pauline moved with Celia to the Midwest to stay with Celia's father.

Around this time, Fraggle started to get into serious trouble in school. When he was expelled in ninth grade, his mother sent him to live with Frank, who was living with his parents in Tennessee. Fraggle finished the school year at a small Catholic school and then returned to his mother's house. When he was expelled again in the tenth grade, his mother sent him back to live with his father. This time,

Fraggle stole Frank's car and ran away. A week later, Fraggle appeared at his mother's house, where he lived until he was expelled from eleventh grade.

By now, Alice had met another man whom she would eventually marry. Fraggle and his new stepfather fought constantly. Just before his seventeenth birthday, tired of getting thrown out of the house, Fraggle decided to leave. He hitchhiked to California. Over the next few years, Fraggle traveled across the country, returning home periodically when he grew tired of life on the streets.

Meanwhile, Pauline had moved back to Virginia and had started to allow Frank back into her life. "He would come visit on the weekends and take me and Celia to lunch and stuff," Pauline said. "Christmas rolled around. Frank bought me a big TV and VCR." Pauline was pregnant again, and Frank helped out around the house after she gave birth. "He cooked all these meals and stuck them in the freezer. Cleaned up my house." Pauline wanted to believe that the counseling had helped. "Celia kind of liked it when he would come around. But we made sure though that he was never alone with her."

One day, though, Celia began to act strangely. "She started screaming when her own father tried to get her to take a bath, something she'd always loved doing, and she started coming out every night with no clothes on," Pauline said. "For a whole week, she wet the bed, something she'd never done before."

Alice learned that Frank had been alone with Celia for about an hour a week earlier. When she and Pauline asked Celia why she was walking around naked, Celia said, "Papaw does this to me." Celia was just three years old.

They called the police, and Celia was interviewed by investigators. Frank denied the charges, but the police concluded Frank had sexually molested the child, touching her vaginal area with his tongue and fingers. Seven years after Frank had been arrested for sexually abusing Pauline, he was arrested and charged with first-degree criminal sexual conduct and lewd act upon a child under fourteen. After spending about a year in jail, Frank was extradited to Pennsylvania for breaking the terms of his probation. He was given a thirty-month prison sentence and served a year and a half of his term.

Frank did make an effort to be a parent again to Fraggle, who hadn't seen his father since he ran away when he was fifteen. Frank came to New York in the spring of 1996. At that time, Fraggle could barely walk; his feet were covered with dozens of open cuts from walking without socks. He had been diagnosed with cellulitis and a fungal infection on his feet. He needed antibiotics and had called his father for the money. "He drove fifteen hours up here to hang out for four hours and then drove fifteen hours back," Fraggle told me, still moved that his father had taken the trip. "He came to give me money and give me shirts and $20. He didn't have a lot of money. He also offered to take me back. He said, 'I came just to see you.' I thought it was pretty cool he came just to see me and made an effort to be a part of my life."

....

IN 1996, local newspapers reported that violent crime in New York was down, but for anyone involved in drug dealing, the Lower East Side was still a dangerous place. During the ten months Stephanie lived on the streets in New York, from January through October 1996, thirteen people had been murdered and twenty-five rapes had been reported in the Ninth Precinct, which extended from East Houston

Street up to Fourteenth Street and from the East River to Broadway. Most of the slayings were drug related.

The park along the East River was dark, deserted, and dangerous, yet Stephanie crossed the footbridge that spanned the FDR Drive sometimes six or seven times a night to get to the park to shoot up. "It was the only place where I didn't have to worry about the cops," she told me. Although Stephanie was not easily frightened, she was often nervous and scared near the river. And she had good reason to be. In October, a man tried to rape a girl who was sleeping by the river with her boyfriend. A few nights later, a man approached Stephanie on the small footbridge and asked her if she wanted to "fuck." Stephanie ran, but the man gave chase.

These incidents terrified her when she was on cocaine and "tweaking." When she tweaked, her hearing seemed to become more acute: She was nervous, hallucinating, and paranoid. Shadows became people who followed her, threatened her; strangers watched her, chased her. Everything and everyone she encountered, whether it was a man in a red shirt or an overturned garbage can, had meaning and was a message sent from the universe specifically to her. If she was alone by the river, she heard the rustle of rats in the garbage or, in the autumn, in the fallen leaves. Often, Stephanie would be in the bathroom at Leshko's shooting coke when she started to "hear" sirens. She heard the police coming into the restaurant, shuffling their feet outside the bathroom door. These hallucinations paralyzed her, and at times she cowered on the toilet for as long as an hour, hoping the police would leave.

By mid-October, Stephanie was shooting more than ten bags of dope and about three bags of coke a day and needed $130 a day to support her habit. To make that kind of cash, she had to hustle. She was always in a rush and always running to meet someone. Two nights in a row, I went out looking for her with no success. On the third night, as I stood on Avenue A, she suddenly ran up to me from behind. "Keep walking, I have to go," she said.

I jogged alongside her, trying to keep up as she told me she was on her way to meet Fraggle, who was hiding by the river. She looked frightened for the first time since I had known her. "There's a guy on the street with a gun looking for Fraggle," she said. Stephanie stopped at a table covered with used books, bent down, and pulled out a small knapsack from underneath. I tried to get details, but she bolted across the street and ran toward the river, calling over her shoulder, "I can't right now. I'll beep you tomorrow."

. . . .

FRAGGLE was in trouble again.

A few days earlier, Fraggle was approached by a group of ticket scalpers looking to hire kids to wait in line for World Series tickets. The scalpers were giving the kids $200 apiece to purchase four tickets at the stadium box office, the maximum each customer could buy, with each kid receiving an additional $80. Fraggle jumped at the chance.

The Yankees were playing. Even though police had arrested thirty-two ticket scalpers over the previous two-day period, scalpers still brazenly hawked legitimate and even counterfeit tickets for the first two games of the series for prices ranging from $250 to $1,700. Some scouted for buyers along River Avenue and the neighboring blocks in the Bronx, others brazenly hustled on stadium property. The scalpers also worked the Major Deegan Expressway near the stadium, the coffee shops, the subways, the parking lots, and the side streets.

Fraggle and nine other kids rounded up from Tompkins Square Park headed for the stadium and joined the line of hundreds of people squeezed together like cattle between two ten-foot-wide barricades. The kids had been instructed to stay together, but the crowds had made that impossible. They had waited in line twenty-seven hours without food or sleep and were just two hours away from the window, when the scalper noticed that six of the kids had fallen behind about twenty feet. The scalper was furious and told them to leave.

Fraggle had not fallen behind and was handed his $200. But he decided, along with the other kids who stayed, that they would give the kids who were sent away $20 apiece. Fraggle snuck away from the line to meet the other kids. But when he couldn't find them, instead of returning to the stadium, Fraggle, exhausted and hungry, ran to the subway. On the train, he collapsed onto a seat, then fell asleep. Hours later, he woke up in Brooklyn, he jumped off the train and took a taxi to Tompkins Square Park. It was nearly midnight, and Fraggle had to stay out of sight. The scalper had warned the kids that if anyone bailed out with the money, he was going to make them an example. When Fraggle saw Stephanie and told her what had happened, they hid at the river, where they spent the rest of the night and the rest of the money doing coke and dope. The next day, Fraggle learned that the scalper's boss was looking for him. Fraggle heard that three other kids had also ripped the scalper off, and that one of the kids already had been threatened by a man who had held a gun to his head.

. . . .

FRAGGLE was sleeping on the sidewalk in front of Leshko's when he woke up to a man kicking him in the kidney. The scalper's boss found him and he wanted his money. "Meet me at nine tonight," the man said. "I don't care if you don't have any money on you, just be here. You can work off the money you owe me."

Fraggle was scared. He had every intention of meeting him, but he never made it. At seven, only two hours before the meeting, a woman from the neighborhood asked him to cop her some coke, lending him her $800 mountain bike so that he could return quickly. But Fraggle took longer than she expected. When he returned to the park, the girl was gone. A few yards away, a member of DOA, a local drug gang, riding his own bike, saw Fraggle and called him over.

Gangs such as DOA, The Bad Boys, Champion, Dead Man Walking, and High Speed along with lesser known, smaller, and less organized crews like Cut Throat, controlled many of the blocks on the Lower East Side. The gangs hired a network of kids with bikes and backpacks to deliver product to customers, often paying them with expensive sneakers and leather jackets. The heroin gangs were known to use violence to quell minor disturbances near drug spots. Members of three of the gangs—Dead Man Walking, The Bad Boys, and High Speed—were also suspected by the police in a number of homicides in the area.

"Hey, man, I've got to find the girl who owns this bike," Fraggle said. He stretched his neck to see if he could spot her on the sidewalk outside the park.

"She went looking for you," said the crew member. "Leave the bike here, she'll be right back. I'll tell her."

"I want to explain why I took so long."

"Get off the bike."

Fraggle thought that the guy was a friend of hers, so he got off the bike and stood beside it, holding the handlebars. Then the DOA crew member motioned to his friend standing nearby. The friend walked over and the two murmured something that Fraggle couldn't hear. In a flash, one of the guys grabbed the bike's handlebars out of Fraggle's hands, jumped onto the seat and rode away, his crew buddy following on his own bike behind him.

Fraggle panicked. Looking around for help, he saw Malcom, a small-time drug dealer. Malcolm was in an especially bad mood; two undercover cops had been in the park all day and were still hanging around. Malcolm had seen Fraggle give up the bike.

"What do I do?" asked Fraggle.

"Go get the fucking bike," Malcolm said. "What are you, a faggot? Go get the fucking bike."

Fraggle stood still. He was scared. He knew that the DOA guys would beat him up. There was no way he was going to get that bike back without getting badly hurt. "Go get the fuckin' bike," Malcom repeated.

Jimmy, a short, muscular man who hung out in the park, had also seen what happened. He knew the girl who owned the bike. "You better go get the fuckin' bike or I'll kick your ass," he said.

Fraggle ran down the cement pathway leading out of the park, chased by the muscle-bound man who now was saying he was going to kill him.

Suddenly, another DOA crew member biked up next to Fraggle and pulled a knife from his jacket. When Fraggle saw the blade, he stopped.

"You better just walk away right now."

"OK, man, just chill," said Fraggle.

"You better just walk away."

"You better go get the fuckin' bike, or I'm going to kick your ass," said Jimmy, who was now standing just behind him.

Fraggle stood frozen, his hands trembling. "Look, chill

out, guys," he finally said.

Jimmy walked up to Fraggle and punched him in the face, landing Fraggle flat on his back. Both Jimmy and the DOA crew member stood over him, watching, waiting.

Fraggle staggered to his feet and immediately started running. He ran up the block to a bar. He pleaded with the bar's manager to call the police. "These guys are going to kill me," he said.

"What the fuck are you doing bringing this shit in here?" the manager said.

"I didn't do anything. These guys are trying to kill me."

"Get out of here. Go out the side door."

"These guys are not just trying to kick my ass. They've got a knife."

"Look, you either go out the side door and take a chance with them, or take a chance with me. Now get the fuck out of here," he yelled.

Fraggle ran to the side exit and out the door. The two guys spotted him, and Fraggle ran into a nearby grocery store.

"What are you doing? Get out of here," yelled the owner.

Jimmy stood outside the front door yelling at Fraggle to come out.

"Look, please, get on the phone and call the cops. These guys are going to kill me." Fraggle began to cry. "Please call the cops."

"I'm not going to call the cops. He has a gun. I'm not going to risk getting shot over you."

"How are you risking getting shot by walking to the back of the store and calling the cops?"

Eventually, one of Fraggle's friends came up to the front door. Fraggle told her to call the police. Jimmy and the other guy walked away.

When the police arrived ten minutes later, Fraggle

explained what happened. The men chasing him were gone, and the police left a few minutes later.

The next day, Fraggle told me that he had learned that the bicycle belonged to a "Mafia guy's niece." He said the mobster was also hunting for him. "Everybody's out here looking for me," he said.

....

FRAGGLE really wanted to stop shooting cocaine, believing it was coke that kept getting him into trouble. Cocaine pumped him up, excited him. It forced him to conjure up new ways to get more money, and made him more willing to take risks. Fraggle didn't believe he could just stop using cocaine, so instead he decided that he would shoot cocaine only if he had enough for a bag of dope as well. The dope acted as a buffer and pulled him back into a mellow state where he was less likely to take risks. Just twenty-four hours later, though, Fraggle had already blown his plan.

"I screwed up," Fraggle told me a few days after having made his decision. "I had a dime of coke and no money to get dope. I should have waited until I could get a bag, but of course I didn't."

That night, Fraggle told me, he split the dime bag into two shots. He took the first one around midnight and then the second shot a couple of hours later. At three, Fraggle was wide awake. He decided to go to Fourteenth Street and First Avenue to sleep, then panhandle in the morning, catching people on their way to work. As he walked uptown, his legs began to feel very heavy and then to ache. At first, he thought he had been walking too much. But his legs kept getting heavier, and his head started pounding, as if someone were banging on his temples with cement blocks. The pain grew so sharp that

Fraggle had tears in his eyes. Eventually, the area behind his ears started to get cold. He felt light-headed and dizzy.

Fraggle lay down in a shallow stairwell on Fourteenth Street. Curled up in a fetal position, he put his head on his backpack, hoping to sleep, but the excruciating pain didn't subside. Suddenly, his heart started pounding harder and more rapidly, and his chest starting cramping. He felt as though someone was squeezing his torso while hitting him on the head with a wooden board.

Fraggle was scared. He tried to tell himself that it was fear that made his heart beat like that, but he knew better. When he started feeling woozy, he began to worry that he was dying. He was just two blocks away from Beth Israel Medical Center, but he couldn't move another step. He dragged himself up from the stairwell, crawled to a pay phone ten feet away and dialed 911. Within minutes, he was throwing up on the sidewalk, doubled over in pain. After what felt like hours, Fraggle saw the ambulance, parked at the corner of Second Avenue, one block away. He started screaming to the paramedics, but they didn't hear or see him. He knew that his only hope of being found was to make it over to the ambulance. Fraggle dragged his body up off the ground and began to walk toward the corner, taking slow, small steps. When he was halfway up the block, the ambulance began to pull away. Fraggle started running after it, screaming. The driver finally stopped.

Fraggle woke up in Bellevue Hospital the next day wearing a white cotton gown and strapped to an IV. He was feeling much better, but the doctors wanted to do more tests. Fraggle liked lying in a warm bed, but he was dope sick. "Plus, I knew Stephanie would be really worried sick about me," he said. "There were too many people after me."

Fraggle put on his clothes and walked out of the hospital.

When he arrived downtown, the needle of the IV was still in his arm, the white patches from the EKG still stuck to his chest.

. . . .

THREE DAYS after Fraggle left the hospital, I found Stephanie dressed in a pair of overalls and a short-sleeved T-shirt, sprawled out on her stomach in the middle of the sidewalk on Avenue A. It was Sunday, late October. It was a cold, cloudy day and looked as though it might pour down any minute. Stephanie lay on a thin piece of cardboard, the lower half of her body barely covered by a crib-sized blanket. With her right cheek flat on the concrete, Stephanie looked near death, her breath so shallow she didn't appear to be breathing at all. Snot had crusted dry near her lip, and she was drooling. I knelt beside her, put my hand on her back, and tried to wake her. Stephanie didn't move.

"She's just a junkie," a man's voice called over my shoulder. "Don't bother with her." He walked away.

"Are you going to call an ambulance?" asked another man.

Stephanie had become increasingly thin over the past month, often looking sickly and weak. That day, she looked worse than I had ever seen her. I feared, for the first time, that she could die on the street.

For the next ten minutes, I continued to try to wake Stephanie, rubbing her back, calling out her name. Finally, she started to move. She passed her tongue across her lips and cracked open her eyelids. Then, she rolled over to her side and slowly sat up, wincing. She was having trouble breathing. She told me she had fought with Fraggle the night before. She had punched him in the face, and he had kneed her in the ribs. I tried to persuade her to go to a hospital to get an X-ray, but she insisted that she was fine. "I earned it last night," she told me. "I really did."

I got her a cup of coffee and sat with her against the wall. She was hungry and asked for some cereal. Leaning on my arm, she pulled herself up, and we walked across the street to the supermarket.

She insisted on Lucky Charms, and we had to go to three stores before we found a box. "It's the only cereal that has blue in it," she said. "I love blue." With her cereal, a quart of milk, and a plastic container from a salad bar to use as a bowl, we walked back to Avenue A, and Stephanie sat on the corner to panhandle. I stood against the wall nearby.

A man walking by stopped. "Hey, your boyfriend ripped me off real bad."

"Yeah, well, I haven't seen him all day," she said. "He's not my boyfriend anymore." Stephanie coughed, her body convulsing each time she drew in a breath.

A few minutes later, another man also stopped.

"Hey, what are you doing here?" he asked.

"Rotting," she answered.

The man said nothing, just turned around and walked away.

Stephanie kept yawning, her eyelids were red and crusty. She looked barely able to hold herself up. Suddenly her eyes widened. "Hey, dude I went to jail with," she called out to a young man crossing the street. She pulled herself up and ran after him, her shoes still untied.

. . . .

PEOPLE were getting tired of Stephanie. Her dope habit had more than doubled since August. She showered less often, her hair now looked stringy and greasy. She rarely smiled, and because she was so worn out, she was more easily irritated and frequently told people to fuck off when someone came by to talk. She was skinny, constantly coughing and crying regularly. Most of the veins in her arm had collapsed. Because it took her longer to inject herself, when she disappeared into a restroom, she stayed locked inside for long stretches at a time. Although many of the local restaurant and store owners had initially felt sorry for her, they now simply saw her as a junkie. She was no longer allowed to use their bathrooms; a few restaurants wouldn't even let her in to eat. The manager of the local laundromat kicked her out, calling her a junkie in front of a room full of people.

Other people on the street were also getting angry at Stephanie more often. Apache had punched Stephanie in the face and threatened to kill her. Apache was black, in his mid-twenties, HIV positive, and always looking for a new sex partner. He went after all the new girls in the park, tempted them with dope, and then tried to get them to sleep with him, most of the time not telling them he had HIV. He masturbated while lying on the grass in the park and sometimes exploded in anger without reason. By mid-October, he was walking around the neighborhood wearing a waist-length, black-haired wig, a gold nose ring, and tight black leather pants. One night, Apache chased Stephanie down the street, stopping only after she ran into Leshko's and begged the waitress to call the police. Two drug dealers were also angry at Stephanie. One was the dealer she stole from in the days before her birthday; she told the other to fuck off after he told her he'd gotten sick of seeing her on the street. He threatened to break her legs the next time he saw her. That same week, she had heard that the police were telling other runaways and homeless people in the park that she was wearing out her welcome, and that she had better find another place to sleep because her continued presence was going to cause problems for the rest of them.

Stephanie also was having trouble making money. People now regularly told her to "go home" and to "get a job" when she panhandled. She twice asked me for money. The first time she asked and I refused, she got annoyed and walked away. The following time, I refused her again, but instead of storming off, she said, with a big smile, "You can't blame me for trying." She never asked me again.

Feeling increasingly desperate, Stephanie began considering opportunities she had resisted because they were either too risky or disgusted her. A guy from Minnesota on a visit to New York had offered to wire her money to transport large quantities of dope back to his home. Another man from Eastern Europe had offered her $2,000 to marry him so he could get his green card. This offer she considered seriously, until people on the street told her anything under $6,000 was a lousy deal.

"I almost left with Louie the other night," she told me one day. "He paid my friend $80 to put his hands down her pants. He tried to do that one night with me. I said to him, 'You pay the other girls a lot more money.' He said, 'Well, you know, there's places I can go for $5.' And I said, 'Well, you know, if you want some nasty crack-addicted bitch that's picking her face and has got open wounds, go ahead. I don't do shit like that.'" She looked at me still disgusted at the idea. "I didn't do it, but I thought about it."

••••

IN THE PAST, Stephanie had felt the risk was too great to sell drugs. Besides, she made good money copping. When she copped, she took money from a client and gave it to a dealer who gave her the dope. If she sold, she would have to carry large quantities of dope and cash. The difference was a lot more jail time. If she was caught carrying five bags of heroin, she would be charged with a misdemeanor, but busted with ten bags or more, she would get possession with intent to sell—a felony. Caught exchanging even one bag of heroin for cash, she would be charged with selling—also a felony. The maximum jail time she could serve for a misdemeanor was less than a year; for a felony, it was a minimum of one year, depending on the quantity of drugs she was carrying.

During the second week of October, Stephanie was arrested again. She was copping from a drug spot that had been under surveillance and was stopped on the street. Again, she was carrying only one bag of heroin. On her way to see the judge the next day, her public defender told her she was wanted: She hadn't attended the drug class assigned to her from her previous arrest. Stephanie stood before the judge nauseous and weak, wiping snot that dripped from her nose with the sleeve of her sweatshirt. Barely able to stand up, she leaned heavily on the desk beside her. A few minutes later, the judge told her he would give her another chance. She could do the drug classes again, but failure to appear would be a mandatory thirty days in jail. The court gave her a voucher and a subway token, but she was too weak to walk to the subway station. Instead, she jumped into a taxi without any money and asked the driver to take her to the Lower East Side. When she got to Avenue A, she got out of the taxi and pretended to look for someone who would lend her money to pay for the ride. When the driver realized that she wasn't coming back, he drove away. One of her dealers saw how sick she was and got her a bag. Stephanie was so desperate that she mixed up the dope and shot it up in plain view while sitting on a stoop on Avenue A. The next day,

Stephanie went to her drug class high on dope. For four hours she sat nodding out, her head bouncing up and down. When the class ended, a man tapped her on the shoulder to wake her up.

She knew if she was arrested again, she would spend time in jail. But she was exhausted from running around copping to make the more than $130 a day she needed to support her habit. If she couldn't score because the dealers were lying low, or she didn't have the money or customers to earn enough to get high, the physical pain she felt was more than she could handle. Although she feared jail, having dope available to her at all times was more important. So when Stephanie was approached by one of the DOA heroin dealers to sell, she agreed.

She sold her first bundle quickly and easily. The dealer fronted her bundles (ten bags per bundle) for $75 that she sold for $100 on the street. She gave him the cash after she sold the dope, making enough for two bags right off the top.

In the beginning, because most of her clients didn't know she was carrying, they still paid her to fetch the drugs, so Stephanie was earning twice as much for each bag she sold. Because she had developed such a large clientele copping and was now able to deliver the goods faster than before, she was able to make a lot of money and get drugs for herself quickly. In just a couple of weeks, she was selling an average of five bundles of heroin a day (fifty bags) and making the equivalent of thirty bags of heroin or $300 a day for herself. On weekends, she sometimes sold as many as ten bundles a day (one hundred bags). Because she was carrying the drugs now, she could do as much as she wanted, whenever she wanted. And over the next month, her heroin and cocaine habit nearly doubled.

. . . .

IT WAS HALLOWEEN. In just a few hours, more than twenty thousand marchers and two million spectators would crowd Sixth Avenue, less than ten blocks from where Stephanie slept, for Greenwich Village's annual Halloween Parade. Later that night swarms of people dressed as vampires and ghouls, fairy-tale characters, and celebrities, including Kathy Lee Gifford, Madonna, Bill Clinton, Paula Jones, Dick Morris, and O.J. Simpson, would dance through the streets. There would be more than a few parading as Mayor Giuliani, one of them holding up a bat emblazoned with the words "Quality of Life," a comment on the mayor's campaign to clean up the city. After the parade, the revelers would disperse into the night, many of them ending up in the East Village.

It was mid-afternoon when I went out looking for Stephanie. She wasn't on her corner, but I headed for the opened box of Lucky Charms cereal sitting on the sidewalk across the street. On the ground beside it lay an unzipped down sleeping bag with a sneaker poking through. Fraggle was sound asleep. Slimy yolk and bits of eggshell stuck to the brick wall a few feet over his head.

I sat down and waited for him to wake up. Fifteen minutes later, his hand pushed the edge of the bag off his face. Still lying down, he told me that he and Stephanie had slept on the corner together the night before, but she'd disappeared hours earlier. She had said she would try to get them both a bag, but she never came back. Fraggle covered his head again and tried to go back to sleep.

A few minutes later, Stephanie appeared. She was dressed in an oversized men's hooded parka, but she was still shivering from the cold. When I touched her forehead, she felt hot.

"Fraggle, Fraggle, Fraggle, listen to me," Stephanie said. Fraggle lay motionless and didn't respond. "Listen, if you go to bed before me, don't lay on top of the blanket like that because it's my blanket and I should have at least a corner of it, OK? I froze my ass off all fuckin' morning."

Fraggle still didn't answer.

"You fuckin' asshole." Stephanie began to pull the edge of the blanket away from Fraggle. "I'm not going to let you take it all," she said, tugging at it.

All of a sudden, Fraggle's arms pushed the blanket from over his head. "You should have fuckin' woke me up, asshole. I sat here till early in the fuckin' morning waiting for you to come."

"You don't gotta call me asshole."

"Take the blanket—I don't care," Fraggle screamed louder, pulling the blanket closer to him.

They were like two children arguing over a toy in a schoolyard; Stephanie grabbed at the blanket, Fraggle clutched it closer.

Suddenly, Fraggle pushed the blanket aside and stood up. He then shoved the blanket hard at Stephanie, knocking her back, and kicked the box of cereal. "You fuckin' bitch. Fuck off," he screamed, his jugular vein sticking out, his neck red. He then kicked the quart of milk. It splashed on the sleeve of her jacket and on her back. Then Fraggle quickly walked away.

Stephanie sat crying. "He does this all the fuckin' time. I have no desire to hang out with him at all. I can't stand the sight of him anymore. I'm tired of fuckin' being screamed at."

Stephanie put her face in her hands and took a deep breath. "I can't take another winter out here if he's going to be like this." More than seventy-five inches of snow had fallen in New York the winter before, twice the normal snowfall for the city. Blizzards downed power lines, schools and offices were shut down, and people glided down major streets and avenues on cross-country skis. Stephanie and Fraggle had made it through that winter by sneaking into apartment buildings and sleeping on the top-floor landings near the roofs, staying in squats and in apartments of kids they met, sleeping on subway platforms or on the trains, and staying up all night drinking coffee in warm coffee shops and diners.

She sat quietly. "I don't even recognize myself anymore," she said. "I used to be a good person. Now look at me." She wiped a tear off her cheek. "I'm dying out here."

.....

TWO DAYS LATER, I saw Stephanie again. She told me that the night before, she had been on the footbridge by the river when a man walked up to her and asked her for a cigarette. He was emaciated, in his late forties, Stephanie learned later, a crack addict.

"I don't have one," she answered.

"Why the fuck don't you have one?" The man took a step toward Stephanie.

Stephanie was scared and took a few steps back.

"I'm going to fuckin' rape you," he said, smiling. "I'm going to give you a head start, but when I get you, I'm going to rape you up the ass."

Stephanie started running as fast as she could. The man stood still.

"You run, but when I get you . . ." The man ran after her, quickly closing the lead Stephanie had on him. When Stephanie reached the housing projects on Avenue D, she ran up to a dope dealer she knew standing on the street. When she told him she was being chased, the man walked her to Avenue C. The man following her eventually disappeared.

Stephanie still seemed shaken the next day as she told me

the story. "When I saw Fraggle and told him how scared I was, did he ask if I was OK? No, all he said was, 'I'm tired of hearing about this shit.'"

．．．．

A FEW DAYS LATER, Fraggle disappeared. He had been gone for three days when I saw Stephanie. Absent, he was more of a presence than when he was around. For days, she had been walking up and down Avenue A asking everybody she knew if they'd seen him. It was possible that he had been arrested, but she feared the worst. "He's got too many enemies out here," she said. "He's probably dead."

Stephanie sat on her corner all day asking everybody who passed by if they had seen Fraggle. She was freezing; Fraggle had sold her sleeping bag for $3.

Later that evening, a woman who worked a prostitution stroll nearby walked up to Stephanie and told her she had heard news about Fraggle. The woman was skinny with stringy hair and had red sores on her face. Her legs and arms had deep purple and black bruises like rotten fruit.

"Hey," she said to Stephanie. "Some kid told me that they saw your boyfriend dead somewhere." The woman knew nothing else and walked away.

Stephanie's mouth and eyes opened wide. She collapsed on the ground. For the next two hours, Stephanie sat on the sidewalk, sobbing. Every few minutes someone came by and sat beside her, trying to calm her down. "It has to be a mistake," one young girl repeated over and over.

Stephanie couldn't bear not knowing if it was true. She stood up and walked over to a pay phone. As she picked up the receiver to dial directory assistance for the number of the city morgue, Stephanie saw Fraggle walking across the street.

At first Stephanie thought that she was hallucinating. "Fraggle," she yelled, dropping the phone. When Fraggle saw Stephanie, he stopped walking. Stephanie ran into oncoming traffic. Drivers honked their horns; others hit their brakes, barely missing her. Stephanie threw her arms around him. "I thought you were dead," she cried between sobs. "Some kid said he saw you dead."

Fraggle hugged her and said nothing.

. . . .

THE NEXT DAY Fraggle and Stephanie sat huddled under a food-stained comforter on the sidewalk, hugging and kissing.

Fraggle quietly sang the lyrics to their favorite song. "Sugar pie, honey bunch, you know that I love you. I can't help myself, I love you and nobody else."

Stephanie was radiant. "He's always singing that song to me," she said, giggling. They looked like they could be in the back of a convertible at a drive-in.

Fraggle stretched over to grab a box of Cap'n Crunch cereal. "We're both cereal people," he said, taking out a handful. "I knew when I first met her and I bought a box of cereal and she loved it. I knew it was love at first sight." Fraggle stood up and said he'd be right back.

As soon as Fraggle left, Stephanie's face grew stern. "He disappeared for three days," she said in a scratchy voice. "He said he tried to kick. He made it till yesterday. But I have mixed emotions about all of this. He said, 'You didn't want me around, so I thought I would leave and see how you feel when I'm not around.' He fuckin' leaves, and I fuckin' miss him and get all worried, and then he comes back." She was angry, relieved, and confused. She felt he had played a cruel joke on her. "What Fraggle did was totally manipulative, but he won't admit that's what he was doing." She took a deep breath. "I thought he was dead."

Fraggle told me later he had gone to Liza's house. Her parents were out of town and she told him he could come by and clean up. He and Liza came into the city every day, shoplifted books, and copped dope before returning to her house in the evening.

Stephanie stood up, holding her ribs. "I'll be right back," she said and staggered away to get a cup of coffee. Jake, a thirty-year-old blond man who lived in the neighborhood, walked over to me. "I tell you, if Stephanie doesn't get out of this situation, her spirit is going to be imprisoned forever, and she'll be a walking zombie. I see it starting to happen."

We talked for a few minutes. Then Jake asked me, "Why don't you take her home?"

Stephanie overhead his question on her way back. "It's not that easy," she said before I could answer. "I'm a junkie. Nobody can just take me home like that. Can I have a cigarette?" she asked Jake, purposely changing the subject. She offered Jake the change she had in her hand.

"The only thing I want from you is a hug," he said. Stephanie leaned forward and gave him a stiff hug, still wincing from the pressure on her ribs.

Stephanie turned her back to him. Eventually Jake walked away.

"I've got to get the fuck out of New York," she said. "But Fraggle has nowhere to go." Stephanie sat down on the ground. "I was a fuckin' wreck last night. After I found out it wasn't true that he was dead, I said screw it. I called Jeanette and told her I'm coming out there. I can't do this anymore. She was ready to get into the car and come and get me because I was such a fuckin' mess. I'm going to try to get on methadone out there." Stephanie started to nod off, sleepy from the dope she'd just taken a few minutes earlier.

Stephanie seemed serious about getting off the street. Leaning against the wall, she opened her eyes for a minute. "I know he's not my responsibility, but Fraggle has nowhere to go. How am I supposed to leave him here?" A few seconds later, she was asleep.

. . . .

IN EARLY NOVEMBER, Fraggle called his mother and told her he wanted to come home. He usually called his mother every few weeks because he knew she worried about him and he wanted her to know he was OK. But this time when he asked to come home, his mother, tired of Fraggle's broken promises, told him he couldn't. "I was crying and told her everything," Fraggle said. He even told his mother he was "sucking old men's dicks" and that he was scared. He told her that he wanted to get a job and go back to school. "She said, 'You always say that.' I guess I've said that a couple of times before," Fraggle admitted.

Fraggle then called his father, who was living with his own parents. Frank's girlfriend lived next door with her daughter and two-year-old granddaughter. Fraggle said that Frank had told him he could stay next door, but only if Fraggle promised to stay off drugs and look for a job. "He just got out of prison, and he wants me to be straight with the law before I come down there," Fraggle said. But Fraggle hadn't gone to court to set the terms of his probation after his release from Rikers, and there was a warrant out for him. Fraggle had no other options. He said he had a friend in Virginia who had her own place, and he would have felt comfortable kicking at her house. "But Stephanie would freak out about me living with another girl."

Besides, no one was willing to pay for his bus ticket and at that point he had no money; whatever he made tricking, he used to buy dope. For the time being, Fraggle was stuck in New York.

. . . .

WHEN BOB ARIHOOD saw Stephanie shivering in a doorway one rainy night, he stopped to talk to her. It was pouring; she was soaked and crying. Bob had been living on the Lower East Side for more than twenty-five years, documenting, through photography, the neighborhood in and around Tompkins Square Park. He had met Stephanie in the spring of 1996, just a few months after she and Fraggle moved to New York. He thought her to be about fourteen or fifteen and even contacted the local precinct to let them know that a little girl was living on the street. "With Stephanie there was no posing, no piercings," said Bob. "She wasn't threatening, like some of the other kids. She also played the game of being the little girl, and people fell for it. She could make you continue to feel sorry for her for a long time and make you want to help her."

But Bob was now worried about Stephanie. He'd seen her body deteriorate and her personality transform. Sometimes Bob would talk to Stephanie, but he usually just left her alone. That night during the second week of November, when he saw her shivering in the rain, he thought she was dangerously close to death. A lot of the people he had photographed had died on the street from overdoses, AIDS, and violence. He feared that Stephanie might be next.

"People are trying to help you get out of here," he said to Stephanie. "Why don't you accept their help?"

Stephanie sat curled up in a ball, crying uncontrollably.

Bob tried again. "I'm sorry to sound like your father, but people are trying to help you. You spend the day running around and buying drugs all day. It's going to kill you."

Snot was running out of her nose. "It's not that easy," she said and continued to cry. How could she explain that her addiction to heroin was keeping her alive? Without constantly chasing after her next fix, she felt she would be dead.

The next evening, still worried, Bob telephoned me. I was spending less time on the street with Stephanie because she had become increasingly difficult to find. When I did find her, she was either too busy or too high to talk. "I think you should know that things are really bad out there," Bob said. "There are some really dangerous people who are angry at her." I had seen so many people threaten Stephanie one day and then act as if nothing had happened the next that I found it increasingly difficult to determine who was a real threat. "Maybe you can do something. She seems to open up to you."

"She won't accept help from anybody."

I told Bob that I would look for her and see what I could do. His final words, before he hung up, resonated the rest of the night. "I've never seen her look so desperate," he said. "She's going to die out there if she doesn't get some help."

The next day, I couldn't find Stephanie. I looked for her the day after and the day after that. On November 16th, Bob called to tell me that Stephanie was leaving for Ohio the next day.

••••

THE NEXT MORNING, I went looking for Stephanie. I walked around the neighborhood for an hour before I found her. She was lying with Fraggle under an unzipped goose-down sleeping bag, on a soiled mattress. Dressed in her hooded ski parka, Stephanie was wrapped tightly around Fraggle to keep warm, but she was still shivering from the cold.

I sat on the edge of the sleeping bag. When Stephanie opened her eyes and saw me, she began to cry. "I don't want to leave," she said. The words were barely audible. "But I have to. Everything's arranged." Jeanette had wired money for a bus ticket to a woman in the neighborhood who had befriended Stephanie. Jeanette would be waiting for Stephanie with some other friends at the bus station in Ohio on the 18th. Someone else from the neighborhood, Sammy, had bought Stephanie three hundred milligrams of methadone to keep her from going through severe withdrawal symptoms during the nearly ten-hour bus ride. At this point, Stephanie was shooting up to twenty bags of heroin and a gram of cocaine a day. The methadone was just enough to keep Stephanie from getting sick on the bus and would probably last until she could get into a methadone program.

Stephanie's pupils were dilated, and she was nauseous. Her joints and muscles were aching so much that she could barely move. She hadn't slept in three days and also hadn't shot any heroin that morning.

"Maybe it will motivate me to get the hell out of here," said Fraggle, trying to be supportive but also hoping that once Stephanie was gone, he would be able to leave as well. "Will you leave the sleeping bag with me?" he added, laughing. Stephanie squeezed him tighter, crying even harder.

Sammy and his girlfriend came by to let Stephanie know that they had secured the bottles of methadone for her trip.

"I want to thank you guys for helping her," Fraggle said.

"I just want to see Stephanie get healthy," Sammy answered. "It's hard core out here. It's just having a heart. I'm not looking for nothing from you guys. You should take a rest too, Fraggle, because you're going to hurt yourself out here. I know you know that."

"She just needs you to support her, Fraggle, that's all," added Sarah, Sammy's girlfriend. She seemed to be blaming Fraggle for all of Stephanie's problems. "Maybe this will be a little inspiration for you, too."

No one spoke, and Sammy and Sarah walked away, promising to return later in the evening.

"Why does everybody think that I want you to be out here in the fuckin' street?" Fraggle asked. "All morning, people kept saying to me, 'And don't you try to talk her out of it.' I don't want you to be out here anymore than you do. Once you're out of here Steph, I'm going to be busting my ass to get out of here. I do not want to sit on these fuckin' streets by myself. I have no friends here. All these people here think I want to stay here. I would have been home yesterday, but I fucked up." A day earlier, Liza's mother had bought Fraggle a bus ticket to Virginia, but he had sold the ticket for dope. He couldn't leave Stephanie on the street alone.

Stephanie knew that this was her last chance to get off the street. She was not going to have another paid bus ticket and enough methadone to make it through a trip back home. She knew that if she didn't leave this time, she might never leave. And she knew that if she didn't leave, she might die.

····

STEPHANIE told me later that she decided she could leave Fraggle after she had caught him tricking. Fraggle often lied to Stephanie about his whereabouts because he knew it upset her when he left to be with one of his customers. Fraggle had left to go hang out with a "friend" from the neighborhood, promising he would be back soon. Again, Stephanie didn't believe him, but this time, high on cocaine, she followed him, trailing one block behind until they got to the bleachers by the baseball field by the East River. Stephanie was about twenty-five feet away when she saw Fraggle bent down in front of a man.

Stephanie started screaming, "I fuckin' hate you. You're fuckin' disgusting."

"Stephanie you don't understand," yelled Fraggle back. "Let me just finish this and we'll talk."

"Fuck you," she said and walked away.

Fraggle told me much later that he was sitting on the bleachers with his legs stretched out, his shoes and socks off. The man he was with was sucking Fraggle's toes. "I know it sounds disgusting," he said. "But that's how this guy gets turned on. I've told Stephanie over and over again, but she won't believe me."

Stephanie told me she had thrown up. "I knew what he was doing, but to see it was a whole different story," she said, convinced she had seen Fraggle giving the man a blow job. For the next week, she was obsessed with the image. "After that, I really didn't trust him. He disgusted me."

About a week later, Stephanie and Fraggle had one of their worst fights, and this time, Stephanie really wanted to hurt him.

They were just outside Tompkins Square Park. As they yelled at each other, Stephanie threw glass bottles at Fraggle, the bottles shattering by his feet. Fraggle jumped the iron fence into Tompkins Square Park to get away. One leg had cleared the fence when a neighborhood kid, who was also a member of DOA, asked Stephanie, "Hey, what's going on?"

"He just kicked my ass," Stephanie screamed, pointing at Fraggle. The DOA member liked Stephanie, but not Fraggle. Stephanie gave him the green light to go after Fraggle, and within seconds the gang member, with some of his crew, began chasing him.

Fraggle, terrified, ran to a police officer for protection. The crew members ran away. Hours later, a rumor circulated on the street that the police had caught up to the DOA boys and had beaten up one of the members. The crew was out to get Fraggle.

Fraggle kept running until he collapsed, exhausted, at the bottom of the stairwell at the Christopher Street subway stop, where he fell asleep. Then he called Liza and went to her house for the next couple of days.

While Fraggle was away, Stephanie realized that she had to leave New York. For the first time, she was really scared. She had grown terrified of everything around her. She knew she was dying. Sitting on Avenue A, she pulled out a piece of paper from a loose-leaf notebook she carried in her bag and wrote Fraggle a letter:

Fraggle,
Well, here we . . . I go again. I promised you that I would never leave again without saying goodbye and I won't. I've looked everywhere for you for the past two days. I hope that we can at least speak to each other before I go. I definitely want to apologize to you for that last fight. It's just that all that anger had been inside me for two days while I waited to talk to you. I did want to ask you about things first but you were never around to give me the chance. I'm sorry things turned out the way they have. But no matter what, even if you hate me forever, I will always love you very much. And I hope that some day you realize that I tried very hard to get back together. But I just couldn't stand being alone all the time, three days at a time, wondering if that was it, if I was never going to see you again. It hurt too much. I couldn't take it.
Love, Stephanie

Stephanie ripped the page from her spiral notebook and left it with Ray, of Ray's Candy Store. When Fraggle returned, he heard that Stephanie was leaving and went to find her. When I saw them, they were clinging to each other.

••••

WHEN I OFFERED to go with Stephanie to Ohio, she nodded yes without hesitation. She had decided to take a late bus so she could spend more time with Fraggle. I left them to spend their final hours together alone and told Stephanie to call me later that night.

By seven that evening, I still hadn't heard from Stephanie. Bob Arihood called me and told me that Sarah, Sammy's girlfriend, and Rachel, a college student who lived in the neighborhood, had been looking for Stephanie all afternoon and couldn't find her.

Already rumors began to circulate: Fraggle had been badly beaten by members of DOA because he had snitched on them to the police; DOA hadn't caught up with Fraggle, but were looking to hurt him; Stephanie had sold the methadone and was hiding.

Two hours later, Bob called again. Stephanie and Fraggle had been found.

I went to Seventh Street and found Stephanie and Fraggle huddled together where I'd left them earlier in the day. Sarah, Rachel, and Bob were standing nearby. Stephanie's stomach was cramping, and she was nauseous and shaking. She had shot only three bags of dope all day. She took a swig of the methadone Sammy gave her for the trip, and within a few minutes she started to feel better.

Sarah walked over to the blanket and bent down. "Come on, Stephanie. We have to go now," she said. It was nearly ten and we needed to catch the 11:30 bus to Cleveland. She and Rachel had been trying for half an hour to get Stephanie up, but Stephanie wouldn't budge.

The two women thought that with Bob's help, they could drag Stephanie away from Fraggle and put her into a taxi to the Port Authority. When Stephanie heard this, she grabbed Fraggle tighter, her arms and legs locked around his body. Stephanie was prepared to fight anyone who tried to move her.

I knelt down to talk with her. "I don't want to go," she said in a voice so groggy it was barely audible. "I can't leave him. I'll be back in a week if he stays." Stephanie was crying. With DOA gang members looking for him, there was no way Stephanie was going to leave Fraggle alone on the street.

"If Fraggle left New York, would you leave?" I asked.

"Yes," she answered, without a pause.

Bob offered to buy Fraggle a bus ticket back home, and Fraggle agreed. If he showed up at his mother's house in Virginia, she might take him back. If that didn't work, Fraggle could stay with his father's girlfriend.

Bob didn't think that Fraggle would actually stay in Virginia, but he knew that getting him off the street would get Stephanie on that bus. "Sometimes when you make that extra effort with people, they turn their lives around," he told me later.

Stephanie and I missed the 11:30 bus, but there was another at two, a local, which meant the trip would take five hours longer. Sarah gave Stephanie and Fraggle some methadone, which they drank out of the bottle. Neither Fraggle nor Stephanie had eaten all day, so we went to Leshko's.

As we sat waiting for the food, I saw how much Stephanie had deteriorated. She was little more than skin and bones. She had a cut over her left eye, and she winced every time she drew a breath. Her arms were covered with dark purple bruises and dozens of scabs, and her clothes were crusted and stained with blood. Shooting up had become so painful that she'd begun shooting just below her armpit.

At 12:30, we took a taxi to the Port Authority bus terminal. Stephanie and Fraggle carried nothing but the clothes they had been sleeping in for weeks, the sleeping bag, and a stained yellow pillow for the bus trip. At the gate, Stephanie and Fraggle sat on the ground and, one last time, made their bed together on the linoleum floor. From a distance, they looked like high school sweethearts traveling across the country.

When it was time to board the bus to Ohio, Stephanie stood up, gave Fraggle a small bottle of methadone, and hugged him. All the passengers boarded the bus except Stephanie, who stood inside the gate, hugging and kissing Fraggle goodbye. Finally, she tore herself away, climbed onto the bus, put her sleeping bag and pillow on a seat, and then again jumped off and ran back to his arms.

When the driver honked his horn at her and turned the key in the ignition to start the engine, Stephanie again pulled herself away from Fraggle and boarded the bus. As we drove off, she waved goodbye, her face pressed against the window. "It just kept getting worse, the longer I was out there," she said. "We got out of here, and that's a first step and that's fuckin' great." She closed her eyes for a second. "But it's going to be a long tough road. Now it's going to be really hard."

Stephanie's hands were caked with dirt, the creases of her fingerprints embedded with grime. She took off her shoes and socks; her feet were swollen and pudgy, like an infant's. But Stephanie was totally relaxed: She had already taken nearly ninety grams of methadone. Within a few minutes, the methadone kicked in even more, and Stephanie fell into a deep sleep. She sat slumped over in her seat, completely limp, her legs stretched out in the narrow aisle, her mouth wide open.

Eight hours later, we stopped in Buffalo to switch buses. As we waited for our connection, Stephanie sat quietly on the cement. "I wonder how I'm going to do it," she said to me. "I'm really scared about seeing everyone. I never want to live like that again. I know I almost died out there." She picked a cigarette butt off the ground, lit it and inhaled.

"That's sad," said a man standing nearby.

"Look, I'm homeless, and I've been sleeping on the side-walk for the last year and a half. If you have a problem with it, kiss my ass." The man walked away. Stephanie giggled.

She slept a good part of the rest of the trip. When the bus finally pulled into the gate in Cleveland, Stephanie combed through her hair with her fingers, then dusted off her stained T-shirt and khaki pants. "I'm scared to death," she said.

She got up, walked down the aisle and off the bus, leaving the sleeping bag and pillow on the seat.

Outside it was cold, only twenty-four degrees. Stephanie didn't seem to notice.

REDEFINE ALONE

Stephanie

alone and content
content to be me ...
Knowing what I've been
            and who I am now
A beautiful woman with
            big brown eyes...
Content with the world ...
    the space
        that I occupy
    no longer occupies me ....
A haven of furry creatures
and brilliant poetry....
    A reflection of almost
every dream realized
    with utter perfection....

TO: NEW YORK

. . . and I remember you in the way the wind blows cold like ice into my veins and I can feel the hard reality of the concrete under my head fade into an opiate induced indifference just before I close my eyes for one last nod and you are etched in my being and in everything that I am and in all the moments where pain exists . . . and for all of this I love you . . . and I hate you for showing me who I am not, and for showing me the oh, so many ways to fall helplessly . . . and you were more solid than any reality I had ever experienced before . . . you with your beautiful concrete apathy . . . like a mother of my very own who nourished me with lies and forgot my name from time to time, but your trains were always there and your tunnels were there and your womb was there and I could hide for lifetimes and days and dream of how you would so carelessly destroy me and to this day when I catch a glimpse of you in the wind my soul shivers and I am forever reminded of home . . .

—Stephanie

TWO

Throwing Shade

Fear

Fear is all I know,
My one true friend.
Dark as midnight,
Light as day,
Presents of the trusted
Sometimes far away.
My liver—poisoned, toxic
My ankles like iron bolts
My sweat glands—shocked
Far beyond repair.
It's not my drug of choice
But something to remember.
Nothing seems to help it.
Fear is always near.

—Juan

JUAN opened his eyes. He was in a hospital bed on Long Island, connected to an IV drip, his cheeks so swollen they looked as though they had been stuffed with tennis balls. Shades of purple and blue covered the right side of his face from hairline to chin. A small cut over one eye was crusted with blood. For a few seconds Juan couldn't remember what had happened. Then, he remembered everything. He lay absolutely still for a while, closed his eyes and sank back into sleep.

It was January 1999. Thirteen-year-old Juan had been beaten up at school because he was gay.

Since June 1998, Juan had lived in several group homes, a foster home, and a teen homeless shelter, and because he had moved so much, he had missed half a year of school. In December 1999, Juan was placed in yet another group home in Queens. Once settled, he was enrolled in the seventh grade.

Just before the semester began, Juan was excited. And nervous. When he met with the dean, he asked if any other boys at the school were openly gay. None were and he was warned to be careful about what he said to his classmates. "I hope the other boys don't give me trouble," Juan told me. "But I'm not going to lie. I'm not going to hide the fact that I'm gay."

Juan hated sports, going to the gym, and talking about girls. He loved performing in plays, changing his hairstyle, shopping for clothes, and singing along to Mariah Carey. His step was lighter than that of other boys, and his movements more graceful and fluid. Like other boys his age, Juan developed crushes, but on boys, and he openly flirted with the ones he thought were cute.

Juan knew other boys who were quietly gay. He understood why they chose secrecy, but Juan refused to hide his own feelings. "Even when I act straight," he told me, "people say I'm flamboyant." Some days when he was teased or taunted for being gay, he was scared; other days he felt he could fight off any attacker. Sometimes, he didn't seem to realize the danger he put himself in; other times, he didn't seem to care.

The morning of Juan's first day of school, he put on his favorite pair of black army pants and a T-shirt. "I wasn't trying to be masculine," he said. "But I was trying not to be a flaming fag until they got to know me." His hair was short, curly and bleached, the dark brown roots about an eighth of an inch long. He thought about dying it black to look less conspicuous, but he decided he liked the way it looked.

The first day, the students seemed pleased to have a new boy in their class. "Everyone was really nice to me," Juan said. "I was the new kid, and everyone wanted to sit with me and get to know me." Some of the kids asked Juan if he was gay. Sometimes he ignored the question; other times, he just laughed and walked away. After a while, he simply snapped the question back: "Are *you* gay?"

The next morning Juan woke up happy to be going to school, and he was looking forward to making new friends. For the first time in a long while, he felt he was finally going to have a normal life: hanging out with kids who accepted him, doing homework, and getting involved in after-school activities.

That day, when one of the girls in his class asked if he was gay, Juan said yes. The news spread quickly. Later that morning, Juan talked back to one of his teachers and was sent to the principal's office. A couple of his classmates told Juan that after he left the classroom, the teacher had called him a "faggot."

When classes ended at 2:30, Juan left to go home. He was walking across the school yard when a boy suddenly came up to him and asked, "Are you a faggot?" When Juan told him it was none of his business, the boy punched him. Juan's books fell to the ground, but he quickly recovered and hit the boy back. A group of girls nearby tried to stop the fight. But the boy cranked back his arm to hit Juan again. A second boy came up beside Juan and punched him hard in the chin. Juan fell, blood pouring out of his mouth onto the concrete. The boy had broken Juan's jaw.

The two boys stood over Juan for a long moment. As they ran away, they yelled back at him, "That's for being a faggot." According to a teacher, the boys had been in trouble before.

Later that afternoon, as Juan lay in a hospital bed, police detectives interviewed him. The attack was deemed a bias crime, and the case went to family court. The school suspended the boys for five days. No student assembly was held after the attack to address the incident.

Juan had been in foster care and under the custody of New York's Administration for Children's Services (ACS) since he was nine. His mother and maternal grandmother were both dead, and he hadn't seen his father in years. The only family he saw regularly was Malcolm, his sixteen-year-old half brother by a different father.

When Juan tried to call his older brother, Malcolm's father often wouldn't let him speak to Juan. Sometimes he yelled at Juan and told him to leave his son alone. He felt that Juan was a bad influence on Malcolm and encouraged him to be disobedient. "I think he blames me for Malcolm being bisexual," Juan said. Malcolm and Juan hadn't spoken to each other for months. "We're not that close because he never listens to me," said Juan. "But he is my brother."

Now in the hospital and facing surgery, Juan wanted to talk to his brother, and he asked the nurse to make the call. When the nurse handed him the phone, Juan sat up, excited. "Hi, Malcolm. It's Juan. I was gay-bashed, and they broke my jaw in two places."

Juan was in pain and mumbling loudly. Remarkably, he was able to make himself understood. Juan asked his brother where he was going to school, how he was doing on the swim team, what he got for Christmas, if he was getting As or Bs in school. When Juan didn't like what he heard, he acted as though he were the older brother. "Now don't slack off, Malcolm," he said. "What do you do after school? You can't go out on weekends? What if I want to see you?" Malcolm told Juan his father didn't want him seeing him. "I'm your damn brother, Malcolm." Juan raised his voice as loud as he could, keeping his lips about a quarter-inch apart. "Do you hear how he curses me out on the phone?" At one point Juan got angry with his brother. "I wasn't about to dye my hair black just to go to school. I'm not in the closet. Do you have any clue how many times I've been gay-bashed?" Juan didn't want to hear anyone even suggest that his behavior had somehow provoked the attack.

Juan switched subjects rapidly and filled his brother in on the highlights of the past four months of his life. He told Malcolm that he was living in a new group home in Queens and spoke proudly of his job as an outreach worker for the New York Peer AIDS Education Coalition, where he received a weekly stipend to educate other kids about HIV transmission and prevention. "I got you something for Christmas." He sounded anxious to please Malcolm. "Were you planning on getting me anything? I bought you a shirt and a pair of pants."

They talked for nearly an hour. After Juan hung up the phone, he cupped his hand around the bottom of his jaw and closed his eyes.

For the next few hours, his jaw aching, Juan drifted in and out of consciousness. He was uncomfortable lying on his back, but the medication he had been given made it difficult to stay awake. By early evening, he was alert again. When I told him the boys from the group home would be visiting before his surgery, he panicked. "Oh, no," he said, covering his face. "I don't want them to see me this way."

Juan cared about how he looked. His eyes were big, dark brown and shiny as licorice; his eyelashes, long and thick. He had full lips and round cheeks. His complexion was a light golden brown, and he kept it flawless by frequently swabbing his face with Sea Breeze antiseptic lotion and dotting it with Clearasil. He changed the length, style, and color of his hair regularly.

Juan frantically pressed the buzzer by his bed. No one came. After a few minutes he buzzed again. Ten minutes later, a nurse walked in. "Nurse, do you have some gauze for my face?"

The nurse hesitated. She seemed confused. Juan explained that he wanted to wrap his face because he didn't want the boys in his group home to see how he looked. The nurse smiled but told him that his face would have to stay uncovered. Juan was disappointed. He grabbed a small hand towel and tried draping it over his cheek. Realizing this was too obvious and very awkward, he practiced holding his hand casually over his face in different positions to cover the swelling. After about five minutes, he gave up. He sat up and looked in a mirror on the wall by the side of his bed. "I look terrible," he said and slumped back into his pillow.

About an hour later, five teenage boys walked into his hospital room. Juan had covered his jaw with the towel, but after aggressive coaxing from the boys, he showed them his face. The boys stepped in to get a closer look. Then they grew quiet.

Juan had been living with the boys for about a month. They teased him regularly and often relentlessly about being gay. Some days it really upset him. But this evening, the teenagers seemed to have sympathy for their housemate. "That's not right, what they did to you, Juan," one of the boys said. He was nearly six feet tall and round. His small head seemed the wrong size for his body. Another boy, his oversize pants slung way below his skinny hips, jumped on the bed, lay next to Juan, and played with the television remote. A third boy pushed buttons on a second remote that operated the bed. With each press, the boy made Juan's upper body, knees, and feet glide up and down. Juan smiled. He liked the attention.

"Yo, we can go get those boys and mess them up," said another boy, stick-thin with gangly limbs. He was short and looked no older than twelve. A couple of the other kids nodded their heads in agreement.

"Beating them up isn't going to solve anything," Juan said. "But I want them to go to jail for what they did." Juan's grandmother had taught him to be nice to people even when they weren't nice to him. "I let God take care of things," he told me later. "It might be twenty years from now, but he'll take care of them."

After the boys left, Juan lay still and stared up at the television screen. He pressed the remote, running through all the channels twice, before turning off the set. The screen went black. Juan was numb. "Stuff like this happens all the time," he told me. "It happens so much I'm used to it."

So often had it happened to Juan and other gay, lesbian, and bisexual youths in foster care that a federal class action lawsuit had, ironically, been filed just one day after Juan was attacked at school. The suit charged that because of their sexual orientation, gay, lesbian, and bisexual youths were routinely subjected to physical violence and psychological abuse in the city's child welfare system. The lawsuit, filed by the Urban Justice Center (a nonprofit advocacy organization for the homeless) and the law firm Paul Weiss, Rifkind, Wharton & Garrison, was the first of its kind in the country. The plaintiffs named in the lawsuit, *Joel A. v. Giuliani,* described experiences of homophobic abuse—from unrelenting harassment to broken bones to sexual abuse—by peers, foster parents, and staff members of child welfare agencies. Their complaints and pleas for protection were either routinely ignored or they were told they invited or deserved the abuse, according to the suit. The plaintiffs also alleged that some group homes for young people had a de facto policy against admitting gay youth, and that city officials had repeatedly ignored pleas by youth advocates to expand services to gay youth. "The defendants' failure to protect members of the class from bias-related aggression results in extreme physical, psychological, emotional, and developmental injury," the complaint read.

As an immediate remedy, the suit sought foster care facilities specially staffed and programmed as "safe houses," and in the long term, staff training to make all placements safe and supportive for self-identified lesbian, gay, bisexual, and transgendered youth of all ages. The suit also requested that ACS develop, implement, and enforce procedures to investigate complaints and harassment against these youths; issue periodic and widespread official policy statements of nondiscrimination based on sexual orientation; and establish a technical support center to address issues affecting these kids.

Within the foster care system, the needs of lesbian, gay, bisexual, and transgendered kids had been largely ignored. In January 1999, out of more than sixty foster care agencies in New York City caring for the nearly forty thousand children in the city's custody, only Green Chimneys Gramercy Residence, a four-story row house on Manhattan's East Side, served gay, bisexual, and transgender youth. Green Chimneys, however, could handle only twenty-five boys, ages sixteen to twenty-one. The only other residential foster program in the entire country specifically for gay youths was in California, and served about thirty-six boys and girls.

Juan had been anxiously waiting for the lawsuit to be filed. Over the past seven months, he had run away from several group and foster homes because, he said, he felt uncomfortable and unsafe. He hoped that the lawsuit would force the city to open up a group home for gay kids his age and was ecstatic when he heard in the hospital that the papers had been filed. "Now they have to find a place for me immediately," he mumbled.

That evening, Juan's jaw was wired shut. For the next few days, he would be able to communicate only with paper and pen. For the next six weeks, he would have to feed himself by squirting liquids through a plastic syringe squeezed between his teeth.

During his stay in the hospital, Juan slept most of the time. The nurse gave him Demerol to ease the pain. When he was awake, he worried that the swelling had gotten worse and that the wires wouldn't be off his jaw in time for him to perform in a talent show at the end of February put on by one of the local drop-in centers for homeless youth. He had spent months rehearsing and wanted to look good on stage. The only thing that kept him optimistic was that he would lose weight. At about 160 pounds and a little over five feet six inches tall, Juan wasn't fat, but he was conscious of his weight and wanted to be thinner.

After three days, Juan was able to speak more easily, although he was still having difficulty enunciating his words. He looked forward to being discharged to his group home the next day. "The boys were nice to me," he said about his housemates who had visited. "I know they feel bad about what happened. I don't think they'll give me a hard time anymore."

. . . .

A WEEK AFTER DISCHARGE, Juan called me from the emergency room. One of the boys in his group home had hit him in the jaw. "Can you please call ACS and tell them I don't want to go back there after the hospital?" He sounded scared. When I told him that he should call the agency himself to explain exactly what happened, he said, "They don't listen to me. They won't do anything if I call. Please call them. I don't feel safe."

I called ACS's Emergency Children's Service office. "Under these circumstances, we expect the agency to transfer the child to another group home," said the man on the phone. "If he makes the request and they refuse, then the state hot line should be called."

I didn't hear from Juan again until the next afternoon. Everything I told him, he already knew. He had been through so many group homes and shelters, he knew the rules and procedures by heart. "I'm OK now," he said. "I still don't feel safe, but I'm going to stay. The lawsuit will force ACS to open up a new group home for gay kids soon anyway."

Juan would have to wait a long time before a new group home for gay youth opened in New York City. Two weeks after *Joel A. v. Giuliani* was filed, a federal judge approved the sweeping settlement of another federal class action lawsuit against New York City's child welfare system. The suit, *Marisol v. Giuliani*, which was filed in 1995 shortly after six-year-old Elisa Izquierdo was beaten to death by her mother while under the city's watch, charged that ACS had failed so completely to protect children in its care, the federal government should put the agency into receivership and let a federal judge determine who would run the city's child welfare system. The *Marisol v. Giuliani* settlement opened ACS to an intense two-year independent scrutiny by an advisory panel composed of child welfare experts. The panel would closely monitor the performance of ACS and issue recommendations and timetables for improving and reforming the agency. Any recommendations the panel might make would not be binding on ACS, and the court could not intervene as long as the panel reported that the agency was acting in "good faith" to implement reforms. Unfortunately for Juan, the settlement also set a moratorium on new class action suits filed during the same period.

But the door wasn't completely shut. The lawyers for *Joel A. v. Giuliani* appealed the settlement in the Second U.S. Circuit Court of Appeals. If the appeal was denied, the plaintiffs could still sue the city as individuals. Either way, Juan had decided he was suing. And he was suing ACS, his legal guardian. He wasn't living in a place where he felt safe, and securing such a place would probably take a very long time.

....

I MET JUAN through the New York Peer AIDS Education Coalition (NYPAEC). I had written a magazine piece about the group in 1995 and had stayed in close contact with a couple of the kids. In the fall of 1998, Angela Echevarria, one of the original peers, told me about Juan. He had been with NYPAEC just a few months, and Angela was struck by his enthusiasm and wit. When Angela told Juan about my project, he called the next day.

We met in the West Village. Juan was cheerfully passing out plastic packets of condoms from a bag to people on the street, reminding them how important it was to practice safe sex. "You want vanilla flavored or mint?" he asked one couple. "Take what you like, because you have to use these every time the mood strikes." HIV/AIDS had killed people he loved. He seemed to take his responsibility working for NYPAEC seriously.

In 1999, every hour, two young people between the ages of thirteen to twenty-one were infected with HIV in the United States. It was estimated that half of all new HIV infections in the United States occurred among young people under twenty-five, and one-quarter of new infections occurred among people ages thirteen to twenty-one. Those youth most at risk for contracting HIV were gay men of color.

NYPAEC was created in 1990 when three organizations (Streetwork Project, St. Clement's Episcopal Church, and Sanctuary for Families) became concerned about the rising level of prostitution and drug use among youth on the streets. The resulting coalition asked clinical psychologist Edith Springer to set up an organization to address the needs of the most difficult-to-reach youth populations in New York

City: street youth, prostitutes, squatters, active drug users. Fliers were posted on the streets inviting anyone interested in doing HIV outreach to a dinner meeting at St. Clement's. More than thirty kids appeared that night, and twelve decided to become peer educators. Juan learned about NYPAEC through a flier he'd seen taped to a wall at a local drop-in center for homeless youth.

Harm reduction was at the core of NYPAEC's philosophy. Harm reduction accepted that drug use was a fact of life and worked to minimize its harmful effects rather than simply ignore or condemn it. The philosophy could be applied to all behavior, not just drug use. It helped young people understand the risks associated with their practices and learn strategies to reduce these risks. Most importantly, it viewed street youth as competent to make their own decisions at their own pace.

By the mid-1990s, there were about twenty-seven active NYPAEC peer educators, and most had spent some part of their lives living on the streets. The group included former and current homeless teens, high school students, squatters, gay, heterosexual, and transgender youth. A majority were African American and Hispanic. Many were active drug users, some prostituted, and about a quarter knew they were HIV positive. The number of active peers varied from month to month and year to year: Some took breaks by choice, some went to college or got full-time jobs, some were hospitalized, still others were incarcerated. From the group's start to the end of 1999, five peers had died—one from a drug overdose, one from HIV, one from an asthma attack, one from a stabbing, another was shot in the head.

NYPAEC peers did outreach wherever they happened to be: in Manhattan, Brooklyn, the Bronx, Queens, and Staten Island; on the prostitution strolls, in squats, parks, strip joints, dance clubs; in agencies, shelters, at transportation terminals; in schools, the foster care system—wherever young people were found. Educators passed out condoms, dental dams, finger cots, lubricants, and AIDS literature, working at all hours of the night to get their message out: If you're going to do it, do it safely.

The peer educators met weekly in two smaller groups to discuss their outreach work and to plan events. They were paid $22.50 a week as a stipend to defray their expenses. For many of the peers, NYPAEC functioned as a family and helped them to stabilize their lives.

NYPAEC peers received extensive training in sexually transmitted diseases, including HIV, education and prevention, harm reduction, and outreach work. Peer educators made presentations at conferences, local agencies, and schools and gave training sessions at health clinics.

"Juan is like a sponge," said Jennie Cassiano, who was then NYPAEC's peer education program coordinator. "He takes it all in. He's tremendously smart. Because he hasn't been in school for so long and is not being challenged in any way, he's constantly reaching out for new information. His ability to take in and process information is extraordinary."

At a meeting to educate foster kids about HIV/AIDS, I saw for myself how much Juan had learned as a NYPAEC peer educator. Juan was able to explain, in detail, how HIV was diagnosed, what T-cell counts meant, what the results were of the latest clinical trials, what vaccines were on the market or being tested, and what testing techniques were being used. He knew how and why infants born to an HIV-positive mother mother could test positive and then seroconvert and test negative months later. He also knew how and when the test for HIV was initially developed. At the session, he described how drugs like crack facilitated HIV transmission: "They fog your judgment and break down your immune system. Also, crack makes your lips dry and crack. You can get it through a broken pipe stem pressed on your lips."

For Juan, NYPAEC was a safe place where he could be himself. As a peer educator, he also felt needed. "There are so many kids out there on their own," he said. Advocates estimated that between 15 percent and 30 percent of street kids were HIV positive. "But if you give them condoms and explain how they can protect themselves, you can help save their lives."

· · · ·

FROM THE TIME he was eleven months old, Juan lived with his grandmother Roseanne and brother Malcolm in a two-bedroom apartment in a housing project near Lincoln Center in Manhattan. As a small child he often asked about his mother. "She left," he was always told. When he was older, he was told his mother was a drug user and a prostitute.

His father floated in and out of his life. A neighbor told me that Juan's father was seldom around because he was in and out of jail. "They were never married," Juan said about his parents. "For all I know, I was a mistake. He'd come around every few years just to say hello. He didn't even know the date of my birthday."

Although Juan's mother came to the apartment periodically to try to get money from his grandmother, who had custody of Juan and his brother, Juan remembered meeting his mother for the first time when he was only six. At that point, she was about twenty-five years old and living in a residential facility in the Bronx for people with AIDS.

Juan's first memory of his mother remained vivid. Early one morning, he and his grandmother had taken the subway to 161st Street in the Bronx. Upstairs on the street, Roseanne stopped to make a call at a pay phone. After she finished, she walked with Juan to the corner and waited. It was foggy, Juan said, and people seemed to drift in and out like ghosts. About five minutes later, a tall woman suddenly appeared across the street. She had thick long black hair and was wearing a ruby-red down coat. Juan knew it was his mother. "I looked just like her," he said. Juan looked up at his grandmother. She was crying. Holding his grandmother's hand, Juan and Roseanne crossed the street. Without hesitating, Juan wrapped his arms around his mother's waist.

During the next year, when Malcolm stayed with his father on weekends, Juan visited his mother at the hospice where she lived, sleeping on a small cot in her room. She coughed all the time, and on some days she was very weak. "At first, she was trying to be so nice to me and trying to spend as much time with me as she could," Juan said. "But then she got strict. She'd be mean sometimes, but it was hard for her because she was sick." Still, Juan liked visiting his mother. "All the people in the hospice loved me. Her best friend spoiled me. He took me out to eat, and we'd go bowling. He was like a father to me."

One day, Juan was told that his grandmother would be coming with Malcolm to pick him up from school to go to the hospital. "I knew then that my mother was going to die," he said. It was lunchtime, just three days before Christmas. As his teacher decorated the classroom for a holiday party, Juan sat quietly and waited.

When Juan arrived at the hospital, his mother was unconscious and on a respirator. Juan placed a gold chain he had bought her for Christmas around her neck, sat by her bed, and held her hand. Each time the respirator filled her lungs, his mother squeezed his fingers. At six that evening, Juan,

Roseanne, and Malcolm left the hospital. Two hours later, Juan's mother was dead. Juan was seven; Malcolm, ten.

At the funeral home, Juan said, Malcolm was so upset he tried to open her casket. But Juan didn't know what to feel. "She wasn't really a mother," Juan said. "She was more like a big sister or an aunt. I cried when she died, but I was crying because my grandmother and brother were crying. To see my grandmother cry was the worst thing in the world." Juan's mother was the second child Roseanne had lost to AIDS. One of her sons had died a few years earlier.

Juan loved his grandmother very much. After school each day, Juan helped her cook and told her about his day. In the evening, he and Roseanne watched *Jeopardy* and *Wheel of Fortune* together, guessing answers along with the game-show contestants. They spent hours talking in her room. "I would always give her hugs and kisses and tell her that I loved her," Juan said. "When I was little, I would lay on her stomach. She was the softest woman in the world."

Roseanne was obese, and when Juan was a child, she used a cane to get around. She also had asthma; her attacks at times were so severe that she would end up in the hospital. After her daughter died, Roseanne's health deteriorated even more. She began to have trouble with her heart and continued to gain weight. "That's when she started to get depressed," said Celia Howard, a neighbor and family friend. "You could see it in her face. She started staying in the house more. She needed a wheelchair to get around."

Roseanne loved her grandchildren and gave them everything they wanted. They watched television all night, and if the other children in the projects took their toys, she'd replace them, even though the boys had been told to keep them upstairs. "They were never disciplined, and they got used to having their own way," Celia Howard said.

Not long after their mother died, Malcolm left Roseanne's to live with his father, who had won custody of the boy. For about two years Juan lived alone with Roseanne. She taught Juan to prepare spaghetti and chicken with rice and peas. Juan also shopped, helped to clean the house, and did laundry. A home attendant came to the house daily to help, and a neighbor often stopped by to clean and cook. At night or on weekends, Juan took over. When his grandmother missed the potty chair she used and accidentally urinated on the floor, Juan cleaned up after her.

When Juan was around nine, Malcolm twice ran away from his father's house because he said his father mistreated him. Roseanne went to court and regained custody. With Malcolm back in the house, the boys fought regularly. "They used to fight for their grandmother's attention," Celia Howard said. "Sometimes she wouldn't feel well, and if they wanted her attention, they would aggravate her. If they couldn't get her attention one way, they would do it another way." Roseanne found it difficult to control them. She screamed and cursed to get them to listen. The boys screamed and cursed back.

About a year later, when Juan was not quite ten and Malcolm was thirteen, Roseanne placed the boys in foster care because of her deteriorating health. For a few months, the boys lived together in a foster home, but because they fought with each other, they were eventually separated. "The lady was old, and she was mean," said Juan of his caretaker in his next foster home. "She spoke only Spanish, and I was miserable."

Juan's first language was English, but he spoke some Spanish, which he learned from his Spanish-speaking neighbors. He thought his father was Puerto Rican but he wasn't sure. His mother's father was Puerto Rican, and Roseanne was American. When I met him, he told me he hated speaking Spanish.

Juan didn't last long in his foster home. Less than a month later, in March 1995, the foster care agency handling Juan's case recommended he be moved to Children's Village, a residential treatment center in Dobbs Ferry, New York. Malcolm joined him two months later.

••••

FOUNDED IN 1851 in New York City as the New York Juvenile Asylum, The Children's Village was originally established as an orphanage for homeless immigrant children.

By the mid-19th century, the tremendous wave of immigration had swelled the populations of the eastern cities. Often jobless and hungry, the new immigrants crowded into dilapidated tenements and cheap lodging houses in cities across the country, struggling just to stay alive. Thousands of their children became known as "street Arabs," named for their Bedouin-like wanderings within the big cities. Many were orphans, their parents dead, jailed, or simply gone. Still others had run away from home, fleeing abuse.

Swarms of these homeless ragamuffins roamed the streets, dodging the police, gambling, fighting, and stealing. Although some supported themselves by selling newspapers, carrying coal and firewood, peddling flowers, and sweeping streets, others became pickpockets, petty thieves, burglars, prostitutes, or extortionists.

In 1869, social welfare reformer Charles Loring Brace, reporting on New York City's "street wandering children" for the *New York Times* wrote, "Their sufferings are sufficiently painful and their numbers so large as to cause to everyone who reflects a profound anxiety about the social and moral future of the City under this steady increase of the 'dangerous classes.'. . . . Some are honest and industrious, others live by their wits and are exposed to incessant and overwhelming temptation. . . . Their number we should estimate as not above 10,000. But 10,000 of such children is a fearful mass of childish misery and crime, and most threatening to the property and moral interests of the city."

The asylum was originally located on 176th Street in Washington Heights on twenty acres extending from Tenth Avenue to Broadway. Children ages seven to fourteen not only lived there but also attended the asylum's school and worked in various jobs that served the dual purpose of maintaining the asylum and teaching them a trade. Under the direction of qualified adults, the children made and mended all their own clothing and shoes; baked the bread; performed the kitchen, dining room, and other household chores; and did all garden and farm work. Some of the children also were organized into a brass band. Children were kept on average one and a half years before being returned to friends or family. If they had no one, they were sent west to the asylum's agency in Bloomington, Illinois. By January 1898, there were 1,048 children living in the asylum; 19 percent were natives of Italy, 10 percent were from Russia, 4 percent were from Germany, and 3 percent from the Turkish Empire and Syria.

In 1901, with social reformers pushing for homeless children to be moved away from the corrupting influences of the city, the institution was relocated to a 277-acre farm in Westchester County, New York, and renamed The Children's Village.

In the decades that followed, The Children's Village evolved into a sophisticated treatment center for orphaned, abandoned, and emotionally scarred children who were victims of abuse and chronic neglect. The agency provided a range of residential and community-based programs, including a shelter for runaways, a crisis residence for children who required short-term psychiatric care, and a child abuse prevention program for the families of children already in care.

The agency's residential treatment center (RTC), situated on a sprawling 150-acre campus in Dobbs Ferry, New York, looked more like an expensive boarding school than the largest foster care home in the nation. About three hundred boys ages five to eighteen made their home in twenty-one small cottages set among rolling hills on a lush, forested campus. In 1999, roughly 80 percent of the boys at Children's Village were African American, 15 percent were Hispanic, and 5 percent of other racial backgrounds. Each child received psychiatric, psychological, and social work services; medical and dental care; voluntary religious education; and year-round special education in the public school located on campus. After an average stay of about two years, nearly half went back to their families; others were placed with foster families or in other residential group homes.

Most boys came to the RTC after several unsuccessful placements in foster or group homes. In 1997, nearly 50 percent of children admitted to Children's Village had a history of psychiatric hospitalizations, nearly 40 percent had a history of suicidal behavior, over 40 percent were abused, and nearly 75 percent had been neglected.

Juan was not quite ten when he was placed at Children's Village. "The boys started bothering me from the beginning," Juan said. "I'm feminine. The way I walk, the way I sit, the way I talk. I've always been different. Other boys have always made fun of me."

Within the first few days, the other boys started calling him "faggot," "plukie," "fudge packer," and "batty boy" (a derogatory term used in Jamaica for homosexuals). After about a month, the teasing escalated to physical attacks. Juan said the boys threw objects at him and attacked him in the shower, his room, at school, and in other areas throughout the property. "Nana used to call me every day," Juan said. "Speaking to her made it bearable."

Juan visited his grandmother every weekend. He didn't want to worry her, so he would tell her he got the bruises playing ball. When Roseanne was too sick to take Juan for the weekend, Juan thought about running away to visit her.

Juan's only friend, Tony, was also gay. Tony entered the foster care system when he was ten because his mother couldn't take care of him. Tony was shy and much quieter than Juan, but he was also harassed regularly. Boys called him names, slapped and punched him, and threw rocks at his face. When he complained, some staff members told him they wouldn't be able to help him if he kept acting so gay.

Juan and Tony performed in plays and sang in the chorus together. In the morning they rehearsed the songs from choir and sang on the way to school. They talked about what they would do when they left Children's Village: They dreamed about getting an apartment together in New York City, being able to dress the way they pleased, and being free to be who they wanted to be.

Juan was at Children's Village less than a year when his weekend visits to his grandmother's came to an end. One January night, Juan was admitted to the infirmary with severe stomach cramps and a headache. He sensed something bad had happened when he was discharged the next day, still sick. Waiting for him were Celia Howard, Malcolm, his social worker, his supervisor, and the nurse.

"Celia took my hand and squeezed it," said Juan, remembering the day. "'You know your grandmother was sick,' she said. 'Well, she passed.'"

Juan's grandmother had had an asthma attack. When the ambulance arrived, the attendants began working on her but were unable to lift her onto a gurney and into the ambulance, so they called the fire department for assistance. Just as the fire department arrived, she died. "I believe in a cosmic connection," Juan said. "When she died, I got sick. My grandmother was pronounced dead the exact same day and time I was admitted into the infirmary."

For the next hour, Juan and Malcolm sat crying. "I didn't eat for a week," Juan said. "I wasn't refusing to eat, I just wasn't hungry. I just sat at the table and thought about my grandmother."

There was no funeral; there was also no one to claim the body. Roseanne's only surviving son was in prison. The hospital was going to send the body to a potter's field, a burial ground for the city's unclaimed dead. At Juan's urging, Celia Howard got in touch with a priest at a nearby church, who called the undertaker who had cremated Juan's mother and uncle. The undertaker went to the hospital and claimed Roseanne's body. Shortly after, she was cremated.

Even after Roseanne's body had been burned, Juan could not erase the image of his grandmother in the morgue. He also wished he had been able to say goodbye. Years later he still felt close to the only person who, he felt, had loved him unconditionally. "I know she's watching me," Juan told me, with a tear in his eye. "I don't really feel like she's gone."

Over the next two years, Juan said, the assaults at Children's Village became more violent, and he described them to me in great detail. A source familiar with Juan's case record said that the files indicate that Juan was continually "victimized" by the other residents at Children's Village and that at one point the incidents were "getting out of hand." There were also indications in the case file that he was "assaulted" by other residents, although there were no specifics regarding the nature of the assaults. A report by an independent psychiatrist who assessed Juan in June 1998 stated, "The available [Children's Village case] records make abundantly clear however, that Juan has been vexed, provoked and at times, physically threatened or attacked as a result of being gay. . . . A September 1, 1997 progress note indicated that Juan was being victimized by his peers on a daily basis."

"This is a hard place to be different," said Markham Breen, director of program development at Children's Village. "There are certain skills kids value a lot, like if you're good at basketball or if you're athletic. That's a big deal. We go to great lengths to promote tolerance of differences. But what we have here in reality is terrible bias against race and gender. And we have big issues with homophobia. When we talk about discrimination, homophobia is always on the top of the list in terms of how viscerally and intensely the kids feel it."

Juan told me he was punched, thrown down a flight of stairs, and cut by a knife. Boys threw rocks and batteries at him as he walked to classes. He said he was frequently taken to the infirmary. Once, in the unit where Juan lived, some children threw a blanket over his head, knocked him down, tipped a locker over onto him, and ran out of the room, leaving him lying on the floor. Another time, he said, as he tried to leave a recreation hall, a group of boys jumped him while others stood by and watched. One boy held Juan, while another punched him in the face. In the end, his face was soaked with blood. Still another time, Juan told me, two boys almost drowned him at the pool. He said he had been threatened by one of the boys while swimming and had even complained to the lifeguard, who assured him that he didn't have to worry. Moments later, the two boys jumped Juan and held his head under water. When Juan eventually struggled to the surface, he coughed up water and vomited.

Juan said he reported these incidents but was told by a staff member that nothing could be done about an incident he hadn't seen. One day when a group of older kids began throwing pieces of wood at Juan in the park, Juan fell while trying to run away and hit his head on the wooden frame of nearby swings. A member of the staff came over to see how badly Juan was hurt. Juan said he had seen the staff member watch the attack, but the person denied witnessing the incident. Juan said a staff member even punished him one day for getting blood on the floor when his nose bled.

When the staff did intervene on Juan's behalf, Juan said some staff members blamed him for the trouble, telling him that he "set himself up" to be victimized because he taunted the other children. Juan said that he was told that he needed to take responsibility for provoking the attacks. When staff members didn't blame him, the intervention was demeaning. After one of the boys threw Juan down a flight of stairs, Juan heard a staff member ask the child, "Why did you do this? I thought you didn't want to touch him."

Although Children's Village addressed homophobia in its staff trainings on prejudice, "the issue of homophobia is one of the hardest training issues," according to Breen. "First, folks aren't always open to discussing it, and second, deeply held personal value systems seem to be the slowest, most difficult thing to change. The problem is not those individuals that speak up and are willing to work with us as much as those who keep their mouths shut and will do what they're going to do and make their little offhand comments. I've identified staff who need additional training through what kids have told me."

At times, Juan was isolated from the other boys. At one point he was restricted from participating in recreational activities, including Boy Scouts, drama group, and swimming, following reports that he had sexual encounters with another resident. According to a source familiar with his case record, the staff felt that they could not control Juan during these activities and could not protect the other children from his sexual advances. On occasion, Juan was kept in the "respite" cottage (a closely supervised, severely restricted residence). Once, he was placed in the cottage for two weeks because he "expressed suicidal ideation" after being assaulted by other children. Juan would also request to be placed in respite on a number of occasions because he felt more comfortable being isolated from the other children. This request was sometimes refused on the grounds that respite was for residents who were deemed to be a danger to themselves or to others.

From very early on in his placement, other residents alleged that Juan had made sexual advances to them. About a year after arriving at Children's Village, Juan was required to participate in a group for children exhibiting "problematic sexualized behavior." During the sessions, Juan felt that the message being conveyed was that homosexuality is bad and that homosexuals try to coerce other people to have sex with them.

But that was never the intended message, according to Dr. Maxine Weisman, chief of psychology at Children's Village: "In these groups, we talk about sex as being a positive thing, but it's also about relationships. We look at sexual behavior among the boys and try to figure out what's going on, so we can prevent some of them from going on and having unhealthy relationships and also to keep them from being victims. It's not healthy for eleven- and twelve-year-olds to be engaging in sex. And we have a policy that there's no sexual activity allowed on campus."

At one point, a Children's Village psychiatrist suggested that Juan be placed in a residential treatment facility run by the Office of Mental Health. Another staff psychologist also recommended RTF placement in order to protect him from being victimized, as well as to prevent him from victimizing others. Juan, however, was never placed in such a facility.

Throughout his stay at Children's Village, Juan felt that being gay was discouraged. He was not allowed to attend the gay pride parade because the staff felt that it was "inappropriate." On Family Day, Juan said he was told he could not invite gay friends because they might get beaten up, but he believed it was because the staff disapproved. "All they want to do is have sex," Juan said he overheard a staff member say one day. Sometimes, Juan was told he was going through a phase, that he just needed counseling to get over his homosexuality. "If you learn one thing here, it's don't be gay," Juan said a counselor told him. "It's the easiest way to get a sexually transmitted disease."

"We do our best to let the kids know that sexual preference is a choice," said Breen. He also said that Children's Village made information on various support groups and organizations that work with gay kids available to the boys on campus. In fact, Juan learned about Triangle Tribe support group for gay, lesbian, bisexual, transgendered, and questioning youth in the foster care system from his social worker at Children's Village. He also arranged for Juan to attend the twice-monthly meetings at Green Chimneys Gramercy Residence in Manhattan. "But I think that a gay kid is going to have a hard time in any group home, except for Green Chimneys," added Breen.

Juan was constantly depressed and sometimes, while

lying in bed at night, he thought about killing himself. He imagined that he was lying in the middle of the road and getting hit by a car or that he was jumping off a fire escape. "I thought, What if I don't die? That would hurt too much," Juan said. He thought about acting crazy and using the medication they gave him to overdose. He did none of these things, but one night, he had had enough. A few of the boys had told the staff that Juan tried to touch them. After the boys produced a sexually explicit note claiming it was from Juan (he said they'd written it themselves), Juan was sent to bed early. He'd already spent weeks isolated from the other boys and was feeling so alone he wanted to die. In his room, Juan ironed his clothes, shined his shoes, brushed his hair, and sat on the sill of the open window. He was halfway out the window before he changed his mind. Another time, he drank a cup of Windex. It gave him a bad headache and made him throw up.

Juan saw his brother, Malcolm, every day. "I walked past his cottage to go to school, and I'd see him playing on the field," Juan said. "But we rarely hung out. He knew I was being beat up, but he didn't defend me because he thought I was trying to hit on other kids. He blamed me." Malcolm eventually left Children's Village to live with his father.

During his third year at Children's Village, although he was too young for the program at Green Chimneys Gramercy Residence, Juan wrote letters to Dr. Gary Mallon, the associate executive director. Juan had met Mallon at a Triangle Tribe meeting. Juan sent his first letter to Mallon in October 1997:

Dear Dr. Mallon,

You should remember me from the triangle tribe. Well anyway, the reason I wrote this letter is because of "distress." The distress I mean is the distress I'm in when I'm being called gay, faget, bitch, girl, whomo. And all kinds of other names that bring me down.

My social worker said that 16 year olds and up are alowed to go there to stay. I dont think thats right, nor fair. As a fact that same night coming back from the tribe my social worker told me I was to grown for my age. And I myself think I get along with older kids better then with little kids. at the tribe I feel comfortable because noone can critacize. Here I feel like limated. I cant talk the way I want, I cant walk the way I want, and so many other things. But there, I would be able to "act the way I want!" Here some times if I act to femanant they just call me so many names, and teese me so bad [I] just go in the bathroom and lock the door and cry. the tears on the paper are from just remembring the times and feeling traped in hell. Maybe if I came there I would be in peace, were [I] wouldnt be called names be critasized. as me being a young adult you might think I would not say this. But I'm "beging" you to let me live there were Ill have somthing in comon with somone els and I can live in peace with out thinking I must act like some one els and be myself with out feeling guilty.

Your friend,

Juan

Five months later, in March 1998, Juan wrote Dr. Mallon again.

Dear Dr. Mallon:

how are you. Im not doing so well. actualy, I'm doing terrable. Mentaly and physically every day I am abused both ways. there is no way I can express my life on this paper but I'll try. I am called all types of names. I have been hit with rocks so bad Ive had to go to the emergency room. and I know what your thinking "so bad". You meen theres been other times? yes! Every day people thow all types of things at me. sometime I just want to die and I dont mean die as in death. I just want to go away some were safe like green chimneys. yes I know I'm to young but I cant wait three or four years. I just cant! please give me a chnace. I promise [I] would be able to live up to any resoncabilitys I would have. I know now your probably getting sick of me asking to come there but I cant stay here.

Sometime when Im in my bed I start to cry and I ask my self why is this happening. I think about what you wrote in your article about being strong. then I break down and cry and think about how safe I felt at green chimneys and how I didnt want to come back here but had to. Oh but what I would do to stay. blood on this paper is the blood from my face bleeding because I was thrown down a fliet of stairs. please accept me their. I cant take it _here_ any more.

The names they call me like "bitch", fagot", "queer," gay bastured and the things they say to me like "you gay bastured you don't deserve to live" and even "you gay fucker, I'll beet the fuckin gay out of you if you look at me." Make me want to go crazy and yet I wonder how another human being can talk to another in such a way. The reason thier are so many mistakes is because I'm rushing so no child will try to take it away and read it so I leave in this letter with this if you were to give me a chance I would prove it to you.

I cant take it anymore.

PS. Please call me or visit me.

He included two phone numbers, four extensions, and his address. Juan said he also wrote numerous letters to ACS administrators, explaining what was happening to him. He waited to hear back.

. . . .

IN JUNE 1998, Juan ran away from Children's Village. That night, ducking behind trees and bushes, he ran through the wooded campus. When he reached the train station in town, he boarded a train for Grand Central Station in New York City. He had only $3 in his pocket. He was thirteen.

There was no safe place for Juan to run.

When he got off the train, he headed to Green Chimneys Gramercy Residence. Too young for the program, he was taken to ACS's Emergency Children's Services placement office on Laight Street. But staff there turned him away; he already had a placement. Juan was told that if he was unhappy at Children's Village, he could go to Covenant House for the night and then speak to his social worker in the morning about getting another placement. But Juan had already told his social worker he was miserable. He felt nobody was listening to him, nobody cared. Juan returned to Gramercy Residence, where, he said, one of the residents sneaked him into his room for the night.

The next morning, Juan walked into the Thirteenth Precinct. When the officer he talked to called Children's Village, Juan immediately phoned his law guardian, the court-appointed lawyer who represented his "best interests and wishes" in the system. She persuaded the police not to return Juan to Children's Village. That afternoon, a judge heard Juan's case and ordered that a new placement be found immediately. Juan was placed in a group home.

Group homes are society's modern-day orphanages. In 1999 about 12 percent of New York's foster children lived in congregate care facilities, including small group homes and large institutional settings, known as residential treatment centers. More than sixty agencies that contracted with ACS operated the homes; ACS ran the rest. Children were sent to group homes only if the court could find no responsible relative to care for them. Group homes housed the abused, neglected, and unwanted, or youth too old or too angry to be placed in foster homes. These young people were among the most emotionally fragile in the city's care.

Caring for these children were child care workers, the lowest paid and generally the least educated and trained of the child welfare practitioners. Child care workers who worked in contract agency group homes generally had only a high school diploma. Median salaries in 1999 were $18,000 for new employees and $22,000 for all other workers, regardless of experience. A report issued by the Special Child Welfare Advisory Panel, created as part of the *Marisol* v. *Giuliani* settlement, stated that in one agency's residential treatment center, "child care staff are earning less per hour than some of the youngsters they take care of make at their after-school jobs off campus." The extent and quality of training also varied widely among contract agencies.

The group homes were supposed to provide psychological and educational services and a surrogate family environment, but child care advocates, not to mention the kids, said that although some group homes provided safe, stable, and healthy environments, others were nothing more than shelters from which kids ran away regularly. In the poorly managed homes, kids were allowed out without supervision after school, remaining on the streets well into the evening, without consequence, as long as they returned by curfew. Kids also complained that in some homes food was scarce, facilities were dirty, education was poor, and violence or the threat of violence was commonplace. Many kids bounced from one group home to another.

At eighteen, most of these teens were on their own. Although in New York young people had the right to remain in foster care until twenty-one, to do so they had to be enrolled in school or in a vocational program. The city was supposed to provide classes on career counseling, apartment hunting, budgeting, shopping, and cooking, as well as a one-time check up to $750 and housing subsidies of $300 a month for up to three years, until age twenty-one; however, many youth got neither the instruction nor the money. Many were unable to attend the classes because of school or work schedules; others felt it was a waste of their time. As for the money, some didn't know about it; others ignored the opportunity.

Just how unprepared these young people were to make it on their own was evident in the nation's twenty thousand youth who aged out of foster care every year. According to the U.S. Department of Health and Human Services, within two to four years of aging out of foster care, only half had completed high school, fewer than 50 percent had jobs, 60 percent of the young women had given birth, and fewer than 20 percent were self-supporting. Studies have shown that a quarter of such young adults spend at least some time homeless and 25 percent of males had been imprisoned at least once within twelve to eighteen months of leaving foster care.

At thirteen, Juan still had many years before he aged out of the foster care system. But he was on the road to becoming another "system kid"—angry and scared, prepared for nothing. For the next five months, Juan ricocheted from one group home and shelter to another, always, he said, fleeing harassment and abuse for being gay. During this time he also discovered a place where he could feel comfortable as a gay male: the West Village. "I felt safe there," said Juan. "I could be me."

. . . .

THE WEST VILLAGE had for years been a haven for teenagers. The scene provided them space to experiment and figure out who they were, without criticism or fear. Gay kids in particular found the acceptance they had never received in their own families and communities.

But during the past fifteen years, the neighborhood's quiet streets had become increasingly disorderly and, at times, unsafe. The transformation began in the early 1980s, when a police crackdown in Times Square drove petty thieves and drug dealers to the western corner of Greenwich Village. When the strip along the waterfront by the piers was opened to allow parking, the area became a breeding ground for criminal activity. "There was free access on and off the highway for drug dealers, so people from Jersey and the five boroughs could make a deal and leave," said Michael Mirisola, president of the Christopher Street Block and Merchants Association and owner of a clothing store on the block. "And what better place to have sex than in the back of somebody's car? It turned into an open market for drug dealing and prostitution."

By the late 1980s, hustlers and drug dealers who had been pushed out of Times Square were calling the neighborhood "Times Square South." Sex shops and X-rated video stores sprouted up along Christopher Street and the highway. Eventually, local businesses along the five westernmost blocks of Christopher Street, which had boomed in the 1960s and 1970s, began to close, leaving storefronts empty and abandoned. The business owners who remained were robbed regularly. In April 1990, a man walked into Mirisola's store, put a .45-caliber gun to his head, handcuffed him, stuck a sock in his mouth, and locked him in the basement. "At that point we had already had about five holdups on the block," Mirisola said.

Although the crime rate was still lower in the Village than in most other neighborhoods in the city, slashings and muggings frightened local residents, and people got caught in the crossfire of drug deals. Gay bashing was also on the rise. Gays were harassed and intimidated regularly, at times beaten. The gay-bashers were predominantly white males, in their late teens to early twenties, who prowled the streets in cars or on foot in groups of three or more. Most used sticks or bats; others used their fists and their feet.

Greenwich Village had always been known for its "anything goes" attitude. But some argued that that tradition of tolerance and respect for differences had contributed to the increased violence. Some residents were reluctant to call the police for help, fearful that an increased police presence would change the Village's liberal climate. "You also had a lot of the old Stonewall veterans who wanted to have nothing to do with the police," Mirisola said. "They told the cops to stay out of the neighborhood, and the cops happily did."

The Stonewall rebellion began in a Greenwich Village bar in 1969. One June evening, police and agents of the Alcoholic Beverage Control Board entered the Stonewall Inn, a gay bar on Christopher Street, and began to throw the patrons out, one by one. Instead of quietly leaving, as they had done for years, hustlers, drag queens, students, and other patrons held their ground and fought back. The door was barricaded with a parking meter, and the agents and police were trapped inside. They wrecked the place and called in reinforcements. The crowd grew. For three days, people protested. The gay rights movement had begun.

In July 1990, when an advertising executive was shot and killed while talking on a pay phone near his apartment on Jane Street, one of the quietest streets in the West Village, the community began to mobilize. Residents of Jane Street and two adjoining blocks hired a private security firm to patrol the neighborhood between eight p.m. and four a.m. every night. To combat anti-gay violence, volunteers joined the Greenwich Village Pink Panthers and organized weekend patrols throughout the West Village. To improve safety on Christopher Street, Mirisola called the Guardian Angels for help. The next month, Christopher Street residents, with Guardian Angels by their side, launched their own block patrol.

Within a year, the patrol, as well as an increased police presence, drastically reduced crime in the neighborhood. Yet residents began to grow concerned about the increasing number of young boys, mostly black and Hispanic, hanging out in the area. Many of these boys seemed to have no homes. They hustled to survive. At all hours of the night, they hawked their bodies on the quiet, crooked side streets of West Tenth Street and tiny Weehawken Street, long a hustling and cruising area. Some stood in shadowed doorways or under street lamps, watching, waiting. Others brazenly hung out on street corners, staring at or waving to passing cars. In the morning, the boys could be found sleeping in front of doorsteps, against buildings, and along the piers.

The high number of homeless boys had become so noticeable by 1992 that Community Board 2, which covered Greenwich Village, began looking for ways to help them. Each of the fifty-nine community boards in New York City represents a specific geographical district and is made up of unsalaried members appointed by the borough president in consultation with the City Council. The boards play an advisory role in zoning, community planning, city budget, and in the coordination of municipal services. "We realized there was only so much cops could do," Mirisola said. "We wanted the cops to deal with the lawbreaking, but they couldn't deal with the homeless kids who were out there until six in the morning."

The board's first effort, the Neutral Zone, was a disaster. Run by the Greenwich Village Youth Council, a community-based nonprofit organization, the Neutral Zone was a Christopher Street drop-in center for gay, lesbian, and transgender youth. "We thought if we could take these kids off the street and put them into a better environment and maybe teach them something and help them get a job, it would be great," said David Poster, president of the Christopher Street Patrol. "But all it did was make the problem worse. We had more kids than ever before coming to hang out." Residents complained the Neutral Zone was so mismanaged that its facility had become the site of all-night parties, drug dealing, and pimping. Three years later, amid allegations that five violent incidents, including a rape, had occurred within its walls, the Neutral Zone closed. (In 1996, the New Neutral Zone, a structured program that provides counseling and referral services for fifteen to twenty young people a day, was opened with new staff on West Sixteenth Street. It has about 125 members, ages fifteen to twenty-two.)

In 1993, a cover story in *New York* magazine, "The Village Under Siege," by Michael Gross, described a neighborhood that seemed out of control: "Local customers are afraid of the waves of unruly people pouring out of the subways and the buses and the PATH trains that converge in the Village in greater numbers than anywhere else in the city, except possibly Times Square. They're afraid of the drug dealers who set up shop in the streets around Washington Square Park. They're afraid of the hip-hoppers from outer-borough neighborhoods whose urban update on *American Graffiti* finds them cruising the Village streets in expensive cars fitted out with trunk-mounted speakers blasting rap music—Whoomp! There it is!—while drivers and passengers get blasted on brown-bagged 40-ounce bottles of malt liquor. . . . Public life there, street life, isn't just meaner these days—it's an aural, visual, olfactory, and sometimes physical assault on simple decency."

The piers became known as the neighborhood's emergency valve. "When there were problems in the neighborhood, they were pushed west to the piers, where pretty much anything was allowed to go on," Mirisola said. "It was like the Wild West. The piers were no man's land." Owned by the state, the piers and the bulkhead were not patrolled by New York City police. The area was dark and had no public telephones. One man had set up a sound system at the end of one pier and sold cassettes to the kids. "It was an all-night party," Mirisola said. "There were hundreds of kids out there. But every now and then, it would flow over to the streets."

The Christopher Street Block and Merchants Association looked to the Hudson River Park Conservancy, a joint city and state agency overseeing redevelopment of the park, for help. The Conservancy wanted to reclaim the waterfront for public use. The agency had already begun to shut down several piers on the West Side for renovation. It had also made the area in front of the piers a no-parking zone. (Cars stopped pulling up to the waterfront only after cement barricades were erected and the Christopher Street Patrol stood behind them for almost a year asking drivers to leave.) In 1996, the Conservancy imposed a midnight to 5:30 a.m. weekend curfew on Pier 45 at Christopher Street and hired security to patrol the bulkhead and the piers.

By 1998, crime was down in much of the city, yet it was startlingly on the rise again in the West Village. Although there had been no murders reported in 1996 or 1997 in the area, there were four murders in 1998, three in August alone. According to the Sixth Precinct, one of the killings, the shooting of an eighteen-year-old, involved a turf battle and prostitutes. Bias crimes were on the rise as well. According to police statistics, bias crimes increased 81 percent, from forty-two in 1997 to seventy-six in 1998.

Kids were everywhere, and it was difficult to know which teens were homeless and which were not. "There are still so many kids patching together existences," Mirisola said in spring 2000. "And when the weather is good, they sleep on the piers or just keep walking or turning tricks. And there are those kids who live with their aunt or something, and they are homeless from time to time. A lot of people will say these kids aren't homeless. I see them early in the morning. There's no arguing that some of these kids have nowhere to go."

. . . .

DURING THE SUMMER of 1998, Juan spent his week-end nights from eleven to sometimes six in the morning hanging out with hundreds of other young people who gathered in the West Village and on the Christopher Street piers. Some wore baggy jeans, loose T-shirts, and combat boots; others paraded around in skimpy tank tops and skintight shorts. They smoked cigarettes; some drank alcohol and got high. Most of the kids were gay, lesbian, bisexual, or trans-gender. "I met other kids like me," Juan said. "It was the one place I felt comfortable." It was also the place where Juan discovered the art of voguing.

Voguing had evolved from the Harlem drag balls of the 1920s. Those balls were held at the elegant Rockland Palace and Savoy Ballroom and attracted many high society and interracial crowds. "Not all the guests were homosexual; many came to gawk," wrote Steven Watson in *The Harlem Renaissance*. "These onlookers ascended a gold banistered staircase to the box seats that ringed the huge ballroom and looked down on the Grand March of ersatz divas promenading beneath a colossal crystal chandelier and a sky-blue ceiling. The women mostly dressed in drably colored loose-fitting men's suits (rarely a tuxedo); whereas the men outdid themselves as extravagant *señoritas* in black lace and red fans; as soubrettes in backless dresses and huge spangles; as debutantes in chiffon and rhinestones; and as a creature called 'La Flame' who wore only a white satin stovepipe hat, a red beaded breastplate, and a white sash." Appropriated from the fashion world, voguing (from *Vogue* magazine) mirrored the hauteur and posturing of "high society."

Voguing entered mainstream culture in 1990 when Madonna's song "Vogue" climbed the charts. Voguing blended gymnastic contortions with the preening moves of fashion models, combining lightning-fast staccato hand movements, whirling arms, swoops, high kicks, and spins on the ground. It was rhythmic and graceful, requiring enormous skill and creativity. It looked like a cross between ballet, kung fu, break-dancing, and gymnastics.

Many of the kids who vogued performed in balls, which were held throughout the year. The ball scene provided a strong sense of community. There was a system of "houses" to which young people more or less apprenticed themselves. More than a dozen houses, including Mizrahi (after the fashion designer), Latex, Infiniti, Ebony, and Vuitton, had twenty to more than one hundred members and functioned as a kind of family. The younger members were known as "the children"; the more experienced who had won trophies at the balls were "legends"; the ultimate authorities watching over everyone were the "mother" and the "father."

Juan was shocked the first time he saw kids voguing on the piers. "I'd seen people walking around with their arms up in the air, but I didn't know what they were doing," he said. He began attending mini drag balls at a small dance club in Manhattan to watch and learn. Juan studied the performers carefully as they "walked," or competed, picking up tips each time. "Voguing is really hard to do well. I couldn't get anyone to teach me, so I taught myself. I just watched and learned."

At the balls, participants competed in particular categories, depending on their gender and characteristics: women (biological females who looked female), butches (women whose features and mannerisms were male), butch queens (all gay men, from "flaming sissies" to macho "straight-acting men"), and fem queens (men who lived full-time as women). Participants vied for trophies for best face, body, and voguing. There were dozens of categories that changed regularly, among them Best Dressed Spectator, Fantasy Cartoon Character, High Fashion Streetwear, Junior Sex Siren, School Girl vs. Working Girl, and Church Lady vs. Crackhead vs. Fourteenth Street Ho'. Competitors who won three or more grand-prize trophies were "legends," forever famous.

Those who walked in the balls could live out their fantasies. They strutted down the aisles as elegant high-fashion models dressed in full-length gowns, prep-school students (of both sexes) wearing knee socks and carrying textbooks, construction workers in hard hats, beauty queens in bathing suits, aerobics instructors in spandex, sadomasochist dominatrices in black leather, roughnecks with gold teeth and gold chains.

"In real life, you can't get a job as an executive unless you have the educational background and the opportunity," explained legendary Dorian Corey, who appeared in *Paris Is Burning*, the widely acclaimed 1991 documentary on drag balls. "In a ballroom, you can be anything you want. You're not really an executive, but you look like an executive. Therefore, you're telling the straight world, 'I can be an executive if I have the opportunity.'"

The criterion by which everyone was evaluated was "realness," the ability to blend in with the straight world. "If you can pass the untrained eye, or even the trained eye, and not give away the fact that you're gay, that's real," Corey said. "The idea of realness is to look as much as possible as your straight counterpart—whether it be a real woman or a real man—a straight man."

More than anything, the ball scene was also about finding a place to belong and be known and recognized. "You have three strikes against you in this world," said one of the drag queens who was the subject of the film. "You're black, you're male, and you're gay. If you're going to do this, you're going to have to be stronger than you ever imagine."

Throughout the movie, the community of mostly black and Hispanic drag-ball participants described backgrounds of poverty and family ostracism. Rejected by their families and society, they longed for acceptance. "A lot of those kids at the ball don't have nothing," said Pepper Labeija, one of the film's drag queens. "They come to balls starving. They sleep at Under 21 [former name for Covenant House], or they sleep on the piers, or wherever. They don't have a home to go to." Still today, many of the kids who walked the balls were on their own. Some shoplifted or prostituted in order to afford the clothes they needed to look "real."

The voguing world also had developed a language of

insults. It was known as "reading," and it too was practiced to perfection. If you could find a flaw in a person—like someone's tacky clothes, messy hair, or overdone makeup—and make a clever verbal insult, you had a good read. Reading only took place within the gay world; when verbal sallies were exchanged between the gay and straight worlds, they were usually intended as vicious insults. "Throwing shade" (giving attitude) was a more subtle form of reading. According to one drag queen, when throwing shade, "I don't tell you that you're ugly. I don't *have* to tell you because you *know* you're ugly."

The verbal battles took physical form through voguing. On the piers for hours at a time, young men practiced their voguing and competed against each other in "battles" in which they shared the floor, dipping, swooning, and swirling dangerously close to each other but never touching. They dropped to the ground and, like a standing blow-up doll that springs up when punched, popped back up in one full swoop, barely grazing the floor. Like double-jointed contortionists, they twisted and turned and flipped their limbs back and forth in robotic yet fluid motions. Emotions were high, and on rare occasions the competitions got so fierce that they escalated to real fights.

By the time I met him, Juan vogued everywhere and often. He vogued while walking down a crowded city street, in the lobby of an office building waiting for an elevator, down the aisles of a drugstore. "You have to keep practicing to get better," he said. The more he vogued, the more confident he grew. "In the balls, I do butch queen and drag realness categories," he said. "But they chop me a lot because they don't know me. The most popular girls get the most trophies—it's just politics."

....

AFTER LEAVING Children's Village in June, Juan bounced from Emergency Children's Services (ECS) to Covenant House to a group home in the Bronx, back to ECS. From ECS, he was placed in another group home in Brooklyn, then went back to ECS and on to a foster home. He ran from the foster home back to Covenant House, then back to ECS. In November, he ended up in a group home in Queens. From there, he was admitted to the adolescent psychiatric ward at Hillside Hospital.

The events of the evening that led counselors at the Queens group home to call the police differ substantially depending on who tells the story. According to one group home staff member, Juan came in late one evening and asked for food. Told that the kitchen was closed, Juan began to yell, break things, and kick the kitchen door. At one point, he grabbed a pair of scissors out of a drawer and threatened to stab a staff member.

According to Juan, he had gone to the kitchen that evening only because it was his turn to clean it. Another boy, with whom he had argued earlier, came in and started antagonizing him. When the boy pulled a box cutter out of his pocket, Juan grabbed a pair of scissors from the table. The boy lunged toward Juan, who pushed the box cutter away with one hand and with the scissors slashed at the boy, grazing his leg. The boy bolted out of the room, tossed the box cutter out the window, and ran to the counselors, telling them that Juan had tried to stab him. One of the youth workers at the group home called the police. The next morning Juan was admitted to Hillside Hospital.

"Once they put the straight jacket on, I swung, and one of the buckles hit the guy in the face," Juan told me a month later. "I wouldn't stop kicking and punching and fighting."

Most of the twelve- to eighteen-year-olds admitted to Hillside Hospital showed symptoms of depression, conduct disorder, adjustment disorder, and attention deficit with hyperactivity disorder. Hillside was considered a short-term facility, and the average length of stay was ten days to three weeks, although some kids stayed six months or longer. Juan was diagnosed with bipolar disorder, and it was recommended he be given Lithium. The diagnosis was based in part on the fact that he was observed traipsing down the hall, flailing his arms and muttering. Doctors said he was "responding to internal stimuli." Juan said he was voguing.

At Hillside, Juan grew increasingly frustrated and frightened. And when Juan felt powerless, he often antagonized those around him. "If you don't do what they tell you, they physically move you," he said. "If you hit back while they're pushing you, they can justify restraining you. And when they wanted to restrain you, they pushed the red button. Then you'd hear across the loudspeaker, 'All available staff, please report to adolescent pavilion. Restraint team needed.' Then these big men who stood outside the door put on their thick gloves and, all at once, came in and bum-rushed me. They threw me to the floor, then strapped me to the bed. They put a sheet made out of net material on top of your body with holes for the hands and feet and then they tie your hands and feet to the bed."

According to Hillside Hospital, restraints were used as a last resort and only when a patient was a danger to himself or to others.

One day, Juan said, he was restrained for refusing to remove a wooden crucifix he wore around his neck. When I pressed him to tell me more, he admitted that when the nurse tried to remove the crucifix, he pushed her, and she fell onto the linoleum floor.

At Hillside, Juan shared the halls with about fifteen kids. Some, on heavy medication, shuffled through the hallways with their heads bowed down as if in prayer. A few simply stared into space. Others had lots of energy and were outgoing and friendly. "Most of the kids seemed normal," Juan said. "They just seemed to be teenagers who had teenagers' problems." Juan didn't know their detailed histories. He heard only their versions of what were undoubtedly far more complex stories about life at home and the reasons why they were admitted. But he felt that many of the teens were hospitalized because, like himself, they were not understood. "It was so sad," he told me. "One boy was there because, while he was drunk, he was making jokes, pointed at his head, and said, 'Bang bang.' And they put him away. One girl couldn't stop crying. Another girl was gorgeous but thought she was ugly and tried to slit her wrists. Another boy was put in because he had seizures and his parents thought he was crazy. Another girl was just autistic. She was so sweet. I used to help her eat because her hands shook so much."

Two weeks after being admitted to Hillside, Juan was released. He was prescribed Depakote, an anticonvulsant, to stabilize his moods, but refused to take it. A few days later, he was transferred to another group home in Queens.

....

JUAN told me he didn't want to be adopted. He was fiercely independent, and I suspected that part of the reason he didn't "want to be anybody's child" was that he could best maintain that independence by staying in the system. "I like being in a therapeutic setting," he told me one day. "It's what I'm used to."

But he liked the system because he knew how to work it,

and he stretched and broke rules regularly. He knew he could go AWOL from a group home for seventy-two hours before his bed would be given away. He knew his legal rights concerning education, clothing, visitations, and employment—and when these rights were being violated. He knew, for example, that he could petition the court to get visitation with his brother if his brother's father refused to allow the visit. Juan also knew he had a right to change his social worker if he felt his needs weren't being met. And he knew he had a right to a Service Plan Review twice each year and a say in his Uniform Case Record. Reviews determined what happened to a foster child in care, and these meetings addressed such issues as visiting a sibling, setting new goals, and problems with placement. The case record was the overall plan that foster care set for the youth. But most of all, Juan knew he had a right to be treated like the other boys and with respect.

Juan's new group home after Hillside was a diagnostic center: Children were evaluated by a psychiatrist before being shipped somewhere else. Although they were supposed to be placed within ninety days, some, usually the ones who were more hard to place, stayed up to a year or longer.

The group home was just a few miles from Kennedy International Airport in Queens and an hour and a half by bus and subway from midtown Manhattan. Bus service was slow and infrequent, and many neighborhood residents relied on vans, often unlicensed, to shuttle them to the subway. The vans, called "dollar vans" because of the one-dollar fare, crammed as many as twenty people at a time in their seats and ran frequently throughout the residential area. The group home, a two-story house with a basement that flooded when it rained, stood at the end of a quiet block, across the street from a swamp.

Ten boys, ranging in age from fourteen to eighteen, lived

at the group home with Juan. At thirteen, Juan was the youngest. The home was staffed twenty-four hours with youth counselors working in pairs for eight-hour shifts. The staff cooked, organized activities, and supervised the boys. During the day, some boys attended classes at a group home down the street, while others were enrolled at a local public school. The boys rotated chores that included cleaning the bathrooms, the basement, the front lawn, and the kitchen. They earned points and privileges, including participation in outside activities. Recreational activities were scheduled in the evenings and on weekends, enabling the boys to go to the movies, roller skate, attend baseball games, and even visit amusement parks.

From the day he arrived at the group home, Juan did not hide the fact that he was gay. He practiced his voguing regularly and sang along to his favorite performer, Mariah Carey. Music seemed to allow him to express emotions that words could not. During one of my visits, he grew so excited when he heard the Spice Girls singing on television that he ran out of the room mid-sentence to see them and started singing along. Some of the boys laughed as they watched him perform, but most just ignored him. On my visits, I saw some of the boys tease him about acting like a girl, but I never saw the staff treat him differently from the other boys.

Staff members who spoke to me about how Juan was treated by the boys and by other staff when I wasn't around requested that I not use their names. "The children were not used to being confronted that close with someone of that sexual preference," a staff member told me. "He was the only gay kid at the group home that came out. I'm not saying there were no other gay kids, but I know if there were concerns with someone and their sexual preference, they would not come out because they'd seen how Juan was being treated.

He was fully out there and had no problem with that. It was even difficult for the staff to adjust."

Ironically, this very societal stigmatization and rejection brings many lesbian and gay youth into the child welfare system in the first place. Studies have found that gay youth face severe social and emotional isolation and are disproportionately forced to leave home. An estimated one-third of gay youth end up in the city's care after being rejected by their families.

An anonymous survey of 4,159 Massachusetts public high school students conducted in 1995 found that gay, lesbian, and bisexual youth were more likely than their straight peers to be victimized and threatened and to have engaged in suicidal ideation and attempts, multiple substance abuse, and high-risk sexual behaviors. The survey found that 25 percent of these students had skipped school the previous month because they had felt unsafe en route to or at school, and 32 percent said they had been threatened with a weapon in the previous thirty days. These percentages were about five times greater than those of their heterosexual peers. As many as 35 percent of the gay youth questioned said they had attempted suicide in the past year, compared to 10 percent of heterosexual kids surveyed.

"From the beginning, we tried to address the feelings the boys had," said another staff member at the Queens group home. "Don't judge him. He's a human being like everyone else. Then it went to another level. There were jokes, and it became a way of accepting the situation. The jokes were constant, and in my opinion it was unhealthy. But Juan took them and threw them off. He's very smart, and he would give it right back. Then the staff fed into it. He needed a group home where he could be accepted for his sexuality. This wasn't the place for him."

In many ways, Juan was just like other boys entering adolescence. His body was changing in size and shape. He was frenetic one moment, lethargic the next. His thoughts at times were chaotic and scrambled. He was self-absorbed, preoccupied with being accepted by his peers, and fought for autonomy. Like other teenagers, he saw the world in black and white; there were no shades of gray. A best friend one day became a worst enemy the next. For adults, this behavior might seem crazy, but for teenagers it is common.

Yet Juan was constantly reminded that he was different from the other boys. "All the boys care about is talking about girls and watching sports on television," Juan said to me one weekend. "I want to watch the Disney Channel and MTV. They don't care about anything I'm interested in." Juan even had the group home rent *Paris Is Burning* because "I wanted the kids to see what I did and understand me better." Although most of the boys enjoyed the film, they continued to ridicule Juan. He felt increasingly rejected and isolated. And it made him long even more for acceptance.

Juan said that every day, someone at the group home commented on his homosexuality. Sometimes, he thought they were just joking; other times he felt they were deliberately trying to hurt him. Adept at "reading" and "throwing shade," he often lashed back with a clever response, without missing a beat. But even when he was being clever, what they said bothered him. "I'm really stressed out by all the comments," he would tell me regularly.

The comments made by staff, however, upset him most. Juan told me one staff member called him a "faggot" in front of the other boys. One day he told me that he was not allowed to go to the gym with the other residents, because "it's a straight gym." Juan said the staff member told him, "I don't want to bring any faggots in there."

"We're the mature ones," a staff member said to me when I asked how Juan was treated at the group home. "How are we going to protect him if we think this way? We have staff members who can't deal with it [homosexuality]. He's very sensitive and sharp, and he can pick up the vibe."

Although Juan liked a few of the youth workers at the home, he felt especially close to Vera Pace. Juan told me that when Ms. Pace was around, he felt safe. "The boys would never try anything on her shift," Juan said. But Juan also liked that she was fair. "She didn't treat me better or worse than the other boys. She also stood up for me when people had problems with me." But less than a month after Juan arrived, Ms. Pace was transferred to another group home.

Juan grew increasingly impatient. He got furious when a staff member blamed him for the harassment he received from the other boys. "They tell me I need to calm myself down," he told me one day. "They think that gay males who act feminine carry on too much. I'm not carrying on—this is the way I act. They can't get it through their skull. They tell me I act like a flaming queen. I am a flaming queen. I'm not acting."

When Juan wanted something, he wanted it immediately. But his behavior varied wildly, depending on who was with him. When Juan was among people who accepted and respected him, he was calm and respectful. He was more willing to accept "no" as an answer as long as he felt he was being heard. At his group home, however, Juan felt nobody was listening to him. He grew frustrated easily and at times yelled at the boys and the staff. Sometimes he felt like he was going to explode. He broke rules regularly and lost privileges almost daily, isolating him even more. When other boys were getting $15 a week for doing their chores, Juan sometimes got as little as $1 a week.

When he did act out, it was hard to know what triggered his behavior. Was he an impatient thirteen-year-old boy with poor impulse control, testing the limits of authority? Or was he a kid stuck in a place he didn't belong, acting out his frustration at being rejected for being gay? Clearly he was both, and the two fed off each other. To complicate matters more, Juan and the boys he lived with were at an age when their hormones were bubbling.

Like most teenagers, Juan developed crushes on others his own age. Only for Juan, the crushes were on other boys. Juan always went on about the boys he liked. And he got excited when one reciprocated his feelings. At the group home, he had a crush on two boys: Derek and Luke. Juan had told me that Derek, who slept in a bedroom above his, tied notes onto a string and tossed them out his window to Juan's room late at night. In the notes, Derek told Juan that he loved him, asking him not to go AWOL because he wanted to spend more time with him.

"I wake up thinking about Derek," he told me. "I think about him all day and go to sleep thinking about him. When he gets into problems in the house, I'm right behind him. The first person that hits him is getting hit by me."

But in front of the other boys, Derek was often mean to Juan. I saw Derek ignore Juan or tease him in front of the other boys when I visited. "He's not really gay," Juan said. "He's just messing with me." Occasionally Derek defended him in front of the boys, but most of the time, he was cruel, calling him "faggot" and "bitch" in front of the others. For Juan, the rejection was devastating. It further fueled his frustration and triggered many of his outbursts.

When Juan liked a boy, he didn't keep it a secret. For many boys, this felt threatening. Some of the boys responded by behaving erratically, like Derek. Other boys were just mean. Sometimes, a boy would falsely accuse Juan of making a pass at him, just to get Juan into trouble. Although other boys could talk to staff or other friends about their heartaches and disappointments, Juan's crushes were not considered appropriate in the group homes where he lived. And after Ms. Pace left, he felt he had no one to talk to about them. One day Juan called simply to tell me that Luke, another boy he liked, had kissed a girl in front of him. "I know he did it on purpose because he was sending me a message, but I have feelings, too."

According to the boys I spoke to who lived in congregate care facilities, sexual encounters between teenage boys in some group homes and large residential treatment centers were fairly common, although the liaisons were rarely acknowledged, primarily because they opened an agency up to formal investigation. Any sexual encounters that were reported were almost always reported as sexual abuse. An Indiana study published in 1992 found that children in residential group homes were ten times more likely to be physically abused and more than thirty times more likely to be sexually abused than children in the general population living in their own homes, in part because 70 percent of the perpetrators were other children. The study, however, dealt only with reported maltreatment. The rates were especially significant, given that in group homes, indifference and fear of reprisal or job loss often resulted in underreporting.

In Florida, David Bazerman, a lawyer representing children in Broward County in a federal lawsuit against the county's foster care system, said in an affidavit in December 1998 that he was aware of fifty instances of child-on-child sexual abuse involving more than one hundred Broward foster children in just the two years prior to giving his affidavit. The official number during that same period was seven, because until what Bazerman called "an epidemic of child-on-child sexual abuse" was exposed, the child abuse hot line didn't accept reports of such abuse.

In New York in June 1999, *Newsday* reported that a nine-year-old boy allegedly was sexually assaulted by three older boys at St. John's Home for Boys in Rockaway Park, Queens, a group home for seventy-five boys ages nine to twenty. The three accused youths, all thirteen years old, were charged with sodomy in Queens Family Court. According to the article, the case uncovered what appeared to be rampant sexual activity at St. John's. (The state Office of Children and Family Services conducted a probe but deemed the allegations unfounded and refused to release details of the investigation.) In August 1999, a New York 1 News investigation uncovered reports of boys, some as young as seven years old, being forced to engage in sexual acts with other boys at St. Agatha Home in Rockland County. New York 1 News later uncovered police reports alleging more than two dozen incidents of sexual abuse at the group home in eight years. (The state investigated the charges against St. Agatha but would not release information as to whether they took action against the facility. According to the city's public advocate, St. Agatha implemented a corrective action plan that included an increase in staff, better staff training, and counseling for children involved.)

Although the study and media reports indicate that the sexual encounters were all forced, the teenagers I spoke to had told me that much of the sexual activity in group homes was consensual. Clearly, the issues were complex. Boys who had been sexually victimized learned from a young age to engage others through their sexuality. For some, the sex was an act of violence, in which they repeated the victimization they themselves had experienced. For others, the sex was connected to a deep need to find the affection and nurturing they had been denied in their families. Often, the boys did not self-identify as gay.

The social stigmatization of being gay was so strong that even adolescent boys who did self-identify as gay developed a number of coping strategies to deal with the discrimination. Some learned to hide it and lived in fear of being discovered. Others denied that their actions were homosexual and explained that their homosexual encounters were either forced or were a phase or were something they had grown out of. Some internalized the hatred toward homosexuals to the point where they participated in attacks on gays. Boys who questioned their own orientation, or hid it, could be the most abusive.

Juan couldn't change who he was, and he didn't want to. "I know if God didn't want me to do this, I wouldn't be doing it," he said one day. "He made me. Does it say anything about gays in the Bible? I know there's a city of gays he destroyed. The only reason he destroyed it is because the person had lust for the angel. I mean that's a stupid reason to destroy a city. You're going to destroy a city because of somebody's feelings? They can't help that."

Juan needed what all other children his age needed: physical safety, friends, respect for his own uniqueness, and support and encouragement to grow and mature. More than anything, Juan craved an emotional connection with someone who cared about him. But because he was placed in group homes where he was continuously rejected and ridiculed, and because he had counselors who were ill-equipped to deal with his issues, Juan's sexual preference became the focus of all the attention he received. "Juan's been in the system a long time," one staff member from his group home said. "No one looked at this kid and said, 'What happened?' He is a mess. He is hurting. He is thirteen—a baby. How many zeroed in on that? Including ACS. He carries a lot of baggage. If you don't deal with the baggage he's bringing in first, and then you put more baggage on top of that, then you forget why he's even here."

••••

WHEN I FIRST MET Juan, he told me he was transgender. "I don't like wearing boy clothes, but it's easier to just be gay in the system," he said. At the time, the message on his voice mail at the New York Peer AIDS Education Coalition said, "You can leave a message for Juan, Jasmine, or Latasha after the beep." Juan was his given name, Jasmine was the name he'd started using in Children's Village. He called himself Latasha when he dressed as a girl. Most of the time, though, he used Juan or Jasmine."

Transgender is an umbrella term that includes everyone who challenges the boundaries of sex and gender. The term includes cross-dressers, transsexuals, intersexed people (those born with both male and female sex organs), womanish men, mannish women, and anyone whose sexual identity seems to cross the line of, or be in conflict with, their anatomical sex.

Being transgender is an expression of gender, not sexuality. A transgendered person can be heterosexual, bisexual, lesbian, gay, or asexual. What they often share, however, is a long-standing feeling of being trapped in the wrong body. Some transgendered people prefer living only part time in their self-defined gender. Many desire to live fully in their self-identified gender. Some go on hormone therapy or go through sex-reassignment surgery. Transsexuals live full time in their chosen gender role, usually on hormone therapy, with a name change and gender identification correction on documents.

In the United States, most reputable therapists and medical doctors who regularly work with transsexuals follow the Harry Benjamin Standards of Care, clinical guidelines relating to hormonal, psychological, and surgical care for transsexuals. The Standards of Care require, for example, a psychiatrist or psychologist to know the patient for at least three months before recommending hormone therapy for adults eighteen and older. Because "gender identity can rapidly and unexpectedly evolve," the Standards of Care recommend that hormones rarely be administered to adolescents younger than eighteen. According to these guidelines, for sex-reassignment surgery, patients are required to have undergone a minimum of one year of continuous hormonal therapy and one year of continuous, full-time, real-life experience as the desired gender. Surgeons also required two letters of recommendation from different mental health professionals experienced in gender identity disorders, one from a person with at least a master's degree, the second from a psychiatrist or clinical psychologist. Even though the Standards of Care are only minimum guidelines and carry no force of law, some transsexuals find the standards too restrictive, even insulting; others find them worth the trouble and look for doctors who subscribe to them. Still others travel to South America or Asia where the restrictions are fewer and the surgery cheaper.

When the guidelines are followed, changing genders is not something that can be done on a whim. It takes time and a lot of money. Gender identity therapists charge from $60 to $100 an hour. Psychiatrists and clinical psychologists generally charge more. One year of regular counseling usually averages about $3,000.

For male to female transition, hormone therapy runs from $60 to $160 each month and usually includes a combination of female hormones (estrogen and progesterone) and anti-androgens that block male hormone production. They are taken orally, intramuscularly, or through patches applied to the skin and are usually not covered by insurance. Although the results vary significantly from one individual to another, it usually takes months for the hormones to begin to have an effect. The changes can be dramatic or barely noticeable. In general, female hormones increase breast size and sometimes redistribute fat away from the waist and toward the hips and buttocks. Over time, sex drive decreases, and erections become infrequent and difficult to maintain. The hormones reduce sperm count and fertility, often leading to sterility. For some, body hair becomes finer and less dense, and the pores of the skin shrink. In general, the body becomes softer, more shapely. To keep the female characteristics, the therapy has to be lifelong, although it is usually modified after two years.

Biological females treated with androgens can expect a permanent deepening of the voice, permanent clitoral enlargement, mild breast atrophy, increased upper body strength, weight gain, facial and body hair growth, male-pattern baldness, and decreased hip fat.

The surgery is major: for men, the internal penile tissue is mostly removed, and the outer skin is inverted and inserted into the body inside out as the new vagina; for women, a double mastectomy, hysterectomy, and phalloplasty—the construction of an artificial phallus. The estimated cost for a male to female sex-reassignment surgery ranges from $7,000 to $15,000. The basic female to male surgery is considerably more, ranging from $40,000 to $70,000.

For males, there is also a tracheal shave (to reduce the Adam's apple), liposuction of the waist, facial surgery (brow shave, jaw reduction, rhinoplasty, cheek implants, eyelid lift), breast augmentation, and labiaplasty. Each surgery costs from $1,500 to $5,000. Because vocal chord surgery is especially risky and not always effective, some men go to speech and language pathologists or take voice lessons to raise the pitch of their voices and to learn to use more typically female speech patterns.

Costing anywhere from $40 to $75 an hour, electrolysis to permanently remove a male beard, and in some cases chest, hand, back, and other body hair, is one of the most expensive parts of transitioning. To remove face and neck hair alone takes from 200 to 400 hours, often taking years to complete.

The total cost for a physiological male to transition to female (including only half of extra surgeries listed and two years of hormones) comes to nearly $50,000. Transitioning, however, usually costs much more.

Some transsexuals know from childhood that their gender identity is in opposition to their biological body, but others are not so clear. "For some, it begins with thinking that they might be gay," according to Kim Kleinman, director of the Creative Gender and Sexualities Clinic at Columbia Presbyterian Medical Center in New York. "The first thing that some people notice is their attraction to men, but there's a feeling that that's not the end of it. For some, there's a feeling there's a second step."

For the first six months I knew Juan, he changed his mind frequently about his gender. One week Juan wanted to be a girl. Another week, he was a gay male boy. He loved shopping for clothes, and he loved wearing makeup. He had a huge black vinyl sack filled with twenty-four color palettes of eyeshadow, dozens of lipsticks and lip gloss, mascara, different shades of foundation, hairspray, and oil sheen. He carefully put together his outfits for the balls and proudly showed me his creations: various miniskirts and short dress-es, tank tops, women's size 10 and 11 shoes and pantyhose. Because the staff at his group homes insisted he dress like a boy, when he felt like dressing like a girl he usually packed his women's clothes in a bag and changed after he left. Those times when he most strongly self-identified as a girl, Juan talked about wanting to take hormones.

The first time Juan took estrogen pills, he got them from a friend. He was told to take the pills once a day, but instead took them twice a day until he started to feel changes in his breasts. "I wanted the Adam's apple to go away, but I didn't want the breasts," he told me. He stopped taking the pills after one month.

Many myths circulated on the street about hormones: Hormones reduce an Adam's apple, change the pitch of a male's voice, affect the way he walks, stop hair growth. In reality, an Adam's apple can only be removed surgically. Also, once a boy's voice changes at puberty, use of female hor-mones cannot raise its pitch. And although some hormone users experience a decrease in facial and body hair, body hair doesn't stop growing. Perhaps the greatest myth is that the more estrogen a man takes, the more female he will look. In fact, the effects of hormones depend on an individual's genet-ic disposition. Some men who take estrogen develop large breasts and hips; others change minimally. If, however, hor-mones are taken before testosterone levels reach their peak, the body does look more feminine, more like a "real" woman. Young people know this, and it drives many of them to start taking hormones at the onset of puberty.

Transgendered kids who spent much of their time on the street in the 1990s often got their hormones through a black market network from other transgendered people, who gave injections at $25 a pop, often with unsterilized needles that they used on multiple clients. Although physicians I spoke to recommended injections no more than once or twice each month, supplemented with transdermal patches or pills, I met many male teenagers transitioning to females who got injections weekly, believing the myth that frequent hormone use would make them look more female. Even when clean needles were used, there were many risks involved in taking hormones without a doctor's supervision. Estrogen, especially at high, frequent doses, increases the risk of heart disease and strokes, and excessive dosages can overtax the liver and cause serious damage. At the same time, taking sex hormones can also cause serious emotional distress. For some people, even taking normally prescribed amounts of estrogen can cause acute depression and sudden violent mood swings.

Like most thirteen-year-old boys, Juan's body was becoming more masculine: his voice was dropping, he was getting physically stronger, and was learning to deal with new feelings of aggression. The hormonal changes were confusing and unsettling. He was surrounded by heterosexual boys and people who told him he looked and acted like a girl even when he wasn't dressed as one. Complicating everything further, Juan was also attracted to more masculine boys. The best way to attract the attention of a masculine, heterosexual-acting boy was to "be" a girl. But whether he expressed himself as a gay boy or as a girl, he was constantly ridiculed, which fueled the confusion.

"I think Juan very much wants to be a girl, but at the same time I don't think he understands the scope of that and what that really means for the rest of his life," said Jennie Cassiano, Juan's supervisor at NYPAEC. "I think he definitely knows he's gay, and he definitely has some gender issues. But I think he's only thinking about the immediacy of right now. I don't think he's thought about the future. It's difficult because he's thirteen. It's easy to know that you're not masculine at thirteen, but it's more difficult to know what you want to do the rest of your life—especially if you have no guidance. Once he's in a home where he can explore, it's going to be a very different story."

Over the past decade, crossing gender lines has become increasingly accepted in popular culture: Professional basketball star Dennis Rodman preened off the court in a bridal gown; Ru Paul, the first drag pop star, was annointed the official M.A.C. cosmetics girl; fashion designers regularly feature cross-dressed models in their fashion shows; and viewers flocked to movies like the *Crying Game* (1992), *The Adventures of Priscilla, Queen of the Desert* (1994), *The Birdcage* (1996), *Boys Don't Cry* (1999), and *Flawless* (1999).

In the "real" world, however, being transgender still carries a tremendous stigma and disapproval. Many transgendered people feel that they are among the last pariahs in a society that has grown more responsive to almost all other minorities. Although homosexuality was once considered a mental illness and wasn't eliminated from the *Diagnostic and Statistical Manual of Mental Disorders* until 1973, a disorder associated with being transgender was still included in the manual's fourth edition in 1994. Even though being transgender per se was not considered pathological, Gender Identity Disorder—"the condition marked by evidence of a strong and persistent cross-gender identification, which is the desire to be, or the insistence that one is of the other sex with significant impairment in social, occupational, or other areas of functioning"—was still listed as a diagnosis. Although inclusion of the disorder was a point of controversy, its inclusion was, at a minimum, suggestive of the pressure society at large puts on transgendered people to conform.

Today, U.S. society still looks at transgendered people as

"abnormal," "sick," "perverted." To many, they are considered freaks of nature. Not generally accepted by heterosexuals or some mainstream gay and lesbian groups, transgendered people face constant discrimination in the workplace, in housing, in health care, in the military, and in prison. Many transgendered people are unemployed or underemployed. They have practical worries, from the mundane question of which gender box (M or F) to check on employment applications to which restrooms to use. Many regularly worry about their safety. Because of their behavior and choice of attire, transgendered people are frequently subjected to verbal and physical abuse.

Juan was especially conscious of this stigma. One day, I picked him up at his group home to take him to a Triangle Tribe meeting. We were running late, but Juan insisted on changing his shirt and pants. When he emerged from his room twenty minutes later, he was wearing the same clothes as when I had arrived. He wore loose cotton pants, a T-shirt, and a gray wool sweater vest. He was also wearing an oversize jacket. I was confused until Juan opened his jacket to reveal "breasts." Under his T-shirt he wore a training bra stuffed with condoms he had inflated. His new breasts were small but noticeable. "Come on, let's go," he said, rushing me out the door. "I don't want the boys to say anything." We left quickly before anyone noticed the lip gloss and eyeshadow.

••••

IN MID-FEBRUARY 1999, more than a month after he'd had his jaw broken, Juan ran away from his group home. He told me he wasn't going back. According to Juan, the problems had started when he tried to leave a few nights earlier to go hang out in the West Village with his friends.

This was not the first night Juan had left his group home to meet friends. Because Juan was not supposed to be out at night unsupervised, he had to find excuses to leave. Sometimes, Juan told the staff that he was doing outreach for NYPAEC. One time, he told a staff member that he was meeting me. I did speak to Juan the night in question and even met him briefly, but I learned days later that he had stayed out all night. When I asked Juan if he had used me as an excuse to leave the house, he vehemently denied it.

Like so many adolescents, Juan had little ability to sort the facts from his feelings. If he felt that something was untrue, then it was. If he felt that a counselor was unfair, then he was. Most of what Juan told me I found to be true, although his perception of an event might differ widely from others who either were involved or had witnessed the same incident.

"Juan lies when he either feels unsafe or he needs the armor of the lies to protect him in some way," Cassiano said. "But I don't think he totally makes up stories. I think they are always half true."

Eventually, Juan stopped making excuses at his group home when he wanted to leave and simply walked out whenever he felt like it. When someone gave him trouble, he used the lawsuit as a threat to get his way. "We were told 'hands off,'" said a youth worker from the group home in Queens. "He was out of control because there were no limits. No rules. Nobody knew how to handle him. What message are you sending to the other nine kids? It was breaking down morale."

That evening in mid-February when Juan decided to go AWOL from his group home, he learned that two other boys also planned to leave the same night. Juan asked them if they wanted to go with him to Greenwich Village. Just as the boys were leaving, a staff member stopped them at the door. According to Juan, one of the staff said to the boys, "Listen, he just wants you to be gay like him, and he wants to have sex with you, and that's why he's taking you. He wants to turn you gay and take you to hang out with a bunch of faggots." At that point, Juan said, another boy got involved and tried to persuade the two others not to go with Juan. When Juan told the boy to mind his business, "he got in my face and started cursing and really threatening me," Juan said. "His nose was touching my nose. He was so close to me, and the staff member sat there and watched. The staff that's supposed to be there to protect me."

After a while, the boy went inside, and Juan and the other boys left.

I spoke to Juan two days later at eleven at night. He sounded exhausted and told me he hadn't slept since he left the group home. "I'm scared to go back," he said. "I really don't feel safe at all. They threatened me. Who knows, the staff might persuade the other kids to do something to me. I don't know what to do. I have seventy-two hours before I lose my bed. I don't want to go back there, ever."

••••

THE NEXT DAY Juan went to NYPAEC, where he spent most of the afternoon on the phone. When Juan wanted something, he called everyone he thought could help him. He started with his group home. The staff member who answered the phone told him the police were looking for him.

"I don't care if the police are looking for me," said Juan. "No. You all are not taking anything into consideration about me moving my room and taking off the one-to-one." Juan had requested being placed on a one-to-one after the attack at school, but now he wanted it off. "She even follows me to the bathroom and stands outside waiting for me to come out. If a boy had his shirt off in the house around me, she'll tell him to put it on because we have 'those people' in the house." Juan had also requested that his room be changed because he said two boys on the first floor had taken things out of his room and were harassing him.

Now on the phone, the staff member from his group home tried to persuade Juan to come back.

"Well, I might come back so the seventy-two hours don't run out, but I won't stay," Juan said. "I want the one-to-one off. She's going to get it if I go back. She's going to get knocked outside her head. I'm sick of it. "

Juan listened for a few minutes and then said goodbye. He picked up the phone again without missing a beat. He tried to call his lawyers handling the lawsuit, but none of them were in. He called his law guardian, but she wasn't in, either. It was Friday and he knew if he didn't go back to his group home, he would have to go to Emergency Children's Services or stay on the street. Finally, he called one of the directors of the agency that ran his group home.

The man had heard what happened.

"How much do you know?" Juan asked. "Well, first of all I don't feel safe there. I don't feel you're taking anything I'm saying into consideration. I'm not coming back unless my room is changed, and the one-to-one is taken off. Simple as that."

The director told him the one-to-one was put into place to ensure his safety.

"I can defend myself," Juan said. "I wasn't raised around a bunch of straight boys and not learn how to fight. But that's not it. My room. I'm not staying in the same room. The two boys I ever have problems with are on the first floor, and you're keeping me there. I don't want them moved. I want to be moved. I want to feel like I'm a part of the population just like everybody else. Just because I'm gay and I've been beaten up in the past doesn't mean that I can't be treated like everybody else and given a chance not to get beat up in the future."

The director told Juan he would call the group home and take care of everything. Juan hung up. He didn't trust that things would change. Ten minutes later, he called his group home again.

"I'm just letting you know that I'm not going to come back until my requests are being considered. I'm not coming back until you do what I ask. I don't want to stay on the first floor anymore. You're going to keep me there. If that's the case, then I just won't come back . . . That is a form of abuse. Thank you very much. It's abuse because you're neglecting my needs."

Juan was told the boys on the first floor would be moved.

"I knew you were going to say that. I want to be moved. I'm not coming back. I want to be on the second floor, and you don't want to put me there."

If Juan felt he wasn't being heard, there was little room for compromise, and he could be manipulative and demanding. It was difficult to have sympathy for him.

Juan listened a few minutes longer, said goodbye, and hung up. He seemed even more frustrated. He called one of his lawyers again. This time he got through. He explained what happened. "Can you get them to do something? I just called the group home, and they said, 'You're not moving to the second floor.' I can't take it anymore, and I'm scared to go back." Juan listened for a few minutes. "I'm just really scared. I just don't know what to do." He sounded panicked. "There's no one I can call."

Juan knew what his options were, and his lawyers couldn't

change them. If he didn't feel safe at his group home, he could go to ECS and eventually be placed in another group home. But the next one could be far worse.

Juan decided to return to Queens. "I need to sleep," he said. "I like having a bed and to be warm. Some kids don't mind being on the street, but I need those things."

....

IN LATE FEBRUARY, Juan performed in the annual SafeSpace talent show. The SafeSpace drop-in center, a five-story former convent adjoining an Episcopal church near Times Square, assisted more than one thousand homeless youth ages thirteen to twenty-four each month. In 1999, nearly 65 percent were African and Caribbean American and 25 percent Hispanic. About 40 percent self-identified as lesbian or gay; 15 percent as transgender. Nearly 80 percent of the young people who came to SafeSpace had spent some time in the foster care system.

Juan visited SafeSpace twice a month, but when he was working on a specific project, like the talent show or the gay pride parade, he dropped in a few times each week. Although the drop-in center provided food, high school equivalency preparation, computer classes, and medical services, Juan went to SafeSpace primarily to hang out with other gay and transgender kids.

Juan loved performing and for months he had been looking forward to the talent show. After he left the hospital, Juan attended rehearsals twice each week with his jaw still wired. When he talked about his upcoming performance, he lit up. He spoke quickly, his arms waving. Days before the performance, he had a hair weave glued to his scalp to give him long curly locks and his nails painted with blue glitter polish and stenciled with Mickey Mouse appliqués.

More than five hundred people sat in the audience at the Roseland Ballroom in midtown Manhattan the night of the event. Halfway through the two-hour program, dressed in an oversize sweatshirt and jeans and carrying a large black shoulder bag, Juan strode out on stage. Over the loudspeakers the song "Iris" from the GooGoo Dolls began to play. Juan began his performance: He pantomimed opening a door center stage, walking into the room, closing the door, and pulling down window blinds. Alone now in this imaginary bedroom, Juan grabbed makeup out of his bag and started to apply eyeshadow, blush, and lip gloss. He let down his long hair and took off his sweatshirt, revealing a sleeveless knit top that hugged his chest and showed off a feminine silhouette, created with two water-filled condoms stuffed into a size A-cup bra.

His "father" walked onto the stage and into Juan's room. When he saw Juan with his long hair and makeup, he knocked Juan to the ground. But Juan didn't stay down long. He stood up, pushed his father away, and packed his bag. As he walked off stage, he waved the gay pride flag.

Juan wrote the skit himself. The lyrics of the song "Iris" reinforced his message: "And I don't want the whole world to see me, 'cause I don't think that they'd understand—everything's made to be broken. I just want you to know who I am." But he told me that he couldn't relate to the character he had created. "In the skit, I don't stand up for myself," he said. "It would have taken a lot more to knock me on the floor. And if someone hits me, I hit back."

I had never seen Juan so excited. He loved being on stage and the center of attention. He felt beautiful as a woman. After the show, Juan decided he would continue to dress as a woman. "I've done all this work to look like this," he said.

"I want to stay this way."

The boys from his group home had seen the show. "They were all nice to me," Juan said. "They wanted to come backstage. They were laughing with me." But Juan was nervous about how they would react back at the group home. For about an hour, he sat in the ballroom as people cleared away the folding chairs that had been set up for the audience. Not until well after midnight did Juan finally get up to leave. He was quiet as we walked to the subway. On the platform, waiting for the train to Queens, he looked worried. "It's hard to be transgender," he said.

When I saw Juan a week later, his nails were all broken, except for one thumbnail, and his hair weave was brushed straight. He was wearing makeup, his water-filled condom breasts, and a short skirt. He told me he wasn't going to keep dressing as a girl. "When this weave wears out, I'm not going to get in drag anymore," he said. "I'm going to dress as a boy."

When I asked him why, he said, "It's really hard being a girl. It's really hard. Keeping yourself up. Getting your make-up and your nails done and your hair. It's too hard."

Two weeks later, Juan again ran away from his group home. This time for good. According to Juan, he had been sitting in the basement when the boys "came down and started messing with me," hitting him and calling him a faggot. "I told one of the staff to call the police, but they refused, then they made inappropriate comments, like, 'You want to call the police because they won't let you suck their dick.'"

Juan said he was so angry that he grabbed a metal dustpan from the house, went outside, and smashed a worker's windshield. A staff member then brought him inside and put him in his room. Some of the boys came in and jumped him.

"They punched me all over my body," Juan said. "I wasn't hurt, but I was scared."

Juan jumped out his first-floor bedroom window, flagged down a dollar van, and hopped the subway turnstile. That night, he went to a friend's house in Brooklyn.

The staff member with the broken windshield pressed charges. The next day Juan went again to the ECS intake center on Laight Street.

. . . .

ECS, ALSO KNOWN AS LAIGHT STREET, was the first stop for children when they entered the system and the place they returned to every time they "failed" at a placement. Most were taken to the white brick office building after a family court judge found that they were in danger of abuse or neglect at home. But some kids, like Juan, walked in on their own.

When kids walked into Laight Street, they passed through a metal detector and were informed of the rules: no weapons, no gang-related talk, no wearing of gang-related colors, no bandanas, no hats, and no smoking. They met with a child evaluation specialist who recommended placement in foster homes, group homes, or residential treatment centers. Infants and younger children, usually matched quickly with a foster home, were moved out in a day or two; teenagers, many of them truants or runaways who were often abused and rejected by their guardians, spent days, sometimes weeks, sleeping in fold-up cots in the office awaiting placement.

At ECS, kids received a small bag with toiletries (comb, tissues, deodorant, Vaseline, soap, baby powder, toothpaste, toothbrush, shampoo), pajamas, underwear, and socks. They were also given new street clothes. The children ate and showered and spent their evenings watching television, playing video games, and, if they chose, participating in organized activities such as lanyard making or group discussions on drug abuse. At ten p.m., the cots were rolled out. The boys were separated from the girls. During the day, the kids were transported by van to the Teen Center in the Bronx, where they continued to await placement. On any given night, twenty-five to fifty kids spent the night at Laight Street. They were supervised by about eleven child specialists, two to three nurses, and six unarmed security guards.

In recent years, ECS had come under fire for not providing prompt and permanent placements. In July 1997, federal District Court Judge Robert B. Ward ordered the city to stop using the downtown office as a makeshift shelter. Ward ordered ACS to make its "best efforts" to stop the overnight stays by November 1. But seven months later, in February 1998, the *New York Times* reported that "dozens of adolescents are still sleeping in fold-up cots in New York City's emergency placement building every week, even after the creation of more than two hundred foster care beds." According to the article, city officials said they had made the issue a top priority, hiring a consultant to study the problem, hiring child care specialists to work at the center, and spending $15 million on new beds. The city allocated an additional $27 million to renovate a building on the campus of Bellevue Hospital Center to replace the placement office on Laight Street. But by March 1999, dozens of children were still sleeping on cots in the placement office.

Juan had been to Laight Street more times than he could remember. He spent most of his evenings in the nursery, away from other boys who teased and threatened him. In the nursery, Juan was calm and helpful. He soothed infants and toddlers when they cried, swept the floor, and heated bottles. A staff member allowed him to sleep in a small room, reserved for mothers with infants, so the others wouldn't bother him. The room, usually empty, had walls made of glass, but Juan didn't mind. "Juan wasn't afraid of the other boys, and he wasn't going to let the kids bully him," said Miranda Cruz, one of the ECS child specialists. "But we had to watch him carefully. We get some very rough kids."

Juan also had trouble with some of the staff. "Some of the staff made remarks about how he acted and about the fact he was gay," Cruz said. "They definitely treated him differently than the other boys. You could tell it bothered him sometimes." One night, a staff member at Laight Street told Juan that he had to stay out of the nursery. "They think because I'm gay, I'm a bad influence," he told me. "I'm leaving and I'm not coming back here again."

But Juan had no place to go. Not quite fourteen, Juan was still too young for New York City's only group home for gay youth.

. . . .

WHEN GREEN CHIMNEYS Gramercy Residence opened in 1984, it wasn't supposed to be a group home for gay youth, but rather an independent living residence for boys sixteen to twenty-one who were aging out of foster care.

The transformation began soon after the city's child welfare administration sent Green Chimneys Gramercy Residence an openly gay teenager. "The kid didn't get beat up, and nobody called them back saying we can't keep him," said Garry Mallon, the associate executive director. "So they sent more gay kids. But there was no acknowledgement that these kids had unique needs or that the staff needed special training. The only thing that mattered was that Green Chimneys didn't call to have the kids replaced and that the kids weren't beat up, and that was good enough."

Mallon first came to Green Chimneys in 1987. During his first week, a group of four boys marched into his office and said, "We just want you to know, in case you were wondering, yes, we're gay. And don't you go try to change that, Mr. New Director. This is the first place where we feel safe." Mallon learned that about half of the boys at Gramercy Residence self-identified as gay. Yet staff members admitted that they had little knowledge of gay people. They told Mallon that when the boys first came, they chuckled and laughed, but soon realized these boys were just like other teens. When the kids talked about their boyfriends, the staff told Mallon they learned to listen and give them advice just as they did with the other kids. "I thought we should maximize this, and we should talk about developing a real program for these kids," Mallon said. He began by conducting training sessions to educate his own staff about gay youth.

By 1987, Mallon had already worked for nearly a decade in the child welfare system and had seen for himself how gay youth faced repeated abuse and harassment. "Wherever I worked, gay kids were at the bottom of the barrel," Mallon said. "If they were spoken about at all, they were spoken about as if they were dirt." In 1990, when Mallon began working on his doctoral thesis on gay and lesbian adolescents in the child welfare system, he was astonished to learn how few of the professionals he interviewed even confirmed the existence of gay teens in the system.

"Everyone told me we don't have any gay kids," Mallon said. "I would ask, 'Out of three thousand kids you have in your agency, not one of them is gay?' One woman said, 'They might be bad, but they sure as hell are not gay.'"

Around the same time, Mallon began talking with the city about opening a separate group home for gay kids. In 1992, the city's Child Welfare Administration (CWA), the predecessor to ACS, conducted a needs assessment study in response to Mallon's request.

A CWA foster care consultant sent the results of the needs assessment to Robert Little, then executive deputy commissioner of CWA. The memorandum stated that "many children who are gay come through CWA's Office of Placement, and it is nearly impossible to identify and secure a proper placement for them." This finding was based on a CWA survey sent to sixty-eight agencies that provided day-to-day care for children in the foster care system. The memorandum stated that some agencies had informed CWA that "gay and lesbian youth who have been in their facilities have been scapegoated by children and staff, which disrupted services to other residents and created a stressful dynamic in the program."

The memo also acknowledged that there were far more gay or lesbian youth in the system than youth workers had identified:

> According to the *Journal of the American Medical Association* (July 1987) article by Dr. Gary Remafedi, 'Working with Gay and Lesbian Adolescents,' as adolescents enter adulthood, about 13 percent of males and 7 percent of females are predominantly homosexual. With a population of 12,851 children between the ages of 12 and 21, it would seem that there are an ample number of children in the system who are of gay and lesbian orientation who may be able to benefit from a program specifically designed for their

needs. Previous research has found that many gay and lesbian youth have needed to alienate and isolate themselves for self-preservation in avoidance of potentially abusive situations. It seems that the inability of agencies to identify larger numbers of this population is indicative of this data.

CWA concluded that a gay and lesbian group home should be formally supported, that training for foster care staff and parents on issues affecting lesbian and gay youth should be implemented, and that certain CWA forms and documentation should be amended to recognize and identify lesbian and gay youth and specific programs for them.

The 1992 findings, as well as the threat of litigation by the Legal Action Center for the Homeless (later known as the Urban Justice Center), prompted Little to write a letter in support of a gay and lesbian group home to the New York State Department of Social Services (DSS), the predecessor to the New York State Office of Children and Family Services (OCFS). Little urged DSS "to give a ready response" to Green Chimneys' request for formal approval and support for a gay and lesbian group home because CWA had "found there was significant need to warrant the support and development of this initiative." At the same time, CWA agreed to hold a half-day conference and create a task force to explore the needs of gay and lesbian youth in New York City's child welfare system.

The resulting Gay and Lesbian Task Force was made up of CWA personnel, executive directors of child care agencies, and advocates for gay and lesbian rights. Their report, "Improving Services to Gay and Lesbian Youth," made public in December 1993, prominently featured Mallon's doctoral thesis, *We Don't Exactly Get the Welcome Wagon: The*

Experience of Gay and Lesbian Adolescents in New York City's Child Welfare System. Mallon's study of twenty-seven self-identified gay and lesbian youth in out-of-home child welfare settings found that 100 percent of the gay and lesbian young people interviewed reported that they had experienced verbal harassment directly related to their sexual orientation; 85 percent said that they had multiple out-of-home care placements; 78 percent indicated they had been replaced or had gone AWOL from their initial placement because they were not welcome due to their sexual orientation; 70 percent said they had tried to hide their orientation from staff and peers because they feared they would be stigmatized, mistreated, or not accepted if the staff was aware they were gay or lesbian; 70 percent reported that they had been the victims of physical violence directly related to their sexual orientation; 63 percent reported that they had been treated differently by staff because they were perceived to be gay or lesbian; 56 percent said they spent some time living on the streets as an alternative to living in a group home or foster home because they felt "safer" on the street. The study also included interviews with seventy-eight child welfare professionals who corroborated the findings.

"The findings strongly suggest," Mallon wrote, "that the presence of verbal harassment and physical violence caused many young people to perceive that group homes and foster homes were unsafe places for gay and lesbian adolescents. Additional findings noted that the absence of training and the prevalence of religious, social, cultural, and personal bias against homosexuality had a negative impact on the treatment and care of gay and lesbian adolescents in welfare settings."

Gay and lesbian young people of color had an especially difficult time addressing their sexuality, according to the task force report. "For Latino(a)s, the coming out process becomes a family and community affair rather than an individual situation," wrote Julia Andino from the Coalition for Hispanic Family Services in a paper included in the task force report. Andino explained:

> The individual who 'comes out' also 'brings out' his/her family and the community. Because of this communal context and a feeling of loyalty to different communities, the individual will find him/herself fragmented, and/or in an irreconcilable state in which being 'different' from mainstream society can have fatal consequences. . . . The triple lives often lived by Latino/a gay and bisexual men/women who interact with the Latino community, the gay and lesbian community, and the heterosexual white community, exposes males and females to varying norms, expectations and cultures which create greater conflict, stressors, and challenge. Strong cultural perceptions of homosexuality as bad, repugnant, or immoral serve to impede the coming out process and drive Latino/a gays and lesbians to hide or deny their sexual orientation.

The task force report concluded that "lesbian and gay adolescents have been misunderstood, neglected, and in some cases discriminated against by the child welfare system. Given that children of color make up 93 percent of the [New York City] foster care population, it is especially disheartening to note that the child welfare system is even less equipped to meet the needs of gay and lesbian youth of color."

Neither Little's letter supporting a gay and lesbian group home nor the findings of the task force seemed to persuade DSS, which was responsible for licensing foster care facilities, to respond to Green Chimneys' request to open a group home for gay youth. Moreover, even after the task force recommendations were disseminated, state forms still included "homosexuality" on a list of foster care program limitations that included psychosis, neurological impairments, juvenile delinquency, fire-setting, drug abuse, and alcohol abuse. (In 1997, the forms were revised, and homosexuality taken off the list.) Despite countless meetings and correspondence with DSS that stretched over most of a year, the state failed to approve the proposed gay and lesbian group home.

During this time, Mallon decided that instead of waiting to open up a new home for gay kids, he would convert Green Chimneys Gramercy Residence into a safe haven. Mallon believed that if he trained the staff at ACS's Office of Placement Services, he would, in effect, get ACS to send to Gramercy Residence all gay youth who came into the system. At the same time, he would be educating ACS staff on gay youth issues.

By the end of 1995, all boys at Gramercy Residence were gay. The residence had become a de facto safe house for a small male segment of the gay, bisexual, and, in later years, transgender population, but Mallon received no additional funding or support to run what was the only such facility on the East Coast.

"I had every gay kid," Mallon said. "Psychotic kids out of the hospital, kids out of jail, kids thrown out, runaway kids. I had a nightmare group, with no support and no additional funding. Kids were going in and out of the hospital. I also had no way to educate them." Green Chimneys received ten to twelve calls a month from both ACS and agencies that contracted with ACS. In most cases, many of the young people already had been through several foster and group homes where they had suffered abuse because of their sexual orientation. But because the residence was open to just twenty-five boys, ages sixteen to twenty-one, many of the referred youth were turned away.

"Everything came to a head in 1997," Mallon said, when Green Chimneys opened on its premises the Audre Lorde High School, a GED program for Gramercy residents run by the Board of Education. "We practically had a riot here. These kids had so many problems and were taking out their aggression on each other. It got ugly." Mallon called the city and asked for help. "They said, 'We can't take these kids.' They essentially said there was nothing they could do to help. It didn't matter how severe their problems were, I had to keep these kids because they were gay."

Despite the city's response, Mallon resumed training for ACS staff. "I thought if I trained their own direct-care people, then the next time I had a situation where a kid had to be removed from the program, I'd be able to at least transfer them to a city-based program that was equipped to deal with gay kids." Mallon trained twenty separate groups of ACS child care workers free of charge. The three-hour trainings were held at Gramercy Residence so the ACS workers could actually meet gay kids. "They didn't come on time, and they were hostile," said Mallon. "It was a waste. Nothing happened. Nothing changed."

Mallon decided he could no longer accept every gay youth sent to him. He began to say no to kids younger than sixteen who needed more supervision than the program provided or who were deeply troubled. He began to replace kids who repeatedly broke rules or endangered other residents.

As the only safe house for gay kids in New York, though, Green Chimneys was forced to accept children it was not prepared to serve. In one case, ACS asked that Green Chimneys take a boy that no other agency would accept. Green Chimneys did take the child, but six months later it determined that he was not suited for an independent living program. In fact, ACS itself acknowledged that this young person required a more structured environment than Green Chimneys could offer, but another eighteen months passed before an alternative placement, in Los Angeles, was found.

In 1997, Bronx Family Court Judge Myrna Martinez-Perez issued a subpoena ordering a Green Chimneys representative to attend a hearing in a case in which Green Chimneys had no prior involvement. At the hearing, Perez ordered Green Chimneys to accept a gay thirteen-year-old boy for an evaluation period, explaining she had no other recourse. But when the evaluation period was completed, the boy remained at Green Chimneys, even though ACS agreed that Green Chimneys was not an appropriate place for the child. ACS also told Chimneys that no fewer than thirty-two agencies, each of which had vacancies and could offer an appropriate level of care, had refused to take the child because of his sexual orientation. The boy stayed at Green Chimneys for an additional five months. He was transferred to a more structured institution only after he set fire to his bedroom.

In May 1998, Mallon again tried to get a new program for younger gay kids off the ground. He wrote a letter to ACS requesting permission for Green Chimneys to open two small boarding homes. Mallon received no response. In September, though, ACS sent out a memo to all of its contracting agencies saying more beds were needed in the foster care system for certain youth, including gay and lesbian kids. Again Mallon wrote to ACS. Finally, in February 1999, a month after *Joel A. v. Giuliani* was filed, Mallon received initial approval to open a group home. He submitted the full proposal for a group home for gay and lesbian youth ages twelve to fifteen. In July, still having received no response, Mallon lost the site for the proposed residence and withdrew his proposal.

By the beginning of 2000, it was estimated that at least several hundred gay and lesbian young people were in ACS's custody. No programs were yet designed to meet the needs of lesbians of any age; gay, bisexual, and transgendered youth with severe emotional difficulties; or gay youth between the ages of twelve and fifteen. Far too many young people remained adrift in a system that had no place for them. Juan was one of those kids.

. . . .

DURING THE SPRING of 1999, Juan bounced from one home to another. For five days, he lived out on Long Island with a Spanish-speaking man who had six other kids living with him. But when one of the kids complained, saying Juan made him feel uncomfortable, Juan left. For a few weeks he stayed in a group home in the Bronx. He left when one of the boys started threatening him. Every time Juan ran away from a group home, he'd either go to Covenant House or return to ECS, where he would stay anywhere from one night to two weeks waiting for his next placement. A few times, though, ECS turned him away. They would tell him, "You already have a placement. You can't stay here." He usually spent those nights on the street or at a friend's house. Daytime, he was usually at NYPAEC.

Juan and I usually spoke every day, but during those few months, he often made no contact for a week at a time. When we did talk, he seemed distracted and irritable. He seemed to be growing up quickly, but there were days when I was reminded he was still so much a child.

Juan was at ECS the morning of his birthday. It was three in the morning when he called to remind me. My answering machine picked up. "I just wanted you to know I'm all right.

I'm still at Laight Street, and it's my birthday. I'm fourteen, and if you want to see me I'll be at NYPAEC all day tomorrow."

The next evening, Juan sounded elated. He was still at Laight Street. "I'm really happy," he said. "They were nice to me today. They gave me a radio. Everybody is being nice to me. This was the best birthday I've had in years."

....

A FEW DOZEN PEOPLE gathered outside ACS headquarters in downtown Manhattan at the beginning of May for a rally on behalf of foster children, organized by the Foster Care Legal Action Project Youth Organizing Group.

The organizers had contacted the media about the event, but most reporters were covering a sit-in a few blocks away, where hundreds of demonstrators had closed down a one-block stretch of Chambers Street in lower Manhattan. Dressed as flowers and plants, those demonstrators were protesting the impending auction of more than one hundred city properties that were being used as community gardens.

Only a few pedestrians stopped to listen to the protesters in front of ACS headquarters. "We are protesting against ACS and its employees who are mistreating our young people in the foster care system," yelled Angelique Jewell, the group's leader. "It's completely intolerable, and the young people out here say that they're not going to accept it any more."

Kids and adults held handmade signs that read "ACS: The C Should Stand for Care," "Foster Care Youth Have Rights Too," "Abandonment and Abuse Happen in Foster Care," "All We Want Is a Little Respect," and "If My Mom Can't Hit Me, Why Can Group Home Staff?"

Standing behind the barricades, the protesters took turns

speaking into a megaphone about their experiences in the system.

"People are scared to speak out," said one teenager who lived in a group home in the Bronx. He had wrapped a shirt over his face because he feared that if ACS or his group home heard that he was protesting, he would be asked to leave. "I'm eighteen and a voluntary placement. They can throw me out if they want." The boy spoke softly at first, telling the small crowd how the staff at his group home restrained kids by hitting them and tackling them to the ground and how his group home was little more than a shelter. But after about five minutes, his voice grew louder and more confident. Eventually, the teenager removed the shirt from his head and exposed his face. People cheered. The boy smiled. "They're supposed to guide us, but they're not guiding us," he said loudly. "The staff ain't doing their jobs. We run amok now. . . ."

One woman who had been in the system sixteen years spoke of being repeatedly abused in a number of foster homes where she had lived. "We're supposed to be put into better situations when we're removed from our families, but for me, it was worse," she said, becoming emotional. "We're treated like animals and given no support." She said she grew up with such feelings of inadequacy that now as an adult in her thirties she had trouble getting and maintaining a job and struggled with depression.

Jewell spoke again, this time about how many foster children lacked food, clothing, and school supplies and how most were unprepared for adult life when they were discharged. She also talked about overcrowding at ECS, poor screening of foster parents, and about the special problems facing teen mothers and gay youth.

When Jewell finished, she handed Juan the megaphone.

He was excited and nervous: "I've been openly gay since I was eight, and I've been in the system since I was nine. From the first day I came into the system I've had problems. . . . I've had people beat me at night in my room, kick me down a flight of stairs, I've had my leg broken, my nose broken several times, my arm broken, and it was all because kids don't understand."

Juan continued for nearly twenty minutes, talking about feeling safer sleeping on the street and on the subway than in certain group homes, and about the emotional pain of constant rejection. "Even now at Laight Street, I'm treated like I'm different. The room I was sleeping in was next to the nursery, and one of the staff came back and told me I couldn't be near the room because the small children were back there, and some concerns were raised that I might molest them. That all hurts me. It's just not fair. ACS needs to know what's going on."

He repeated himself occasionally, but he was passionate and convincing. "My lesbian and gay brothers and sisters— they're suffering, they're dying. I was deprived two years in a row to go to the gay pride parade. My RTC claimed it was a sexually inappropriate parade, which was not true. Just because a person wants to take a different road in life, some people feel that they can hurt them. I'm urging you to use whatever influence you have on ACS, and to use it now. I believe people's lives depend on it. I have a friend that called me two nights ago and told me he wants to leave. I said, 'Where do you want to go?' and he said, 'Up there,' and I said, 'Where?' He said, 'Heaven.' He said he didn't want to live anymore, and I asked him why, and he said he was getting out of the shower at a group home and a group of boys came out and beat him. He said the nurses refused to take pictures of the welts on his body because they looked so bad.

The place where he is refuses to test him for HIV.

"I'm trying not to let all these things affect me mentally, but they are. I feel like I'm wasting my life in ACS. I haven't been to a real school in years. Before ACS, I was going to school, I was well fed, I was never beat up."

Juan finally stopped when someone pulled him aside and asked that another person be given a chance to speak.

Half a dozen people walked up to Juan when he was finished. They shook his hand and complimented him on his courage. Juan loved the attention. "I'm with ABC-TV," said one woman in her early twenties. "The newsmagazine 20/20. Wow. Your story is really great," she said with a big smile. She seemed excited.

"Thanks," said Juan, also smiling. "We're working on a show, and we'd love to interview you." She gave Juan her business card. Two more people were waiting nearby to speak to Juan. "Please call me," she said, before walking away. "Your story is really great."

Juan liked the idea of being on television. But a few hours later, he had forgotten all about the young woman.

. . . .

JUAN spent increasingly more time on the street. By mid-May 1999, he was smoking cigarettes and marijuana, and he shoplifted. He tried crack once, but hated it. He also started taking hormones again; this time he got them from a friend in Brooklyn who worked for an escort service. Juan was supposed to go to Brooklyn weekly for the injection and pills, but at a cost of $100 a month, he took the hormones for just a couple of weeks.

Nearly all of Juan's friends were gay or transgender. He had met them at the balls, in the West Village, or in group

homes. Some lived in stable homes; others worked the prostitution stroll. Juan liked being around young people who
had a home and family, things he longed to have himself. But
it was also a painful reminder of what he lacked, so Juan also
often gravitated to people who had it worse than he did. He
could help and counsel them, and it made him feel good.

The more time Juan spent on the street, the less I saw and
heard from him. Previously, when he was between group
homes, he seemed vulnerable, very much a child. But as his
life became increasingly chaotic and he spent more time with
people on the street, he seemed distant and angry. During
May and June, sometimes I didn't hear from him for a week
at a time, and when we finally did speak, he was withdrawn
and unresponsive. If I pressed him to talk, he just said,
"Everything's fine." During those periods, if we went out for
a meal, he was often impatient and difficult, sometimes asking the waiter where his food was just minutes after he
ordered. He no longer said "please" or "thank you." Rarely
did he let his defenses down.

One thing he did seem to care about was testifying in
family court against the boys who had attacked him and broken his jaw in school five months earlier. Yet the day before
Juan's court appearance, he learned that there was an outstanding complaint against him (filed by the group home
child care worker whose windshield Juan had broken),
meaning there was a good chance Juan would be arrested if
he appeared in court to testify. If Juan were arrested, ACS
could then decide not to assume custody for him. In that
case, he could be remanded to the Department of Juvenile
Justice and end up in a detention facility. Juan had never
been arrested. He wasn't going to risk it. When Juan didn't
appear in court to testify, the case against the two boys was
dismissed.

Other adults who had contact with Juan over the year also began noticing the changes. "He's becoming more streetwise," said Cassiano. "We've had a lot of people who try to scam here. Juan's never been one of them. But within the last few months, he hasn't been at his group home, so they're not feeding him. He's like, 'If I go to NYPAEC, maybe I'll find something to do for three hours, so I can get lunch money and carfare,' and he's developed that mentality. And that comes along with being on the street because you start to say, 'What are my resources and how can I get to them?'"

During this period, Juan began talking more frequently about his "dates" out on the prostitution stroll on West Fourteenth Street.

Juan had told me months earlier he had prostituted, but I wasn't sure if he was telling me the truth. Everyone on the stroll knew Juan. He was often out there doing outreach to the girls, handing out condoms at all hours of the night. I thought he might be telling people that he was turning tricks in order to be accepted. At times, I wondered if he just wanted me to react. He knew I would be upset. He liked having someone worry about him.

"Don't worry," he told me one day. "I've only been out there twice, but I made $400 each time. A lot of girls don't like me out there because I steal most of their dates because I look so real." Juan said he got six to eight dates a night, charging $50 or more each time. "If they look rich, I charge more. One of the guys was an executive with Toyota. Most of the guys want you to take their thing out. A lot of them want to give you blow jobs. And they want you to fuck them and to be the man—while you're in a wig and high heels."

Juan admitted that working the stroll was dangerous. "I always bring a knife and Mace with me," he said. "And I can tell the strange ones. I won't get into a car with old strange guys. I try to do it with my friend to tell him which car I'm going into and have my friend take the license plate number. We try to get really organized. When me and he are together—when I go on a date, she stays and when I came back, she goes out on a date. She's a boy just like me."

Juan also told me he didn't have intercourse when he worked. "I don't get in most of the cars because they want me to fuck them, and I'm like, 'Sorry,' and they just drive away. Some of them say, 'Give me head.' I'd be like, 'How much? $20? Sorry. $30? No.' I say, 'Try $50.' Most girls will do it for $20 but I won't. I got into one car, and all he wanted to do was to talk dirty to me. The other night, some guy just pulled up and gave me money. He rolled down his window and gave me $20 for nothing. I swear to God. My friends just rolled on the floor."

At first, Jennie Cassiano also had doubts that Juan was prostituting, but he always seemed to have money. "I think it's possible he gets involved with older men who give him money," said Cassiano. "But I don't think he works the stroll. I think he wants attention. I think he knows what's out there and knows the drill, and I think he's thinking, 'I'm fourteen, and if I tell someone that I'm prostituting, it gives me more attention. People look at me and talk to me or even yell at me, but at least I'm getting attention.' Also, I've never had young people his age blankly comment about prostituting as if it's nothing."

But by the beginning of the summer, Cassiano and I started to believe that Juan did in fact work the stroll when he needed money. One girl who used to prostitute told me she had seen Juan pick up dates. By then, Juan spoke about going to the stroll as if he were going to the store. He told everyone he was prostituting. "I only do it when I really want something—like a new pair of sneakers—really bad," he said. "Like if I have a ball coming up and I'm working a certain category and I need to be dressed really good."

. . . .

THE "FEM QUEEN" STROLL was in the meat market on the northern edge of the West Village. Although prostitutes had once confined themselves to Fourteenth Street west of Ninth Avenue, since the mid-1990s prostitution had spilled over into the residential streets further south. With names like Nature, Precious, Mahogany, Coffee, and Divina, the girls who worked the stroll ranged in age from thirteen to over forty, but the vast majority were between eighteen and twenty-five. The girls worked long hours, often until the early morning. Their dates took them to a hotel or parked in a lot or on one of the side streets along the highway. On a good night, girls who dressed well and took care of themselves made $500 and up, charging as much as $50 for a blow job. Other girls, usually crack addicts who worked the streets closer to the water, charged as little as $5 for the same service.

On summer nights, cars often lined up along Ninth Avenue looking for girls: men in shiny Mercedes, Volvos, Lincoln Continentals, and in stretch limousines. Many of the license plates were from New York and New Jersey, some from Connecticut. A few of the cars had medical doctor's plates. A couple had empty baby seats. The cars crawled slowly down the street, then sometimes circled back around the block two or three times. When a car stopped, a girl or group of girls walked up to an open window. One of the girls usually jumped in.

Prostituting was dangerous work, although many of the girls didn't seem to worry. "We protect ourselves," said Coco, one of the girls who worked Fourteenth Street. "Don't forget, we're men. We can beat them worse than they can beat us. The real problem is the cops—not the johns." When someone spotted the police, the news spread quickly. Within seconds, the block cleared and stayed clear until it was safe to return.

Police sweeps were common. Most nights, police arrested two to five girls; some nights as many as ten. In 1998, officers from the Sixth Precinct made 351 prostitution-related arrests on the transgender stroll; all but four were transgender. Roughly 90 percent of the arrests were for loitering for the purpose of prostitution. The other 10 percent, for prostitution, occurred when police staged undercover operations and posed as johns. To get arrested for loitering for prostitution, the girls had to be seen engaging single motorists or single male passersby in brief conversations. Usually, the police arrested a girl only after they had seen her do this at least three times. But even when the girls were arrested for loitering, they never stayed locked up very long. Most of the time, the girls spent one night in jail, often opting for community service instead of jail time. The top recidivist in the Sixth Precinct, arrested about seventy times, usually received between twenty and thirty days of jail time when convicted.

Coco was a regular on the stroll. At eighteen, she was stunning, making good money on Fourteenth Street and living in the basement of her mother's house on the edge of Bedford Stuyvesant in Brooklyn.

Born a male, Coco began dressing in women's clothes when she was eight. For as long as she could remember, she knew she was gay. She kept it hidden until she was fourteen. "After my parents found out, they tried to keep me trapped at home," she said. Her mother, a devout Baptist, was devastated. "'How could you love a man?' my mother screamed. 'Don't you know what gay people carry?' She started crying.

'How can you do this to me? What about grandchildren?'"

Her father, a preacher, tried to change his son's mind. "One day he came with the Bible," Coco said. "He took me to McDonald's and read me the Romans. 'Man should not be with man.' We were sitting outside in the drive-through. When he was finished, he asked, 'Did I change you? Do you have a new sense of mind?' I said, 'No. You believe what you believe, and I believe what I believe.'"

Coco and her parents fought regularly, and by fourteen, she began to run away from home. Initially, she left only for a few nights, but over time, the flights from home grew longer. She skipped school. Sometimes she stayed on the streets; other times she stayed with friends. She began drinking and doing drugs regularly. She told me she also tried committing suicide on three separate occasions.

Eventually, Coco's mother filed a PINS petition on her. A Person in Need of Supervision petition can be filed by parents, police, teachers, or relatives if an adolescent under the age of sixteen has repeatedly engaged in a series of noncriminal behaviors (truancy, running away, staying out late). Kids who have a PINS petition filed on them can be placed in foster care unless their behavior changes. Fearful of ending up in foster care, Coco stopped running. But at home, Coco felt like a prisoner. She said her mother gave her no money, not even lunch money for school. So Coco began prostituting on the male stroll on West Tenth Street. When she learned that she could make more money on the transgender stroll, she started working Fourteenth Street. "I would make the money on the men's stroll and buy skirts, stockings, boots, and a wig and go to the fem queen stroll," she said. With the money, she began to buy hormones.

When I first met Coco in 1997, she was living most of the time as a female. With high cheekbones and long legs, when she dressed up, she was striking. She had plastic surgery to make her nose smaller and had bleached her skin. She was prostituting a couple of nights a week, she said, to make money for clothes and to get her hair and nails done regularly. She told me she wanted to stop working the stroll and would stop when she had a full-time job.

Over the next two years, Coco got her high school equivalency diploma, worked in a law firm and at a local college, and enrolled in two training programs, one in computers and one to become a home health aide. But even with training, getting a job wasn't easy. She had to use her legal name, Leon, to fill out job applications. When she dressed like a woman, which she felt more comfortable doing, she didn't always get the job, and if she did, she told me she experienced harassment and discrimination. When she dressed as a man, she was ridiculed because she was effeminate. In 1999, she was still working the stroll.

One late night, I asked Coco what type of men picked her up. We were sitting in a bagel shop, drinking coffee to stay awake. She thought for a moment and said, "Everyday people." Then she pointed to a man standing by the counter. He was white, in his late thirties, wearing jeans and a T-shirt. Then she pointed to another man, wearing work boots and a shirt that said Con Edison on it. She continued to point to every man in the coffee shop—a young black man in his late teens; an old man with gray hair and long straggly beard; a man in a three-piece suit. "One of those, one of those, and one of those. All types of men. Doctors, lawyers, bums, construction workers."

She took a sip of her coffee, put back the lid, and stood up. "I've got work to do."

....

ONE NIGHT IN MAY, Juan called me around eleven to tell me he was on the stroll doing outreach to the girls. By the time I arrived, which was well past midnight, he had already handed out about thirty condoms, nearly all of his supply for the evening.

About a dozen girls stood on the corner of Fourteenth Street and Tenth Avenue. Some looked like professional basketball players with cover girl faces. Vinyl miniskirts and spandex shirts hugged their curves. One woman, her enormous breasts barely caged by a frayed black nylon bra, wore an undersized neon blue nylon shirt, the buttons undone to her navel. Her hips, injected with silicone, bulged out from a tiny waist. Another woman, also large, wore a black leather skirt that didn't quite cover her bare buttocks. Some of the women were stunning, their makeup expertly done, their hair coiffed, and their bodies sensuously proportioned. They accessorized with shiny belts, dangling earrings, and delicate necklaces. They looked elegant, until you noticed the size-12 feet squashed into three-inch high heels.

A car with four men in their early twenties drove by slowly. Nine girls, standing together, stepped toward the men and paraded up and down the street like models on a runway. The girls gently nudged each other to the side to give the men a good look. They waved and posed as if for a camera.

"That boy's going to be mine tonight," said one girl, slinking towards the car.

"Word," said another girl, impressed by her confidence. She kicked her leg up high like a Bob Fosse dancer, almost striking another girl in the face with her jumbo-size stiletto heels.

One man smiled. "The girls are out tonight," he yelled. The car kept moving, and the girls waved goodbye.

Juan was sitting on the stoop with Delilah. Delilah was

born a biological male, but began taking female hormones when she was sixteen. Tonight she wasn't dressed in drag, only in jeans and a T-shirt. She was in her twenties, Puerto Rican, and lived with her mother. "I'm not getting in drag tonight," Delilah said with a heavy Spanish accent, holding a black nylon knapsack. She looked up and down the street nervously, searching for police. "I'm not taking any chances."

A white car drove by with two men in the front seat. "That's why I'm not getting dressed," said Delilah, pointing to the car. "Those are cops. They work out of cabs also. They sit in the backseat, and they're also drivers."

Delilah let out a sigh. She'd been out for nearly two hours. "My mother's making me stressed," she said. "I found out she's in menopause. I said, 'No wonder the bitch has been cursing me.' So now I'm helping her out. I'm understanding about her menopause. I say, 'You got your pills—you're taking your pills? If you don't take your pills, you give me a bitch attitude, and I don't like that Miss Thing.'"

A man walked by as Delilah was talking. Mid-sentence she got quiet and stood up. The man was wearing skintight white pants. His shirt, also tightly fitted, showed off his muscular arms.

"OOOhhh, my God! Is that all *your* cake?" said Delilah loudly to the man.

"'Cake' means 'ass,'" Juan said, translating for me.

"Cookies and cream, honey," yelled Delilah as the man walked by. "I ain't got no cream, but I got cookies."

Delilah continued talking about her mother. "I love my mother to death, but when she be in a bitchy attitude, I can't handle it. She knows what I do, but she don't like me to come out here. But I like dressing up. I feel good dressing up." Delilah stood up and moved her hands up and down her hips. Delilah told me she had taken hormones for four years but had stopped a few years earlier. She still had small breasts. "My mother knows, but my friends at home, they don't know what I do. When I come out here, it's my business. At home I dress like this—in jeans and a T-shirt—like a boy. But when I dress like a woman, I feel good. I have a lot of guys after me when I dress like a woman, but when I dress like this, no one talks to me."

Delilah told me she had lived in Florida for a few years and returned to New York a year earlier. She now lived with her mother and had her own room and telephone. She also brought dates to the house. "When I want someone to come to the house, I tell them to come over at 11:30 because my mother goes to sleep at ten. At 11:30 she's out—she won't even hear the door open. I go into my room, do my thing, get paid, and when I see you, I see you."

A man in his early twenties crossed the street. He wore baggy jeans and a T-shirt. "Come here, mama," he said smiling and gesturing to Delilah. "I want to talk to you."

"He's so cute," whispered Delilah over her shoulder as she jogged toward him. The two spoke for a few minutes and then walked down the block.

Five minutes later, Juan waved to a woman across the street. Venus was big, about six feet tall, with very large breasts. The white cotton dress she wore was loose and sleeveless. A thick silver necklace rested below her collar bone and matched the bracelet on her left wrist. Her straight black hair, a weave, hung well past her shoulders; her make-up looked professionally done. Juan said Venus was in her twenties. I couldn't place her age. She could have passed for twenty-five as easily as forty. Venus was originally from the South but had spent most of her life in New Jersey. This was her first summer in New York.

"Are you going to the Latex Ball, grandma?" Juan asked.

Sponsored by the Gay Men's Health Crisis, the Latex Ball was the largest of the dozens of transgender balls held in New York City every year. People came from all over the East Coast to attend.

Venus nodded and started voguing. "Walk with me," she said. "Walk with me," she said again. Juan started voguing beside her, waving his arms in all directions. "Word," said Venus in approval.

"I'm 'moning [taking hormones], grandma," said Juan as he continued to vogue.

"I'm not."

"You're not 'moning anymore?"

"I haven't been 'moning for four years."

"You look fab."

"It's all illusion." Venus stopped voguing and tossed her long black hair over her shoulders. She was a strikingly beautiful woman, although genetically male. "When are you getting up in drag?"

"Soon," Juan said. "When I get my cleavage."

"Cleavage doesn't make a bitch."

By two a.m., about a dozen girls were out on the stroll dressed in drag. Those who came earlier dressed as boys had slipped into the dark side streets and in doorways of abandoned warehouses to put on their stockings, high heels, makeup, and wigs. One girl had transformed herself in the subway station nearby.

Juan joked about getting a date. When he saw that I wasn't amused, he said he would never "disrespect" me by doing that because he knew I would worry too much. By three, I decided to go home. Juan left as well. He said he was spending the night at a friend's house.

• • • •

TWO WEEKS LATER, I went with Juan to the Tenth Annual Latex Ball. More than three thousand people packed the Roseland ballroom for the event. Sponsored by the Gay Men's Health Crisis, the evening was free, and included a full dinner buffet as well as fashion and voguing competitions into the wee hours of the morning. The event, which prohibited alcohol, was an opportunity to educate people about HIV prevention. Dozens of organizations handed out free food, condoms, and information on safe sex.

For weeks before, Juan had talked about what he was going to wear, changing his mind daily. The night of the ball Juan spent two hours getting dressed. He put on white stockings and white high-heeled shoes. Then he took two condoms, blew them up, and taped them with clear packaging tape to his chest to give him B-cup breasts. His outfit—a short, white satin skirt with a scarlet red, six-foot-long sash he wrapped like a halter around his chest—looked elegant and smart. Once he was dressed, he crammed his curly hair into a pageboy-style wig. His makeup, done by Jennie Cassiano, was flawless.

When he finished dressing, Juan looked like a diva. With a small spaghetti-strap shoulder bag, he walked out the door, excited and confident. On the street, as he hailed a cab, men stopped to admire him.

"You look beautiful," said one man wearing jeans and construction boots.

"You have a lovely evening, miss," said another man, respectful and polite.

Juan smiled and graciously thanked his admirers. Before walking into Roseland, he glanced at his reflection in a window and adjusted his hair. He wasn't performing in the ball, but he was ready to be seen.

· A stage with a long runway where the contestants would

compete was set up in the middle of the room. Rows of fold-up chairs for the audience filled quickly. Several dozen transgendered people stood in the back of the room ready to walk. Some were biological women with short-cropped hair who were dressed as males; but most were men dressed as women. They wore long sequined gowns, futuristic outfits with plastic tubes and aluminum foil, designer business suits, fishnet, lace, feathers, leather, vinyl, and silk. Like Juan, they were dressed to look real and to be noticed. For the next eight hours, they would sashay down the runway to pounding music and cheers or jeers.

As Juan walked through the crowd, he gracefully accepted the accolades of friends and acquaintances. He looked stunning, and he knew it.

· · · ·

AS SUMMER APPROACHED, Juan seemed preoccupied only with the events of the moment and didn't seem to care where he lived. He was bored and antagonistic, depressed and impossible to reach.

He left one group home after about two weeks because he claimed they tried to medicate him. "I was eating my egg salad sandwich and peeling the crust off and [the pill] was right there," he told me. "It had Paxil written on it. I got pissed and threw the sandwich on the floor."

He left another group home after a week because "the boys were mean. Nothing really bad happened, but I felt uncomfortable. They put me with the worst boy in the house."

While staying at a third group home, Juan said boys from the neighborhood threatened to beat him up. Juan frequently left this group home for days at a time, fearful of getting jumped by the boys on the block. Some nights Juan stayed on the street. For a while, he even stayed at a friend's apartment, but left after a couple of weeks. "He smokes crack all day, and the place is filthy," he told me. "There's food and bugs everywhere."

Eventually, Juan grew so tired of moving around and so desperate to lead a normal life that he even called one of the administrators at Children's Village. "I was thinking," Juan said to the man on the phone. "The problems I had in Children's Village were probably 100 percent minor compared to the problems I'm having now. I told my allocations worker a couple of days ago that Children's Village is probably the best program as an RTC in all of New York City. I was wondering, you all wouldn't take me back, would you?"

When Juan was reminded that he had asked to be removed, he lied. "Not really," he answered. "I was going to stay, but my lawyer just snatched me up."

For the next five minutes, Juan tried to persuade Children's Village to take him back. He spoke about missing a year of school, having his jaw broken, and bouncing from one group home to another. "I'm in the city and I'm at risk for drugs, gangs, prostitution, and all that stuff," Juan said. "I want to be a normal kid, and I can't do that here. I'm sick of it." After about ten minutes, Juan hung up. He was told that Children's Village would contact Juan's ACS caseworker.

When I asked Juan if he really thought that his days at Children's Village hadn't been so bad, he said, "No, they were really bad. But I've heard there are more gay kids there now. Maybe it's gotten better."

Juan, at fourteen, seemed worn out. "My life sucks," he told me. "It's hard being me."

. . . .

WHEN JUAN CALLED me in early July 1999, he sounded ecstatic, something I hadn't heard in his voice for months. "You're never going to believe where I'm moving to?"

Juan had been placed at Green Chimneys Gramercy Residence. Garry Mallon had decided to bend the age limit and give him a chance. Juan was thrilled. "I can't talk. They're coming to get me now. I'm so happy."

Sidewalk Supa Model

There she goes again slayin' that catwalk,
her hair, uncoiling down her toasted honey back.
The onlookers stare in contempt, with a slight
feeling of envy, as the highest bidder
signals her to make an outstanding pivot.
And off she goes, with a price tag dangling round her neck.
Sidewalk supa model.

Next up, we have another priceless beauty,
sporting the newest trans fashions by E.
Her foot and eye wear, glistening in the flashing lights.
Gliding down the narrow walkway . . .
"Tits and hips an ass, oh my"
"Tits and hips an ass, oh my"
She's untouchable.
Sidewalk supa model.

Painted dolls.
Lovely children.
Lips glossed to a sickening attraction.
She's ovah and she knows it!
Sidewalk supa model.

Her shadow faded with an arc,
skin touched flawless, powder light.
"Perfect, phab, eat it girl.
Work, yes, mhm, that's right."
Economic prima donna;
she'll have it all you'll see,
Men groveling at her ankles;
got the business to a T.
Sidewalk supa model.

—Juan

THREE

Dissed

IT WAS OCTOBER 1996, mid-morning. A steady flow of people moved through the Port Authority. Men in suits with smoothly creased trousers, unscuffed shoes on their feet, and newspapers cradled under their arms walked quickly, and with purpose. Travelers lugging oversize backpacks and duffel bags lingered by ticket counters and departure gates. Others, unshaven, shuffled around in secondhand clothes, asking for a cigarette or spare change.

A man in his early twenties handed out photocopied fliers that read "Stop the Disneyfication of Times Square." A construction worker in a hard hat and work boots grabbed one, skimmed it, then walked away, dropping it crumpled on the floor. In a coffee shop just opposite the men's room, three girls, all very blond, all about sixteen, sat slumped in their seats, laughing and munching on bagels with cream cheese.

Minutes before, Dakota had gone into the men's room to brush his teeth, shave, wash under his arms, and put on a clean T-shirt he'd picked up earlier from his sister. He settled his baseball cap low on his head to hide the fact he needed a haircut and tucked his T-shirt neatly into his jeans. When he came out, he looked purposeful, energetic. No one would have guessed he was homeless.

At the bathroom entrance, an old man, his face hollow and unshaven, his pants threadbare at the knees, held out his palm and asked for change. Dakota nodded. The man withdrew his hand and nodded back. They'd seen each other before.

Dakota walked over to where Cedric sat, on the steps not ten yards away. Cedric was asleep. Their bags—a knapsack, duffel bag, and two plastic bags—were more than three feet off to the side.

Dakota shook his head. "Cedric," he called out. "What are you doing?"

Cedric jumped. He was supposed to be watching the bags. Stuffed with sweaters, T-shirts, pants, and two blankets, the bags held everything that he and Dakota owned.

"I was just resting my eyes," Cedric said.

"You can't afford to rest your eyes," Dakota said. He walked over to the bags and moved them closer to where Cedric was sitting. "They have to be open twenty-four-seven. Anyone can just walk away with our stuff. And then what?"

Dakota and Cedric had spent the night riding the subway, and they were exhausted. The evening before, they had tried to get beds at the Fort Washington men's shelter in Washington Heights, but Cedric had been told that he wasn't in the computer system. The last time this had happened, the clerk eventually found Cedric's name. This time, they told him he would have to go to East Thirtieth Street, to the city's central intake shelter for homeless men. But it was well past midnight, and Dakota didn't want to leave his friend alone. They headed for the subway with neither money nor tokens. When they explained their situation to the token booth clerk, he let them board the train without paying. They slept about three hours before they were awakened by rush hour crowds.

"Cedric, I've got to think for both of us," Dakota said, the pitch of his voice rising. A few hours earlier, when Dakota had gone to use the Port Authority bathroom, Cedric had disappeared. "When I come out, he's gone. He's running behind someone else, and everybody leaves me stranded out here. He's worried about the next cat, and the next cat ain't doin' anything for neither one of us. I'm tired of this."

"I was only gone for ten minutes," said Cedric quietly, his head turned away from Dakota. That time, he had followed two undercover cops as they chased someone to the entrance of the Port Authority and then watched the arrest.

"I could have stayed in my bed at the shelter last night instead of being in the street because I care. You don't give him a bed, I'm bouncing with my brother. I do all that to get this from my brother, for the next cheeseburger. That's what he is, a cheeseburger, a cheese dog. Anything that has to do with cheese." Dakota smiled. He made himself laugh.

Cedric bowed his head.

"All he had to do was wait there while I was in the bathroom." His voice was getting louder. "I come out the bathroom and no Cedric. No nobody. I'm walking down the block looking for him. He says the cops were harassing this other kid, and he leaves me." Dakota waved his arms in disgust and turned his back to Cedric.

Cedric lifted his head and turned to Dakota. "I didn't leave you," he insisted. "I was still in the Port, walking around. I was standing right there." Cedric pointed a few feet away. "I didn't see you come out."

Dakota took a deep breath and turned around. "All you had to do is knock on the door—a simple little thing." His voice was calm and steady. Then he turned away and shook his head. "No word, no nothing. It really hurts for my brother to dis me like that." Dakota became quiet. He began to pace back and forth in front of Cedric, growing increasingly agitated each time he turned back around. "I can't keep going through the bullshit. I can't get myself all stressed out, screaming and yelling. Over what? If you don't want to do something, don't do it. But don't tell me you're going to do something and not do it."

Dakota started to say more, but stopped. He doubled over coughing, his face a foot from the ground. His body shook from the spasms.

Cedric sat silently, staring ahead. Nicknamed "Tiny," he weighed well over two hundred pounds. His face was small and round like a baby's. His thick, oversize eyeglasses made his head and eyes seem even smaller. He wore a black wool knit cap, pulled low on his forehead. When I asked him exactly how much he weighed, he said he was embarrassed to talk about it—that he was like a girl about his weight.

"We're splitting up," Dakota said. "I don't need the problems. I'm doing bad already. I don't need other people to hold me down, too. Everything I had, he basically either lost or destroyed it. How much more can I take?" The pitch of Dakota's voice was so high that he was practically squeaking. "We go to sleep, and he's holding some cookies that's supposed to be ours, but he eats them. Do you think he said, 'Well, let me save half because I know he wants some.' Nope. Who had to suffer? Me. He's eighteen years old. I'm supposed to say OK, no problem. I told him next time he violated me, he's going his own way. I cannot deal with this no more."

For a few minutes, neither Dakota nor Cedric said anything. People walked from all directions in and out of the station. Some scrambled by quickly, others strolled through at a slow, steady pace. A black woman, about twenty, wearing skintight jeans that zipped at the ankles, large pink plastic rollers in her hair, and turquoise vinyl house slippers, walked by. She smiled, and waved to Dakota. He stared at her, but said nothing.

When a woman caught his eye, Dakota usually stopped dead in his tracks, stared directly into her eyes, and gave her a deliberate once over. Most women kept walking; some smiled. Dakota's gaze at this girl, though, was different, colder. She didn't seem to notice that Dakota was not pleased. She kept walking, smiling.

When she was some distance away, Dakota's jaw dropped open in disbelief. "She dissed us yesterday and then got the audacity to speak to us today."

A day earlier in a small park just a few blocks away, Dakota had asked the same woman for a cigarette. She told him that she didn't have any more, even though he had seen her handing them out to other people. "Everybody thinks I'm some joke," Dakota said, disgusted. "Is there a sign on my back that says I'm an idiot? You going to sit in the park and ignore me, and then now, you want to lean up all over me and tell me how cute I am? You ain't speak to me yesterday, and all of sudden you want to be friends with me. Don't conversate now, keep it real."

Dakota started to walk away from Cedric. "I cannot survive out here in Midtown. I'm not coming down here anymore. I don't need other people to hold me down. I'm doing bad already. I'm starting to get stressed. I can't take much more. I'm going back to the Bronx to do my thing. I cannot survive out here."

. . . .

TO DAKOTA, the Bronx was home. He grew up there and had sold drugs there—mostly crack cocaine. At ten, he was enlisted as a drug runner. As he grew older, he graduated into selling, eventually even holding up drug dealers. By the mid-1990s, however, New York police intensified their efforts to rid drug-infested neighborhoods of dealers and gangs. Many of Dakota's friends had gone to jail or been killed, the victims of drug deals gone awry. After nearly a decade in the drug trade, Dakota got out. When I met him, about a year later in 1996, he was homeless.

Dakota had two younger sisters, Tamara and Keisha. Their mother had died four years earlier, Dakota said, while giving birth at a hospital in the Bronx. Tamara told me their mother had died of AIDS. "Dakota knows how she died," she said. "He just doesn't want to face it." They had also lost their aunt and their young cousin to AIDS.

By 1996, HIV/AIDS was the leading cause of death for mothers of young children and adolescents in New York State. That year, an estimated 4,500 children under twenty-one lost their mothers to AIDS—almost three times as many children who'd lost their mothers to cancer, and fifteen times as many children whose mothers had been killed in motor vehicle accidents. Since 1981, roughly 28,000 children, about 25,000 of them from New York City, had been orphaned due to HIV/AIDS. Many of these children came from poor families and lacked adequate housing and health care. When a mother became ill, lives already in disarray were further disrupted: Children skipped school and failed classes; some stopped going to school altogether to care for the sick parent. When a mother died, families often dissolved. Young children were shuffled from one relative's house to another or placed in foster care. Adolescents, harder to place, were frequently left to fend for themselves. Sometimes the teens, already disconnected from society, families, and institutions, chose to stay on their own, and instead forged connections on the street.

After their mother died, Dakota, Tamara and her infant son, and Keisha separated and moved from one living situation to another, often staying in the homes of relatives or friends. But these arrangements were tenuous and unstable, and, on occasion, when they had nowhere else to go, the girls lived in shelters and Dakota on the streets. During this time, Tamara had a second child, and both her children were taken away from her and placed in foster care.

"Some of my family members is cool," Dakota told me. "Then they get all grimy after awhile. They say, 'You can stay with me—it's cool.' Then you'll come in and catch them talking, 'That nigger needs to get the fuck out.' But you're struggling. The job don't come overnight. 'Did you apply?' they ask. 'Yes, I did.' They say, 'Then why didn't they call you?' 'I don't know why,' you say. 'What do you want me to do? I can't make that man hire me.' When someone puts you out and tells you to leave, you can never go back. If they could do it once, they could do it again."

After years of living apart, Dakota secured a place for himself and his sisters. "We were staying in a big house with a lady my brother knew," Tamara said. "She was alone and wanted company." But by late summer 1996, the woman decided she no longer wanted all three siblings in her apartment. Tamara and Keisha decided to go to Covenant House in Manhattan. Dakota knew little about the emergency shelter, but he decided to join them. He thought that Manhattan would be a good place to start over.

· · · ·

I MET DAKOTA about ten days after he left the Bronx. It was midnight, and he was standing in a doorway up the block from Covenant House. The large concrete compound, formerly a women's state prison, is located on Tenth Avenue and Forty-first Street. With Times Square to the east and the Hudson River piers to the west, the building stands between one of the busiest parts of the city and one of the most deserted. At the time, the crisis shelter had 137 beds and was the largest emergency youth shelter in the city. In 1996, more than six thousand young people under twenty-one went to Covenant House looking for a bed and food. Most were black and Hispanic, coming from homes within fifty miles of New York City. Many, like Dakota, were from the Bronx.

Dakota had small almond-shaped eyes that seemed quickly to size up his surroundings. His squat yet solid frame was hidden by a full-cut, black vinyl jacket. His black baseball cap covered his eyes.

That night, we spoke for only a few minutes.

Two weeks later, he paged me and asked to meet.

We met at the Port Authority. As Dakota talked, his friend Cedric stood quietly at his side. Dakota told me he had been thrown out of Covenant House after about a week because, he said, he was "too old" for the program. He told them he was eighteen but had no identification to prove it because his wallet had been stolen during a hold-up. To prove his age he had brought in a letter from the assistant principal of his junior high school. The letter stated that Dakota was born in 1977, making him nineteen. "But the letter wasn't good enough, and they kicked me out," Dakota told me. "I don't have ID, and they kick me to the curb."

Dakota and Cedric had met at Covenant House, arriving within days of one another. Cedric's mother had thrown him out of her house in Brooklyn. "My mother's like Burger King—her way, right away," Cedric said. "When I was living with her, the job didn't come fast enough. She kept telling me to do this, do that. I was supposed to be the man of the house. I've been going to the store, cooking, cleaning since I was little. I'm tired of doing all that stuff." Cedric told me that his mother smoked crack when he was young and that his father had been in and out of jail while he was growing up, forcing him to take care of his younger siblings while he was still in grade school. He also told me that his mother had thrown him out of the house six times before he finally decided to go to the crisis shelter. "I couldn't sleep on the streets in Brooklyn because everyone there knows me." This time, he said, he wasn't going back.

At Covenant House, Dakota and Cedric became fast friends. "I first thought Dakota was one of them project kids," Cedric said. "He's one of those kids I stayed away from when I was growing up. I'd go in after school and do my homework and stay in the house until the street lights came on. But he was cool."

After Dakota was thrown out of the shelter, he continued to hang out in the area, and Cedric sneaked him food. Now, only a couple of weeks after meeting, they were talking as if they had known each other for years. "We made a pact that if we ever had to leave Covenant House, we would be there for each other," Dakota said. "When I got kicked out, I told Cedric if you ever get kicked out, turn around, and I'll be right there. I'll make sure you have somewhere to go."

A few days later, when Cedric got into a fight with another kid and was told to leave Covenant House, Dakota was waiting. "I told him I'd be there, and I kept my word."

· · · ·

DAKOTA AND CEDRIC had no idea where to go for help once they were asked to leave Covenant House. Their options were limited. In New York City, two types of housing were available for homeless youth: emergency and transitional.

In 1996, there were only 173 crisis beds in emergency shelters in New York City—137 at Covenant House. Generally, these thirty-day short-term shelters provided primary health care but were not set up to provide the extensive mental health, drug treatment, or specialized health care services needed to stabilize youth with multiple problems. Adolescents repeatedly cycled through these facilities. Eighty percent of these crisis beds were in Manhattan. None were in the Bronx.

Covenant House, a nonprofit Catholic-led agency, was the city's only emergency shelter that accepted youth over eighteen, but the program was not appropriate for all teens. A sizable number left because they couldn't abide by the agency's rules, which banned drug use and imposed a curfew; some left quickly on their own, others were kicked out after a number of infractions. Adolescent illegal immigrants often left because immigration legislation enacted in 1996 made it extremely difficult for counselors to help them access services. Openly gay or transgender teens sometimes left because they were harassed. The average length of stay for all youths was about two weeks.

The only other option for homeless youth over eighteen was transitional independent living programs. In 1997, there were a total of 322 beds available in seven such residential programs in the Bronx, Brooklyn, and Manhattan; of these beds, more than half were at Covenant House. Youth were usually referred by service providers, and the waiting lists for these programs were often long. Each program also had restrictions based on age and gender: only three of these transitional facilities provided services to non-HIV-positive young women without children.

Youth like Dakota and Cedric not connected to social

service agencies were usually not even aware such programs existed. But even young people who knew about them often stayed away. Many emergency and transitional shelters imposed what some youth workers themselves believed to be unrealistic requirements. All shelter programs prohibited the use of drugs and discharged youth who used drugs, yet most did not provide drug treatment services. A young person who had been incarcerated or had outstanding warrants, even minor ones, such as turnstile jumping, also faced serious obstacles in getting or maintaining either emergency or transitional housing.

After Dakota and Cedric left Covenant House, the only place they could go was into the adult shelter system.

. . . .

NIGHT AFTER NIGHT, around eleven, Dakota and Cedric walked to the Thirtieth Street men's intake shelter on First Avenue. There, they lined up, were assigned numbers, and waited, sometimes for hours, with dozens of other men in a crowded smelly room, to find out which of the city's 7,400 shelter beds were available for the night. Many of the men were addicted to drugs, others to alcohol; some were mentally ill. Some had just gotten a bad break. Most were sleep deprived and wanted only a bed for the night. Usually by one a.m., but sometimes later, Dakota and Cedric boarded a bus to their assigned shelter. If the shelter was full when they arrived, they stayed on the bus, waiting to be taken somewhere else. If beds were available, they lined up again and waited for their names to be called. If someone didn't have a number, he was told to leave. Those who stayed were searched and walked through metal detectors. Then each man was given a sheet and a blanket, and was assigned a cot.

The next morning, sometimes as early as six, depending on the shelter, they were sent out on the street again.

Some shelters provided bus service back to Manhattan in the morning, but most did not. If they had no money, the men had to trek sometimes three to four hours on foot back to Manhattan, where they spent the day until it was time to go back to Thirtieth Street. One morning, Dakota and Cedric walked more than six miles through the streets of Brooklyn, over the Pulaski Bridge to Long Island City in Queens, then over the Queensboro Bridge to get back to Manhattan.

The men were always exhausted, sometimes getting no more than an hour of sleep. "You've got to sleep with your coat on, your shoes," said Dakota. "Everything has to stay on you. You want to get comfortable, but you can't because you're scared that when you wake up, your stuff will be gone. You can't even take a shower because it is so freezing cold. Even if you want a cold shower, by the time you get to the shelter, you're so tired that you just end up going to sleep. You can't take one in the morning because in the morning, they just want you out." In shelters from Manhattan to Brooklyn to the Bronx, Dakota and Cedric had seen bottles broken over heads and razors slice through clothing and skin. They had seen men hanging around outside and sometimes even inside the shelters smoking crack and shooting dope. "You sleep with one eye open all the time," said Cedric.

One October night, around midnight, the three of us walked together to the Thirtieth Street intake shelter. When they walked at a brisk pace, they could get to the shelter in forty minutes. That night, the trip took a little more than an hour.

Dakota and Cedric took turns acting as navigators, mapping their way across town. "You always take a different route each night in case someone's watching where you're going," Dakota said. "You have to observe everything because someone else is observing everything, too. They see you walk, and they may not like you. You come back thinking everything is peaches and cream, and you get your ass jumped upon. If they're scheming on you, they won't see you if you come back another way. You come up behind them and take the upper hand. There are always people out there who want to hurt you."

Dakota's concern was not simple paranoia. As a child, he told me, he was stabbed with an ice pick and shot in the leg. He had seen a young girl get shot in the face. In grade school, Dakota would leave school at different times of the day, changing his routes home and the places where he hung out. He also learned to carry single-edged razors in his pocket and in his mouth. "The one in my mouth is to spit out," he said. "You spit it in the face. If you're real close and making threats, I will spit at you. Then you're going to get hit in the face, and as you grab your face, I have time to grab the second one."

Now, he was schooling Cedric. "You can't depend on people who say, 'Yo, man, come by if you need anything,'" Dakota told Cedric one day. "You've got to learn how to do without them. I never had friends. Just people I knew."

"Then why would they tell me that?" asked Cedric.

"They tell you things 'cause that's what you want to hear and then once you hear it, they don't have to do anything. Go tell them you need a quarter, a cigarette, or that you're hungry. They'll say, 'Oh, man, I've just got $2, and I'm going out.' Or, 'A situation came up. Come back later.' They always say, 'If you need something don't hesitate to ask me,' and then when you do ask, they put you on the back burner. You get in a situation when you really do need that person, and that person's not there for you. That shit really hurts."

Dakota was determined to teach Cedric to depend on no one. A month later, he drove the lesson home. They were walking from Wards Island to Manhattan when halfway through the more than three-hour trip, Dakota told Cedric he was going back. Cedric was upset. "You promised," he told Dakota. "You gave me your word."

Standing in front of Cedric and smiling, Dakota said, "Now you see what I'm talking about? I can give you my word, but I can renege on it."

It was a test to see if Cedric had understood Dakota's message. But Cedric had failed. When he said that he was also going with Dakota, Dakota scolded him. "You're supposed to say, 'OK, you don't want to go, I'm going to continue about my business.' In other words, don't depend on me because I'm not going to be there all the time. One day, you and me are going to separate, and you're going to have to survive on your own."

That night as we walked through Midtown, Cedric listened, like a little brother, to Dakota's advice and his plans for the next day. "Dakota does his share more in terms of us taking care of each other," Cedric told me. "I'm no fool, but the little things get right past me. He tells me, 'Don't do this, do that.' It keeps me on my toes."

Now past midnight and about halfway to the shelter, Midtown, not quite deserted, was eerie. A sliver of moon gleamed between buildings. Shadows slid in and out of doorways. An occasional groan or moan seemed to drift in out of nowhere. On one block, a man smashed a bottle against a brick wall, the bits of glass sparkling on the ground like diamonds.

There wasn't much to look at. Most of the stores we passed were dark, some protected by heavy metal gates. So when we walked by the bright fluorescent lights of a gourmet food shop, Dakota and Cedric stopped. The street glowed with brilliant neon signs in Korean and English promoting a string of Korean restaurants and karaoke bars.

"We haven't had anything to drink since yesterday," Dakota said suddenly. "We need some water." He walked into the food shop, and Cedric and I followed.

The store was empty, except for a Korean man, possibly in his late forties, who stood behind a stainless-steel counter. Pastries, cookies, and frosted cakes sat underneath glass domes on his right side. A refrigerated case filled with bottled water, flavored and plain, sparkling and still, lined one wall. The fluorescent lights reflected off the chrome surfaces throughout the shop.

I stood by the front door, and Dakota and Cedric walked up to the man at the counter. "Excuse me, sir," said Dakota. "Can we please have some water?" The man stared blankly at Dakota. He seemed not to have understood.

Dakota repeated his question, a little louder and more slowly, enunciating his words carefully. This time, the man quickly motioned to the refrigerated case to the bottled water.

"No, can we have a cup with water?"

The man stiffened, and he stared straight at Dakota, almost through him. Dakota and Cedric looked more relaxed than tired. They looked back at the man and patiently waited for him to move.

Ten long seconds passed.

Eventually, the man leaned over a nearby sink to his left, turned on the water, and filled a paper cup, which he abruptly handed Dakota.

"Can I have one too?" asked Cedric.

"Only one cup. I have to close," said the man quickly,

waving his hand to the door. He looked nervous.

"We ain't trying to rob you," said Dakota. "We just want a cup of water. We're thirsty. Have you ever been thirsty?"

The man motioned for them to leave. Dakota and Cedric slowly walked out. Dakota remained quiet. After a moment, he said, "Water is free, and they won't give it to us. It's incredible. They look at us like we're going to rob them."

Dakota and Cedric were soft-spoken and polite when they asked for the glass of water. But it was late, and the shopkeeper was alone.

Relations between blacks and Korean store owners had been strained since the late 1980s when a number of over-the-counter disputes had turned into boycotts of Korean businesses. When the man saw two black males walk in his store, wearing baggy pants, their hats pulled low on their heads, he felt threatened. Dakota and Cedric felt they were being accused of something they hadn't done.

Stalemate.

Half an hour later, we arrived at the shelter, and Dakota and Cedric joined the line snaking outside the shelter. To pass the time, they talked about their costumes for the Halloween party coming up at the end of the month at a drop-in center. "We can put a cap over our head and tell people to give us their candy," said Dakota. "We can be stick-up kids." They started laughing.

"We can go trick-or-treating," Cedric said cheerfully. "The candy will come in handy down the stretch."

. . . .

WE MET REGULARLY at the Port Authority and hung out in the surrounding blocks of Times Square. The explosion of the sex industry in the 1970s had brought worldwide attention to the neighborhood. Increasingly, teenagers had become part of the main attraction.

In 1976, the *New York Times* reported on the dangers facing young runaways who came to New York on their own. "They often come into town at the Port Authority Bus Terminal, a few blocks from the midtown area that is the nucleus of the city's rapidly expanding illicit sex business," one article described. In that piece, Capt. Francis Daly, head of the police department's Youth Aid Division, observed, "Frequently a girl comes in and wanders around bewildered and apparently lost and is quickly approached by a recruiter who offers her a place to stay and maybe some drugs. A few days later she is working in a massage parlor or working the streets."

The next year, a *New York Times* front-page story, "Pimps Establish Recruiting Link to the Midwest," reported on the "pipeline"—an organized system in which New York-based pimps recruited girls in Minnesota and transported them to New York. One police lieutenant from Minneapolis estimated that in 1976 alone, four hundred teenage girls from Minneapolis and nearby communities had been picked up by pimps and sent to New York. Eighth Avenue became known as "the Minnesota Strip," and the nation began to take notice.

A year later, *Time* magazine reported that New York had the biggest juvenile prostitution problem in the country. "Police estimate that as many as 20,000 runaway kids under sixteen are on the city's streets, and many are available for commercial sex. Some 800 pimps prey on these youngsters, provide them with food, clothing and lodging—and demand total loyalty and almost all their earnings in return."

The image of the blond, Midwestern teenage prostitute was reinforced and promoted by Father Bruce Ritter of

Covenant House, who used compelling stories of white run-away girls to raise money for his homeless youth shelter, which, as in the 1990s, sheltered mostly kids from New York City. Thanks in part to intense media coverage and aggressive direct-mail efforts, Ritter's campaign to rescue young girls from "sleazy" pimps generated lucrative compassion among the public. Covenant House's fund-raising campaigns were so successful that in thirty years the organization grew from two flats on the Lower East Side in 1969 into a $90 million corporation with sites in sixteen cities across the United States and in five cities in Central and Latin America.

"The media loved the story—pimps picking up young girls at the bus station from the Midwest," said Sgt. Bernard Poggioli of the Port Authority's Youth Service Unit (established in 1976). "But the reality was that about 80 percent of the kids involved in prostitution at that time in Times Square were black and Hispanic from the five boroughs of New York. And they were prostituting long before the cameras came." According to Poggioli, most of the teenagers were fleeing unhappy homes or had been tossed out by their families. "And the pimps didn't come to the bus station looking for the girls. Instead, other girls did the recruiting. A girl who worked the street might meet another girl and then invite her to move in with her. Then the girl would introduce the new girl to her pimp."

Responding to the growing number of pimps and prostitutes in the area, the "Pimp Squad" was formed to persuade prostitutes to turn in their pimps. "Attention, Prostitutes of New York," read the typewritten fliers the seven-member police unit distributed along the streets of Midtown Manhattan. "Are you tired of giving up your money to your pimp? Getting beat or bashed when you don't make your trap? Living on $5 a day while your man snorts the stack up his nose?" The campaign was designed to mimic the tactics used by massage parlors to entice customers off the street and into their establishments, but unlike those fliers, the Pimp Squad leaflets offered to help contact concerned parents or relatives.

While women worked along Eighth Avenue, young men claimed Forty-second Street. A form of prostitution involving "hawks," men who picked up young boys, and "chickens," boys as young as ten, thrived inside the pinball arcades of Times Square. Many of the hawks were white middle-class men who drove in from the suburbs. Although most of the boys were ten to fifteen years old, Hispanic or black, and from poor families in Harlem, the Bronx, or Brooklyn, some were white and from middle-class families. Often lonely, and looking to escape from an abusive stepfather or a future that promised them dead-end jobs, they fell prey to older men who offered them not just affection and cash but also a chance at upward mobility.

As street prostitution, drug dealing, and hustling flourished, visits by both tourists and New Yorkers to Times Square's theaters, hotels, and restaurants dropped significantly. "Times Square has traditionally been the entertainment mecca of the country," said William Daly, director of the Mayor's Office of Midtown Enforcement. "But in the early 1970s, people were afraid to go to the theater. In order to get to the theater you had to walk through an onslaught of pimps and prostitutes—if you see the movie *Shaft* [the original from 1971], there's some truth to that. The theater generates the most revenue for the city. Most people who come to New York will go to the theater, but Broadway was doing very badly."

In response, representatives of businesses, the theater industry, and residents of the neighborhood formed the

Mayor's Midtown Citizens Committee and pressured Mayor Abraham Beame to reclaim the area. In 1976, the city, in the middle of a fiscal crisis, turned to the federal government for funds to establish the Midtown Enforcement Project (MEP). In addition to improving conditions in Times Square, the agency, through its legal unit, strove to develop new legislation that would facilitate the closing of massage parlors and sex shops.

"A lot of the storefronts were massage parlors, and they would just take the clients off the street," Daly said. "They would walk right in and be out in ten minutes. More often than not, the guys would walk out without their wallets, so in addition to having prostitution, you also had robbery, and there was murder and mayhem. Massage parlors were firebombing each other. It was really serious."

Drafted by MEP, the Nuisance Abatement Law, passed by the City Council in 1977, clearly defined what practices were "public nuisances" and streamlined the process of closing down the parlors and other establishments. Within the first two years of operation, fifty-two public nuisances, primarily houses of prostitution, had been closed. In 1979, federal funding for MEP expired. The city took over funding the agency, which was renamed the Office of Midtown Enforcement (OME).

In 1979, a class-action lawsuit, *Callahan* v. *Carey*, brought on behalf of the city's homeless, led to a landmark decision by the State Supreme Court that established a legal right to shelter in New York, and policymakers turned their attention to the homeless. The displacement of people due to fire, evictions, abandonment, demolition, and condominium conversions, coupled with a shortage of inexpensive rental housing, had left an increasing number of families with no permanent place to live. In 1984, about 50 percent of individuals served at city shelters were there for the first time. By 1986, there were about 28,000 homeless people in emergency shelters in the city. An additional 40,000 people were believed to have no shelter citywide. Children were the fastest-growing sector of the homeless population. Overwhelmed by the growing numbers of homeless families, the city's Human Resource Administration (HRA) began placing families into vacant hotels, a number of them in the Times Square area. OME warned HRA that moving families to Times Square meant the agency was putting children in harm's way. City officials, however, felt they had no other option.

The OME's warning proved true. "Almost immediately we began seeing prostitution," Daly said. "Our investigators started seeing kids coming out of the hotels and going into the arcades. The reason it was so noticeable was because the kids who were involved were so young. There were several instances of mothers pimping their own kids. Most of them were boys, because the boys weren't afraid to go out to the street. Some were as young as eleven and twelve." A few of the cases were profiled prominently by the media, generating public outrage.

In 1985, Mayor Edward Koch designated the director of OME to chair a Juvenile Prostitution Task Force. The Port Authority's Youth Services Unit and the police department's Runaway Unit intercepted troubled youth in the area; social service workers tried to identify underage prostitutes and either reunite them with their families or offer them alternative lives.

By the late 1980s, the crack epidemic was also raging in neighborhoods across the city, and Times Square had been hit hard. Drug dealers and crack users claimed the streets. Sex with teenagers was still very much available, although the solicitation was less visible. The Port Authority was a popular meeting place for pedophiles, again usually white, offering cash to primarily young black or Hispanic males. Kids strolled back and forth along the railing in an area of the bus terminal on the second floor known as the "meat rack" as the johns checked them out. The boys, many of whom smoked crack, mostly worked alone or pimped each other, getting more money from the johns to point out other teens. They used the terminal's pay phones to conduct business, calling johns standing at a phone across the corridor to see if they were interested in kids standing near them.

In February 1989, a *Newsweek* story on the Port Authority, "A Nightmare on 42nd Street," described the terminal as "a vortex of hopelessness, crime and despair." The piece reported, "For a commuter on his way home to New Jersey, a stop at the second-floor men's room in the main concourse can be an adventure only slightly less scary than a visit to the Tatooine bar in *Star Wars*. Around the urinal, unshaven men in overcoats linger over cigarettes, adding smoke to the pungent aroma of disinfectant and diesel fumes that permeates the building. In the stalls, voices argue over sex and drug transactions. By the exit door, vials of crack are exchanged over prolonged handshakes. In a far corner, a teenager curses as he burns his finger heating up a piece of 'rock' with a glass pipe. 'I'll do you for a nickel, mister,' whispers a Hispanic boy who looks around twelve, offering himself for $5."

For young people, especially those from the city, Times Square in the late 1980s and early 1990s was an exciting place. Here, black and Hispanic kids who lived in the boroughs and were accustomed to being the target of suspicious stares could themselves stare at awkward out-of-towners. They hopped the subway and flocked to Forty-second Street on weekends to play video games at the arcades and take their pick of more than a dozen movies at all-night theaters for $3.50 a show. They chose between kung fu flicks (*Dragons Forever*), slasher films (*Slaughter High*), blaxploitation reruns (*The Mack*), X, XX, and XXX movies (*Pretty Peaches*), campy cult classics (*Pink Flamingos*), or first-run Hollywood fare (*Mo' Better Blues*). The streets were lined with magazine and video shops, massage parlors, live sex shows, and video jerk-off booths, where workers ran around with mops and flashlights cleaning up the floors. Merchants sold pirated videos and counterfeit identification cards beside street preachers who recited dooms-day prophecies from the Bible. Drag queens in horse-hair wigs and Spandex leggings strolled past hustlers who suckered people with three-card monte games. Old shoeshine men gave spit shines, and young black boys break-danced, executing impromptu dips, drops, and spins next to a shoebox filled with change. Pickpockets were everywhere.

But by the mid-1990s, everything had changed. In 1993, the Walt Disney Co. agreed to put up $8 million toward the renovation of the New Amsterdam Theater; other developers quickly joined in to reclaim Times Square. The area that was known for porno theaters, chain-snatchers, hustlers, video parlors, and all-purpose eccentrics became an urban theme park swarming with tourists, bellhops, and babies. The big clean-up ushered in a swirl of new theaters, glitzy video arcades, overpriced theme restaurants, double-decker tour buses, and construction cranes.

The Port Authority Bus Terminal received a makeover as well. In the 1980s, homeless youth slept in small groups in "cardboard condominiums" erected outside the terminal and in warm niches, corners, and emergency stairwells indoors on cold nights. Outreach workers knew where the kids hung out, and offered food, condoms, and other social services. But in December 1991, the city initiated Operation

Alternative. The emergency stairwells were locked, and areas where homeless people once slept were sealed off. Bathrooms and lighting were improved, and signs posted throughout the terminal prohibited sitting or lying on floors or stairs, panhandling, and smoking. The pay phones no longer accepted incoming calls, making it more difficult for drug dealers and hustlers to conduct business. A Duane Reade drugstore replaced the fast-food restaurant that had been a popular pickup spot for pedophiles and a hangout for the homeless. Coffee shops that had offered 99-cent meals were replaced with upscale shops and cafes like Timothy's World Coffee and Au Bon Pain. By the late 1990s, approximately 125 Port Authority police personnel were assigned to the bus terminal, making it one of the most heavily patrolled areas in New York City.

The Youth Services Unit covered the terminal in two-person teams (a plain-clothes cop paired with a social worker) and escorted kids unable to explain their presence to their office. Established as an alternative to the criminal justice system, the unit worked with several other social service agencies. In 1996, the unit questioned 4,062 young people. More than half were from New York; 68 percent were black or Hispanic. Runaway and homeless youth learned to keep moving to avoid arousing suspicion.

Crime in the area was down considerably and tourism was up. According to the Times Square Business Improvement District, from 1993 to 1997, crime plummeted 49 percent. At the same time, three-card monte scams were down 91 percent, ticket scalpers down 60 percent, and pickpockets down 76 percent. In 1997, an estimated twenty million people visited Times Square, spending up to $3.6 billion, and that figure was projected to climb significantly as the transformation continued.

Young people, especially homeless kids, were particularly affected. Cheap arcades and fast-food hangouts had been squeezed out of the area, and outreach workers had to look harder to find homeless kids. Kids who prostituted moved to the more dangerous prostitution strolls uptown. Kids like Dakota and Cedric kept moving to avoid being noticed. "They're still out there," one youth outreach worker told me. "You can't see them anymore, but they're out there, just trying to hang on."

Dakota often noticed other homeless young men at the Port Authority leaning up against walls and hanging around the exits. "I know how some of these guys make money out here," said Dakota. "But, I ain't never letting a guy in the back door. I don't play those games. If I don't have a place to stay and you offer, you can do this to me or I can do this to you, see you on the train. The train ain't doing no harm to me and I can be free. I don't sell my body. Never have. Never will."

Even with all the new changes, Dakota and Cedric managed to make the Port Authority their home base. In the public bathrooms, Dakota and Cedric washed up and changed their clothes. They befriended the cleaning people who worked at the terminal, realizing quickly they would be needed as allies. They even cultivated relationships with some of the police officers who patrolled the area. The Port kept them warm when the weather was cold outside, but more than anything, it was a haven from the streets. Cedric, especially, enjoyed his newfound sense of freedom. "I've always done what everybody else wants me to do," he said. "Now I do what I want to do."

And what they did was hang out. Dakota and Cedric spent their days riding up and down the escalators, walking back and forth through the terminal, taking different routes to make the day more interesting. They watched the passersby and listened. Like sportscasters, they commented to each other on the ways people walked, dressed, and wore their hair, speculating where they had been and where they were going. They watched teenagers play video games in the game room upstairs, and on those days they had spare change, they played the games themselves, exploding with each target hit and point scored. It all made the time pass.

At night, Dakota and Cedric hung out near the Emergency Red Cross Shelter for Women and Children, down the street from Covenant House. In the early evenings, they accompanied shelter residents, baby strollers in tow, to a local laundromat where they all played cards. Then, before the women's nine p.m. curfew, Dakota and Cedric, wheeling laundry carts and carrying diaper bags, escorted the women back to the shelter. After nine, Dakota and Cedric stood on the sidewalk to "conversate with the ladies," who flirted with them from behind iron-barred windows above. Dakota was a charmer. He spoke gently and smiled. Cedric, less smooth, said less and laughed more. The women smiled and teased and made dates to meet them again the next night. Sometimes Dakota and Cedric returned videos for the women or, like anxious suitors, brought them candy or cookies they had stashed in their pockets after visiting a local drop-in center for homeless youth. By eleven, though, Dakota and Cedric had to leave. They had just enough time to walk across town to the homeless men's intake shelter.

None of the women ever knew where Dakota and Cedric were going. In fact, few people who knew Dakota knew he was homeless during those months we met at the Port Authority. When Dakota bumped into people from his old neighborhood, which he did regularly, he told them he was just "chillin'." Dakota saw how others judged homeless people, holding them responsible for their circumstances: If they lost a job or an apartment, they had behaved irresponsibly. If they couldn't get another job, something was wrong with them. Dakota didn't want to be judged. He didn't want homelessness to define him. "I know it's nothing to be ashamed of," he told me. "Everyone goes through bad periods in their life. But most people don't look at it that way."

Cedric was less thoughtful, more practical. "The one good thing about being out here," said Cedric, was that "there's no curfew."

. . . .

A FEW MONTHS AFTER I met Dakota, I started to question his age. David Marzette, assistant principal at the junior high school Dakota had attended in the Bronx, believed Dakota was four years older than he had told me. So did one of the school's counselors. His records, however, had been transferred to another school.

Many kids on the street lie. They lie to get what they want—food, shelter, money, companionship, drugs, attention. They lie to avoid trouble or to keep what they have. Sometimes in order to be noticed, they create a past in which they were beaten or sexually abused. Other times, they create a past that doesn't include their fathers beating their mothers, or their uncles raping them, or their mothers dying of AIDS. Their lies make them feel better, stronger.

I didn't confront Dakota about his age until I was able to see his arrest record, months later. The arrest record listed two dates of birth, one in 1973, the other in 1977. When I asked him to tell me which was true, he answered calmly: "OK. I was born in 1977. But I have ID, birth certificates, and Social Security cards that say I'm anywhere from nineteen to twenty-eight." He explained that he had been carrying these different IDs for years and that being able to "prove" he was older meant he couldn't be detained for truancy.

Each time I pointed out inconsistencies between what he had told me and what I learned talking to other people, he elaborated in creative detail: how he had smudged his fingerprints the first time he was arrested; how he had gotten his landlord to verify his age incorrectly after another arrest; how he had obtained a phony birth certificate; how the computer had confused his name with his father's; how he planned to burn the tips of his fingers off to change his fingerprints. He produced an explanation for everything, and he answered my battery of questions without hesitation or frustration. "I know it's very confusing," he told me. "I sometimes get confused myself." He was persuasive. He never admitted he was lying, and appeared convinced of his own explanations.

"I don't know if Dakota even knows what's real," his sister Tamara told me. "I don't know what he believes. I've known him all my life, and I've tried to know who he is, but I still get confused because one minute he's this way, and the next minute, he's telling me some story."

I learned much later that Dakota knew what he was doing. Living on the streets for years, Dakota had cultivated, out of necessity, an ability to con other people. Lying about his age was the only way he felt he could get the help he needed to turn his life around.

Older youth like Dakota who aged out of eligibility for services were expected to make it on their own. Yet many "adult" street kids, having spent much of their lives passing through programs and institutions that repeatedly failed them, didn't have the education, job skills, or the emotional maturity to live independently as adults. Many had never known anything but violations of their person; for some, oppressing others was simply a natural way of behaving. Hurt by and alienated from society, which they felt they were never a part of, their anger often flared without warning, usually in ways more destructive to themselves than to others. Without structure, routine expectations, and effective communication, these older youth were not prepared for the practical and social demands of the working world. Even when they were able to find a job, they knew little about managing or budgeting their often minimum-wage earnings, making it difficult for them to maintain stable housing.

For many older youth, even accessing public assistance was not an option. Many street youth did not have access to basic documents such as birth certificates, Social Security cards, and other materials required to process an application for public assistance. Although caseworkers were supposed to instruct youth how to acquire identifying documents, some workers refused to open a case or, if they did, denied claims simply because youth had no identification. If a homeless youth had outstanding warrants, as many street youth did, he or she was immediately disqualified. Because public assistance considered all people residing in a household as a single case, if a young person was sleeping at the home of someone who was also on public assistance, he could no longer apply for it.

But even when they were eligible for assistance, homeless youth were easily intimidated by caseworkers, missed appointments, and failed to follow up on the application process. "The Eligibility Verification Review is brutal," said Lori Weinstein, former Entitlements Counselor at The Streetwork Project, a drop-in center for homeless youth. "Some of the workers are confrontational, judgmental, or insensitive to the kid's situation. Some give the impression, from the moment you walk in the door, that they think you're lying. Kids get confused and contradict themselves. They end up just walking out." With welfare reform, the rules of eligibility were continuously changing, making it increasing difficult to get public assistance.

Dakota knew that he needed help getting off the street. He also believed that he wasn't going to get that help in the adult shelter system. He had heard from other kids on the street that he could get counseling, medical care, and help getting on welfare from Streetwork.

In 1997, every month an average of 275 homeless and street-dependent youth, twenty-two years old and under, walked into The Streetwork Project drop-in center, just five blocks away from the Port Authority. Here, clients were assigned caseworkers and received a variety of services, from food, clean clothes, and a shower to acupuncture and help in getting into high school equivalency programs and accessing public assistance. Youth could also attend a number of weekly groups, including an HIV/AIDS support group, a transgender support group, or a meditation group. Because Streetwork didn't turn away active drug users and allowed clients to determine their own needs and set their own priorities, Streetwork was always busy.

At twenty-three, Dakota wasn't eligible for Streetwork. So when he showed up at the drop-in center, he told them he was eighteen. "The only way I know how to survive is to beat the system," he told me. It took months for them to discover he had lied.

. . . .

IT WAS LATE OCTOBER. At one o'clock in the afternoon a message came through on my beeper: "This is Dakota. Can you meet us at the Port at two?"

When I arrived at the Port Authority, Dakota was upset. Cedric stood a few feet away from Dakota, glancing sideways at him every couple of minutes. He seemed to be waiting for something to happen.

That morning, Dakota told me, he and Cedric had gone to Covenant House because he had learned that someone at the shelter had called his sister a bitch. Said Dakota, "I went up to the kid and said, 'You're going to apologize.' He said, 'I'm not apologizing to no one.' The kid walks away, and then ten minutes later, a police car drives up. The kid comes out of nowhere and says, 'It's the guy in the black hat.' The police officer pulls out his gun and tells me to get up against the car. I told him I'm not going to turn around because as soon as I turn around he's going to cuff me." Dakota had been told by a legal aid lawyer to keep his hands in the air if an officer stopped him so that the officer would know that he wasn't reaching for a weapon. "He can do whatever he wants when I'm not facing him or giving him the opportunity to plant something on me if I turn around. Then the cop called me a wiseass, and he turned me around and pushed me up against the car. The other officer grabbed Cedric, and then they frisked us both."

"I couldn't believe it," Cedric said. The pitch of his voice was high. "We were just standing there doing nothing."

Even if Dakota and Cedric could be made to understand that the teenager, feeling threatened, was justified in calling the police, they were outraged that the police officer had drawn his gun. Cedric seemed scared, but Dakota was furious. As Dakota retold the story, his expression hardened. He'd lived that moment many times before.

"'Where is your gun?' he asked me," Dakota continued. "'I don't have no gun,' I said. There was no gun. The cops had to let us go."

Getting guns off the street had become one of the New York City Police Department's top priorities after Mayor Giuliani took office in 1994. The police increased the number of people they stopped and frisked for weapons, often using minor violations such as fare-beating and public beer drinking as a pretext for a pat-down. The philosophy behind the campaign was sociologist James Q. Wilson's "broken window" theory. "If a factory or office window is broken," Wilson wrote, "passersby observing it will conclude that no one cares or no one is in charge. In time, a few people begin throwing rocks to break more windows." In other words, even the smallest crimes cannot be tolerated because they lead to bigger crimes. New York cops found out quickly that many of these lawbreakers were wanted on warrants, were carrying illegal weapons, or provided intelligence on other crimes. The New York Police Department's "zero tolerance" policing became a way to catch serious criminals. But as it drew praise from older residents of troubled neighborhoods, the aggressive form of patrolling generated numerous complaints of harassment.

Much of the work was done by the elite Street Crimes Unit. Created to take guns and drugs off the street, when the unit was expanded in 1997 and then again in 1998, it was credited for taking more guns off the street than any other unit in the department. But in 1998, of the 27,061 people frisked by the unit, only 4,647 were arrested, meaning more than 22,000—about 80 percent—had not been armed. The year before, of 18,023 people searched, only 4,899 were arrested. The vast majority of people being "tossed" were black and Hispanic men.

Dakota had been regularly stopped and searched by the police, whether or not he was doing something illegal. It was demeaning and demoralizing. Like so many other males of color, he came to believe the police were there not to protect him but to set him up.

When he was young, Dakota dreamed about becoming a policeman. He loved playing cops and robbers and watched TV cop shows like *Barney Miller, Kojak,* and *Starsky and Hutch.* "We young kids looked up to older guys we knew who were in their twenties and decided to become cops," said Dakota. "We wanted to be like them." But now, Dakota had little respect for the police. "Today, it's all about the money. They're all crooked. They're all trying to make a dollar. It's in the papers every day."

Some days Dakota flew off the handle, ranting about abusive and crooked cops, and his anger and his blanket statements made it easy to dismiss what he was saying. But what he said about the police was based on what he had experienced himself and seen in his own neighborhood.

Tales of police corruption in New York City filled the newspapers in the early 1990s, after Mayor David N. Dinkins appointed retired judge Milton Mollen to look into allegations of police officers shaking down drug dealers for money, guns, and drugs. In public hearings in 1993, the Mollen Commission brought to light charges of widespread brutality and drug trafficking in two precincts in central Brooklyn and the South Bronx. In 1994, more than thirty police officers were arrested in the Thirtieth Precinct in Harlem on charges ranging from assault to drug dealing. A year later, in the Forty-eighth Precinct in the East Tremont section of the Bronx, the precinct that covered the neighborhood where Dakota had grown up, sixteen police officers were indicted on charges of robbery, burglary, larceny, the filing of false police reports, and insurance fraud.

The Mollen Commission concluded that "police brutality seemed to occur, in varying degrees, wherever we uncovered corruption, particularly in crime-ridden, drug-infested precincts, often in large minority populations." The Commission noted that the most serious abuses involved patrol officers protecting or assisting drug dealers, and involved in robberies, beatings, perjury, and falsification of records. It also found that the NYPD had failed to monitor or discipline officers accused of brutality and that the "code of silence" had hampered internal investigations.

Private citizens were increasingly registering their complaints. In 1995, the Civilian Complaint Review Board, an independent agency charged with monitoring and investigating police wrongdoing, received 5,618 complaints, up from 3,580 filed in 1993. The majority of complaints were reported by blacks and Hispanics.

The issue exploded in 1997 when Haitian immigrant Abner Louima, picked up by the police after a scuffle outside a nightclub, was taken back to a Brooklyn precinct station and brutalized so badly that he ended up in the hospital. Police officers had sodomized Louima with a wooden stick, puncturing his intestines. Louima, it turned out, had no criminal record and had been trying to stop a fight when the police arrived.

After the police left Covenant House, Dakota and Cedric went to Streetwork. Dakota needed to talk to his counselor, and he wanted an acupuncture session, hoping both would calm him down. Acupuncture was used to detox drug users, to calm cravings, and reduce stress. The ultrathin silver needles helped Dakota relax.

Dakota had not expected to be turned away. But Streetwork was simply overloaded. Because of the high volume of kids who frequented the drop-in center, they could meet their counselors only once a week on their assigned day.

To Dakota, however, Streetwork's workload didn't matter. "I needed help at that moment, but it wasn't my day," Dakota said sarcastically. "They slammed the door in my face."

Dakota then went back to Covenant House to see his sister. They refused to let him enter, he told me, because he had threatened one of the kids. They told him that if he didn't stop coming around, his sisters would have to leave.

"If anyone threatens my sisters, that's it," Dakota added as he recounted the events of the day. "You can bother me a hundred times, but don't bother my sister."

Dakota seemed fiercely protective not only of his sisters but of all women. He defended young women he knew even casually, friends of his sisters or girls he met at Covenant House who were yelled at or insulted by their boyfriends. He told me that he had seen his father beat his mother so much that the experience turned him into a staunch defender of the opposite sex. "That's what I've been doing all my life— defending females," he told me. "If a guy disrespects a girl, I'm going to get up there and take care of it. He's a man, and females can't take it from a man."

When I was around, he seemed eager to help women in need. I had seen him assist an elderly woman carry her heavy bags through the Port Authority to the street to get a cab. He regularly helped women carry their baby strollers up flights of stairs. On the subway, he offered his seat to women of all ages and to small children. Being chivalrous made him feel good. The women always responded with gratitude, kind words, and a smile. At the same time, helping people he considered weaker made him feel stronger.

Dakota grew increasingly agitated as he recounted the events of the morning. When he finished, he muttered something under his breath, turned his back to me, and began pacing. I'd never seen him so angry.

"So now they're trying to push my buttons," he said. "If my sisters get kicked out of Covenant House, there are going to be problems. I will blow Covenant House up."

He stopped and took a deep breath. "This is what I'm trying to avoid, the aggravation and stress," he said. "I don't care if they threw me out, so what? But now you're talking about throwing my sisters in the street. I told my sisters—so help me God if anything happens to my sisters—Covenant House is going to have problems. I'm going to go to jail. I'm going to do my time. That's all I have left. They can't take that away from me." Dakota continued to pace. "That's the worst thing they could tell me—that I can't see my sisters."

Cedric walked up to Dakota and placed a hand on his shoulder. "There are a lot of young people that want to be bad boys," Cedric said. "If you really wanted to, you would have already done it." His voice was soothing, persuasive.

When Dakota got angry, Cedric was usually able to calm him down. Cedric reasoned with him quietly and calmly and Dakota listened. For this reason, Dakota often referred to Cedric as his guardian angel. "I think the Lord sent Cedric to me to make sure I stay out of trouble," he told me one day.

But on that morning Dakota didn't seem to be listening to his friend. "That's the worst thing they could tell me—that I can't see my sisters. They don't own that whole block."

"Chill man," Cedric said. "Calm down, calm down. Let me talk to you." The two stepped aside for a minute, and Cedric talked while Dakota listened, nodding his head. "I understand where you're coming from," Cedric said. "You're absolutely right, but do you want to be dead? Do you want to go to jail?"

For a minute, Dakota was calm, then without warning, he became agitated again. "I don't care if I go to jail," Dakota repeated over and over, further fueling his anger.

Again, Cedric put his hand on Dakota's shoulder. Again, Dakota calmed down.

"You're right, Cedric. I don't need this aggravation." Dakota took a deep breath and bent his head down. About fifteen seconds later, when he lifted his head back up, he seemed calm, his face relaxed. He smiled and nodded toward Cedric. "That's my guardian angel."

. . . .

THE NEXT DAY, Dakota told me about Cujo. "When I get angry, I have this little guy who comes out. I'm like the Incredible Hulk. I have two personalities. I have the good side, and this evil side that takes over. When I get heated, I have ways that I can control the 'beast'—that's what I call him. He goes by Cujo." The name came from a 200-pound rabid Saint Bernard created by Stephen King. "He's stronger than Dakota. Everybody keeps saying it's my conscience. When I was real young, they said I was emotionally disturbed. I was depressed all the time, and they said that I was a threat to myself. I didn't know anything about Cujo then. I discovered him in seventh grade, when I tried to throw a teacher out the window."

Many street youth, especially those who had suffered abuse, were masters of dissociation: removing themselves emotionally and psychologically from what was happening to them. It helped them to cope with physical, emotional, or sexual violence. The most extreme form, Dissociative Identity Disorder (DID), formerly known as multiple personality disorder, is believed to be a psychological response to trauma, including abuse, profound neglect, and the witnessing of violence or death. And although most psychiatrists and psychologists agree that true DID is rare, lesser degrees of dissociation are not uncommon.

"He comes out whenever I get mad—whenever somebody tries to push my buttons," Dakota said. "I've been in situations where I almost snapped a kid's neck, and I almost broke a kid's spine. Soon as he gets what he wants, I relax, Dakota looks around and says, 'Uh oh, what did I do?' But it's too late. Everything goes red in my face. I don't see nothing. He takes over my body. Sometimes I remember what he does, sometimes nothing."

Dakota told me that when he was nine, he once got suspended for almost breaking another boy's arm. The fight had started over an ice cream sandwich, and Dakota remembered nothing of the incident afterward.

"He was on the verge of coming out yesterday," Dakota said. "I wanted to burn Covenant House real bad. I controlled him yesterday, but I was shocked I could."

It was impossible for me to know if Dakota faked Cujo altogether or whether he actually did black out and lose control. The truth was probably somewhere in between. I didn't know what he himself believed.

Whether Dakota believed in Cujo, Cedric felt certain he'd seen him. "There was a time yesterday when I was really nervous," Cedric confessed to me when we were alone later that day. "Sometimes when he gets mad, something happens to his eyes. And then he gets red. Never in my life have I seen a dark-skinned person turn red."

. . . .

THROUGH HIS SISTER, school teachers, and social work and court records, I gradually pieced together the events of Dakota's childhood.

Dakota was born in New York City in 1973, but the family had moved to Louisiana when he was still an infant. Dakota remembered little about his early years, except that they moved a lot and that his mother worked as a home aide and his father as a janitor.

When he was about nine years old, Dakota, his mother, and two younger sisters moved back to New York City. His father had left for New York three weeks earlier to find work and a place to live. But when they arrived in the city, they waited for two nights at the Port Authority before their father arrived to take them to what Tamara described as a crack house in Harlem. About a week and a half later, Dakota's mother left her husband and took her three kids to live with her two sisters, Ruth and Rose. Ruth had her own children, and Dakota and his family crowded into his aunt's two-bedroom apartment in the Bronx.

For the kids, especially for Dakota, living with Aunt Ruth turned out to be a nightmare. According to Dakota and Tamara, their aunt was crazy. "All the sisters had mental health problems," Tamara told me. "Including my mother." Tamara said Ruth hid all the pots and pans after she and her family arrived, forcing them to heat their cans of ravioli on the radiator. Once, Tamara told me, all three sisters began fighting, wildly hitting each other. When Dakota tried to jump in, Ruth grabbed him and tried to throw him out the window. He was ten at the time; the window was five stories high.

A few months later, in the middle of the night, Ruth came into the living room where all the children were sleeping and set fire to a curtain they used to divide the room. "She did it really fast," Tamara remembered. "The flames were everywhere. My mother and us, we just panicked. We started throwing buckets of water on them. All the time Ruth was saying 'Burn, baby, burn!' That's when we realized we had to leave."

Dakota had told me about the fire on more than one

occasion. Each time, though, he was unemotional and related just the bare facts. When I pressed him for details, he stopped. He still got flashbacks, he said, and didn't want to talk about it. After that night, the family moved into a shelter for six months—until they got an apartment in the East Tremont section of the Bronx.

Throughout Dakota's childhood and adolescence, his father drifted in and out of his life, disappearing for long periods at a time. "My father started fuckin' up when I was young," Dakota said. "One time when I was about six, he told me, 'I'm going to get you a Casio [keyboard] for your birthday.' He had two checks in his pocket. One was for $800 and change, and the other was for $300. I was waiting and waiting. Birthday came and birthday left. No Casio. What did he do with those checks? He cracked them up. He blew all the money on crack." When Dakota's father was around, Dakota said, he beat up his mother regularly. "I'd seen my father try to break her arms and her legs. She'd turn green, purple, and red from the beatings."

Tamara told me her father hit her regularly. He said he hated Tamara because she looked like his mother. Tamara was very pretty with almond-shaped eyes, high cheekbones, and dark skin. Tamara said her father even instructed Dakota to beat her. "My father used to tell him, 'If the bitch don't do what you tell her, you knock the shit out of her and fuck her up,'" Tamara told me. "So Dakota would say, 'Tamara, get me some soda,' and I would say no, and he would beat me because he always listened to what my father said when he was young. I was always walking around with bruises and black and blue marks."

Dakota, named Kevin by his mother, was two years older than his seventh grade classmates in his Bronx junior high school. "Dakota always had the most peaceful demeanor and the most charming smile," said Rosalind Turner, a drug prevention specialist at the school. "His good manners would get him anywhere. Even today, he's a quiet person and shows respect."

But she knew that Dakota also had a temper. "Once he gets emotionally upset about something, he will definitely try to hurt somebody," Turner said. Another grade school teacher remembered him hitting a teacher with a chair.

In seventh grade, Dakota started skipping classes regularly, missing almost fifty days of school. Administrators referred him to a special program within the school that addressed truancy problems, and he and his family began counseling.

Research has shown that when children see or even hear a parent being battered by someone they love—and if the assaults happen again and again—they can develop symptoms of post-traumatic stress disorder (PTSD), including emotional numbness, flashbacks, and a kind of hypervigilance, as if they're constantly waiting for the other shoe to drop. Children with PTSD suffer from phobias, separation anxiety, and oppositional disorder (a pattern of negative, hostile, and defiant behavior that lasts more than six months and causes significant impairment in social, academic, or occupational functioning). Many of these children have difficulty forming friendships and developing academically. Children who repeatedly witness abusive behavior also learn that violence is effective at resolving problems.

Dakota's social work and psychiatric records confirmed that he had been affected by the violence he witnessed at home. When he beat up two classmates he believed had stolen money from him, a social worker noted that she felt that Dakota was afraid of his father and fearful of leaving his mother alone with him. After Dakota had received a failing report card, another social worker also mentioned Dakota's fear of his father's reaction.

"Violence was a predominant theme of the interview," a psychiatrist wrote in one evaluation when Dakota was in seventh grade. "Dakota has a fatalistic expectation that sooner or later he will kill someone who triggers his rage and that sooner or later he will be killed. No thoughts of a suicidal nature, and the homicidal thoughts involve no homicidal planning. No overt thought disorder or disturbance of perception noted. In addition to the anxiety and anger, there is an acknowledged depression." The doctor's primary diagnosis was conduct disorder, aggressive and unsocialized, with a secondary diagnosis of borderline personality.

Less than two weeks later, another psychologist noted, "Dakota appears to have a very poor self-image and to have great conflict over aggressive feelings and wishes. At times, his anxiety over aggressive feelings can disrupt his reality temporarily and can lead to periods of impulsive acting out. It should also be noted that Dakota can recover from these disturbed episodes quite quickly. Dakota sees interpersonal relationships as involving considerable conflict and aggression. . . . However, separation and loss are recurrent themes, as are the expectations of men that women be devoted to their needs. Dakota views men as capable of reacting violently when women do not live up to these expectations." There was no mention of Cujo in any of the reports.

When he was about fifteen, Dakota was transferred to a Bronx day treatment center for children with emotional problems. Eventually, he grew tired of being scrutinized by therapists and social workers and dropped out. "They kept telling me I had a lot of problems," Dakota said. "I agreed. I wanted to know what we can do to solve these problems. We weren't getting anywhere."

Dakota and his sisters were in junior high when their mother started getting sick. Tamara said her mother knew she had AIDS but never told her family. For two years, Tamara assumed she had a lingering cold. Tamara had already had her first baby by then. She'd gotten pregnant in seventh grade, she said, the first time she'd had sex. "I was eight and a half months pregnant, but I didn't even know," said Tamara. "I didn't have a stomach. I wore all my clothes. I wore my bikini. I went to the pool. My hips were getting bigger, but I thought I was just gaining weight."

Tamara's school teachers were also stunned when they learned the news. "She went home after school one day and had the baby over the weekend," Turner said. "Nobody had any idea she was pregnant."

Tamara took two months off from school and then returned. Her mother took care of the baby during the day, and Tamara took over in the late afternoon. But when Tamara's mother developed pneumonia, Tamara stopped going to school. "I cooked, cleaned, fed my mother, fed my son, did laundry, and took care of my sister and my brother," she said. "I had to take care of things because nobody else would do it. My brother and sister weren't even going to school. It was hard, but I did it."

About four months later, Tamara's mother died. She was thirty-six years old.

"After their mother died, it was over for those children," Turner said. "The whole family fell apart. They had nowhere to go." Turner said Dakota never fully recovered from the death of his mother. "Dakota tried to help his mother the best he could, trying to be the father, and then she took sick and died. He tried to take charge of the family after that, and there were a lot of problems."

According to Tamara, Dakota, then eighteen, grew

increasingly violent after their mother died. "Every day Dakota used to tell me and my sister, 'If you all don't come back here with money, you all can't come in.' If things weren't going right with his girlfriend, he'd just take it out on me and hit me. One time I could hardly walk."

Dakota never told me he had hit his sister, but he did admit that he had "got caught up in cocaine" with his aunt Ruth sometime after his mother died, but stopped after about a year. "My face looked like it was just shriveling in," he said. "I was sniffling all the time and not eating. It wasn't me. I didn't go to no program. I just stopped." He still smoked marijuana. "Everybody smokes weed," he said.

After six months, Tamara took her son to Covenant House. When a case worker asked her where her guardian was, she responded, "I have no guardian. My mother's dead. My brother beats me all the time. I have nobody."

Tamara felt safe at Covenant House. She was there for about six months while she waited to be moved into a subsidized apartment when her sister Keisha asked her to move back home to the Bronx. Tamara agreed. But nothing had changed. After a few months, the teenagers lost the apartment.

Over the next three years, Dakota and his sisters separated, moving more times than they could remember. They lived at their aunt Ruth's apartment, at other relatives' apartments, at friends' places, homeless shelters, and even on the street. At times, Tamara had to settle for living with physically abusive men just to be able to keep a roof over her and her son's heads. During this time, Tamara became pregnant with her second child.

When I met Tamara in June 1997, she was twenty-one and said that both her children were in kinship care, living with their fathers' families. Their fathers, she said, were in jail. Tamara told me she wanted her children back desperately.

But Tamara was unlikely to win back custody soon. A few years earlier, Tamara was arrested for carrying a fully loaded .38-caliber revolver and sixty vials of crack in the bottom of her baby bag. According to court records, a woman called the police after Tamara's sister Keisha, with a gun in her waistband, threatened her, stating, "I'll blast all of you." The woman told the police that Keisha then walked over to Tamara's baby stroller and placed the gun in the baby bag. When the police arrived, they searched the bag and found a gun and cocaine. Tamara's fingerprints were never found on the drugs or the gun. She denied ever knowing who had placed them in her bag. Tamara was convicted of criminal possession of a weapon in the third degree and was sentenced to five years' probation.

In the years after his mother died, Dakota became a father himself. He had two children, neither of whom I ever met. His children lived with their mother, but Dakota told me that because he didn't get along with her current boyfriend, he hadn't seen them in months.

Dakota hardly saw his own father. For many years, his father had a steady job as a janitor, but Tamara said that "he lost it all because of crack." Since then, he had been living in shelters. Once when Dakota and Cedric had been shuttled to a shelter in the Bronx, his father appeared at breakfast the next morning. "My father said to me, 'I don't mind if you're in a shelter,'" Dakota told me. "'But I don't want you in the same one as I'm in. I know everybody here, and it don't look right.'" Dakota told him that he would try to make sure it didn't happen again.

After his mother died, Dakota kept in touch with Marzette and Turner from his junior high school. "He's been having a rough time," Turner said. "When I saw him last year, he said he'd been breaking into buildings at night for a warm place to sleep and getting chased out. I told him to go back to the hospital for treatment. The last time I saw him, he looked very weak and sick. If Dakota doesn't take care of himself, it's going to be the end for him."

. . . .

WHEN I FIRST MET DAKOTA, all he seemed to want was to stay out of the drug trade and start over. "I've been selling drugs since I was ten," he said. "The only other job I had was through a summer youth program when I was fourteen, and I quit. I quit after one week because they were trying to bust my chops, and for that little bit of money it wasn't worth it. I said, 'I can make what you're giving me in three weeks in an hour selling drugs.'"

East Tremont, where Dakota grew up, was among the five poorest of the city's community districts: In 1996, 48.5 percent of households had an annual income less than $10,000. In 1998, the fifteenth City Council District, which included East Tremont, was ranked among the poorest in the city in terms of quality of life. The district had the second highest number of hospital asthma admissions in the city (1,776 compared to a city average of 676) and was one of ten districts with the most AIDS cases. Fifty-four percent of district residents over twenty-five lacked a high school diploma, and only 27 percent of middle school students had reading scores at or above grade level.

In the mid-1980s, when Dakota was a teenager, the city's youth unemployment rate hovered around 30 percent. In some neighborhoods in the Bronx, the rate was considerably higher. But those figures counted only those who were attempting to find work; a significant percentage of young people were not even trying. Many of the jobs that were available were low paying and offered few opportunities for developing careers. In 1987, four out of five of the city's black teenagers did not have jobs.

For kids like Dakota, the drug trade offered economic opportunity. But more than money, it offered status and power. Moving up the drug hierarchy gave young men a sense of accomplishment they never found in school or in minimum wage jobs. The handfuls of cash they found themselves making increased their self-esteem. Actively recruited by local dealers to work as lookouts and couriers, they worked more cheaply than adults, were treated more leniently than adults by the criminal justice system, and took more risks than adults did. Increasingly, many of these children carried guns. As they got older, they learned to shoot.

I was never able to figure out how much of what Dakota had told me about his drug dealing was true. He told me lots of stories and told them eagerly, easily, but he wanted me to listen and be interested so I would want to see him again. And I noticed inconsistencies in his accounts. Usually, however, when I asked him to repeat a story months later, new details explained the discrepancies.

Dakota told me he was ten when he became a drug runner for the first time. "I used to run for everyone in the building," he said. "I knew all the spots because people I knew worked them. I would buy for people because they knew me. I usually made $20."

Two years later, crack surfaced on the streets of the Bronx and spread quickly throughout the city. In November 1985, a front-page article in the *New York Times* reported its arrival. The new drug was produced in "factories" where the cocaine powder was processed into pure crystals, or "rocks," and then packed into small plastic vials resembling perfume samples. The crack sold on the street in New York ranged in cost from $2 to $50 depending on the number of rocks in the vial.

The new drug was far more addictive than cocaine, and its addictive properties were, according to *Newsweek*, "a marketing breakthrough" for pushers: "When smoked, cocaine molecules reach the brain in less than ten seconds, the resulting euphoric high is followed by crushing depression. The cycle of ups and downs reinforces the craving, and according to many experts, can produce a powerful chemical dependency within two weeks." Crackheads, as they soon became known, needed another hit within minutes and compulsively binged until they ran out of money or collapsed into exhausted sleep. They were paranoid, excitable, and often took dangerous risks. Users stole from everybody—from family, friends, employers—to pay for the next "pipe." Women, "crack whores," often turned to prostitution to get money. They hung out in crackhouses where they gathered for smoking binges that often lasted for several days. Families often broke apart. In the late 1980s and early 1990s, the ranks of the city's foster care system swelled.

The crack business began as a cottage industry but brought in outlandish amounts of cash. "The only equipment needed was two glass coffee pots, a hot plate, a pair of scales, and a case of baking soda," *Newsweek* reported. The magazine described a police narcotics squad raid of a crackhouse in the Bronx in June 1986 to explain how the business worked: "Records discovered in the raid led to the drug ring's factory in an apartment building next door. . . .The suspects had about two pounds of crack worth about $150,000 in the room. They also had more than 16,000 plastic vials that are commonly used in New York to package crack for sale. . . . Luckily, the suspects were caught totally off guard—for they had a small arsenal of loaded weapons that included a rifle, four pistols, and two machine guns. The 'factory,' police said, probably served no more than a 10-block area."

However lucrative, the crack business was also dangerous: Shootings were commonplace. Many of the casualties were adolescent men. From 1985 to 1991, the annual rate at which men fifteen to nineteen years old were being killed nationwide jumped 154 percent, according to a study by the Centers for Disease Control and Prevention. Virtually all of the increase in homicide, 97 percent, was attributable to the use of guns, the study found. At the height of the crack epidemic, the Forty-eighth Precinct, which covered East Tremont, reported one of the highest murder rates in the city: the yearly death toll routinely ran as high as forty homicides—compared to twenty-four in 1996 and fourteen in 1997.

Dakota told me that when he was twelve, he started seriously thinking about carrying a gun. One evening, Tyrone, a drug dealer, came to the family's apartment and asked Dakota to meet him around the corner: He wanted Dakota to sell some clothes. But Dakota and his mother had gotten into an argument earlier in the day, and she told him he could go only to tell Tyrone they would have to meet another time. But before Dakota opened the front door, he and his mother heard the shots. Tyrone had been gunned down on the corner. Had he been out there earlier, Dakota might also have been killed.

"I knew I had to survive. It wasn't going to happen being Mr. Nice," Dakota said. And surviving meant proving himself over and over again. "It was all about respect on my block growing up. Any kind of disrespect is a reason to fight. You can't walk away. People say that you're a pussy, and you have everybody doing the same thing to you that one person did. You have to prove yourself. My mother always wanted me to stay in the house. If I'd done that, I'd be dead now. I would have never survived on the streets now if I'd been stuck up in the house all those years. I had to be out there and learn."

Dakota learned quickly to act tough, unconsciously creating a hard shell—almost another self—in order to navigate through "routine" life in his neighborhood. "My attitude started changing," Dakota said. "I used to go to school and be like, 'Fuck you. Fuck the teachers. Fuck all of you. You all going to still get paid whether you teach us or not.' Nobody expected me to make it this long." "Fuck everything" became his prevailing philosophy.

Two years after Tyrone was shot, Dakota bought his first gun for $100—a shotgun. In Dakota's eyes, having a gun was necessary for protection, settling disputes, and gaining respect. His mother didn't know he had hidden it in the house until she got into an argument with a man who'd come to the door. When the man became angry, Dakota went into the closet, assembled the shotgun, loaded it, and put it up close to the man's face. "You get away from my door," Dakota yelled. "Don't fuck with my mom, or I'll kill you in the hallway."

His mother made him sell the shotgun. "She thought I'd sold it for money," Dakota said. "But I sold it for two .25's— smaller guns." Dakota kept the guns under his mattress, the bullets separate in a drawer. "I wasn't going to get rid of the only thing that was going to protect my life. I wasn't afraid of nobody, but you can just go outside and be shot for nothing. If I'm going to go outside and you're beefing with the next person, if you're shooting at him, I'm going to shoot back. I ain't going to be running and try to call 911 and wait hours for the police to come and ask a thousand questions."

As Dakota got older, he wanted to make more money. "Everyone was getting new $90 sneakers every few weeks," said Dakota. "I didn't need new sneakers every week, but if I was going to hang out with the fellas, I couldn't be all tacky. I had to look good, too. I needed more money, and it just happened. That's how I got into the stickup game. One guy saw I was quiet and that I was trying to get money. They schooled me. They always try to get the young guys to do the hard-core stuff."

Dakota told me he did his first stickup job when he was about fifteen. "We never robbed people," he said. "We always robbed drug dealers—the coke spot, the dope spot. Nobody usually dies, and you get everything. Drug dealers are the best jobs because they aren't going to go to the police."

He explained how it worked in great detail: "I would be the buyer. I'd go into a crackhouse, and let's say I want $400 worth of pure cocaine. We usually used four people if there are two in the house. If it's three in the house, we go seven deep. Everybody had a gun. One guy turns around to get the coke. The other guy is watching me. Then there's another knock on the door. The guy watching me gets up and goes to the door with a gun in his hand. All of a sudden four niggers butt in on you. The other guy at the table turns around. I turn around and put the gun to his head. I tell the guy at the door if he doesn't drop the gun, I'm going to kill his friend. He doesn't want to see his friend die over no bullshit, so he drops his gun. We snatch everything off the table, all the money from the drawer, tie them up. We do it smooth, sometimes hit them in the head with a gun and knock them out, walk a block where there is a car waiting, and go. We always had it set up. I'd get the chance to go in. One of us would go and scope the house a week or two days before." Once, he told me, they'd come out with $50,000, then divided it, depending on the roles they each played.

Dakota stopped doing stickups, he said, because some people left to join other gangs and others started getting killed. One guy, he said, had been shot in the chest twice and died; another friend had been shot in the back three times but survived.

I never knew how much he embellished his accounts to make a better story. When I asked him what he had done with the thousands of dollars he had made doing stickups, he told me he gave some to his mother and some to his friends. But the bulk of it, he said, he gave to a family friend.

Of all of Dakota's stories, this one seemed the most fantastic. "This lady's watched me grow up, and I used to give her a lot of money," he said. "I used to tell her I was working and asked her to hold it for me. Right now she has money that belongs to me, but it's in my children's name. Now I have about $26,000. She has it in an account. If anything happens to me, she lets my kids' mom know. If my kids need anything, the lady will give them money. When my kids turn eighteen, they each get half. I signed a paper that I would not receive a penny under any circumstances because I didn't want to blow it. Every four years, we do another contract." When I asked him if I could meet this woman, he said he would have to ask her. Each time we met, I reminded him, but although each time he promised he would ask, he never did. I still have no idea if she exists.

Dakota's sister had told me that Dakota had for years "been involved with drugs and guns." Dakota's arrest record confirmed his involvement in the drug trade. Before I met him, he had been arrested twice for criminal possession of a controlled substance. The first time, a police officer caught him in the middle of a drug deal. The officer had seen Dakota take crack vials from under a rock and exchange them for cash with two buyers. When Dakota was arrested, officers discovered seventy-three vials of crack stashed under the rock. Less than three weeks later, Dakota was arrested again. This time, the crack vials were in a brown paper bag sitting on the sidewalk. The officer said he saw Dakota remove objects from the bag and hand them to people on five separate occasions before arresting him. Three of those times the officer said he saw the people hand money to a third party standing just a few feet away from Dakota. Both charges were felonies, but Dakota pleaded guilty to lesser misdemeanor charges and was sentenced to thirty days in jail for each case.

"I got out because I had too many close calls," said Dakota. "The last time, I got away with the skin of my teeth. I went from place to place. The police took everything. I had $9 on me. I said, 'All right. That's a sign. He let me get away this time.' But I know I got to chill. I can't do it no more."

Now more than a year later, Dakota was homeless in Midtown. Far from starting over, he was repeatedly asked to sell drugs and to work the streets as a "lieutenant." The drug business, like any other, had structure—the titles changed with the times, the drug, and the operation, but there was an army of unseen workers: CEOs, lieutenants, distributors, chemists, lab operators, labelers, runners, enforcers, and street dealers. In the crack hierarchy, the lieutenant had runners who made the actual sale. The runner delivered the money from the client or the street dealer, depending on the operation, to the lieutenant, who then supplied the package of drugs that was run back to the client. The runner got a cut from the sale, but the lieutenant got more. "They're paying crackhead money," Dakota told me. "But I ain't no crackhead. They want to pay me $30 a day. I ain't hearing that. I've been in the game too long to get paid that kind of money. My life is more important than that."

. . . .

IN EARLY NOVEMBER, Dakota and Cedric started sleeping on the subway at night. The train was warm, and they felt safer underground than on the street or in a shelter. "If we're out in a box, someone could beat us up, and no one would come to our rescue," Dakota said. "There's always a cop around on the subway. They kick people out if you lay down, but at least they're around." They hopped the trains usually around midnight and passed out until the morning rush.

Crime was down throughout the city, but a number of quick-fingered thieves still worked the subways at night. Referred to as "lush workers" by some police officers, these pickpockets tiptoed up to their drunken or drugged-up victims, slit open their pockets, and grabbed whatever fell out. Most of these petty thieves used box cutters and double-edged razors, which, in expert hands, could be used to slice a pocket silently, leaving the skin untouched. Some worked alone; others used accomplices as a lookout or for diversion. Cedric had once lost four tokens through a small, neat slash in his pocket.

When we boarded the A train one night at eleven p.m., the car was still crowded. A woman stood leaning by the door, her two small kids tightly gripping her jean-clad thighs. Two teenage boys with backpacks stood beside three French-speaking tourists holding a *Guide de Routarde* on New York. Another woman, her belly stretching the zipper of her skirt, wobbled on too-high heels.

Over the next hour, the train quieted; the seats cleared. The train rumbled from the Port Authority uptown through Washington Heights to Inwood, then back downtown and over to Brooklyn through Bedford Stuyvesant and East New York, then all the way out past Kennedy International Airport to Rockaway Park in Queens. Then it rolled back and started again. By three a.m., there were eight of us in the car. Everyone looked exhausted. One man stank from urine; another from alcohol; two others sat with their eyelids half closed, their heads nodding. A man in his twenties twitched nervously and paced up and down the car until finally settling in a corner where he fell asleep, his body finally at rest.

Cedric and Dakota slept soundly. Dakota sat scrunched up, his feet on the seat, his knees pulled tightly up against his chest, the hood from his sweatshirt over his eyes. Beside him, Cedric sat slumped forward, his head resting on the green canvas backpack that lay on his thighs. Two other bags were placed on the seat beside him. With the motion of the train and the passing of time, they drifted about a foot away from him. They would have been easy to snatch.

Suddenly a group of five teenage boys marched in from the car ahead. They stood by the door at one end of the car and surveyed the group. One nervously peered through the window into the adjacent car. They huddled together, then separated. Two stops later in East New York, they stepped off. Cedric sat up, his eyes still closed, then sprawled out on the seat, his feet up. Within minutes, his mouth drifted open. He snored lightly.

At four, a man with a cane who appeared to be in his sixties sat beside Cedric, directly across from me. He wore a suit jacket over a white shirt that was noticeably wrinkled. About a half hour later, he stood up, and as he waited for the train to stop, he leaned over and shoved a $10 bill in my hand, then walked to the doors. Scrawled across the bill was a phone number and the words "Call collect."

By six, people dressed for work began to board the train. By 7:30, the car was crowded. Long before he opened his eyes, Dakota was awake, listening to the noises around him—the screeching wheels, the rumbling doors, the morning chatter. By the time we reached the Port Authority at eight, Cedric had been nudged awake by the crowds. Still drowsy, Cedric stood up, and, as Dakota walked toward the doors of the train, Cedric followed, as if sleepwalking, quietly behind.

. . . .

DURING THE FIRST FEW MONTHS I knew them, Dakota and Cedric met me three to four times a week. If they were going to be late, they always paged me. At first, this surprised me. Later, I realized it made sense. Both Dakota and Cedric were trying to start over, Dakota especially. He wanted to make changes in his life, and he saw me as part of the package.

Early on Dakota and Cedric spoke to me often about wanting to find a job. Dakota was a high school dropout. Cedric had his high school equivalency diploma, which he got after he was kicked out of a technical school in Brooklyn. They said they were willing to do anything to make money. "I can't just sit on the street with a cup," Cedric said. "Never will I do that. If I can shake my hand, I can do something." Dakota told me he would sweep floors to keep out of the drug trade.

At one point, they seemed to be making a serious effort. For about a week, Dakota and Cedric walked into fast-food restaurants like McDonald's and drug stores like Rite Aid and filled out job applications, putting the Streetwork address and phone number on their applications. They expected to find a job quickly and grew discouraged when it didn't happen. As the weeks passed with no response, they stopped hoping.

The longer they were on the streets, the less finding work was a priority. Survival quickly became a full-time job. Walking all day and not sleeping much at night, they were always exhausted. They spent most of their energy finding food, looking for a place to rest and thinking about where they would spend the night.

Dakota worried a lot, especially about his health. He coughed all the time and although he said he didn't know if he had tuberculosis, at Covenant House he had been given Isoniazid, a drug used to both prevent and treat the disease and had been told to continue the pills for six months.

Although tuberculosis was on the decline in New York City, with 2,053 new cases in 1996 (compared to 3,811 new cases in 1992), the city still had five times the national average. Because tuberculosis thrived in crowded, poorly ventilated places, it was epidemic among certain populations— seventy-five times more common among the city's homeless. Some patients were treated with the wrong drugs or dosage or they failed to take the full course of treatment (from six months to two years) or took fewer pills than prescribed, leading to the emergence of drug-resistant strains of the disease. Some strains of tuberculosis were so resistant to antibiotics that the only effective treatment was surgery.

Dakota also needed glasses. He was severely nearsighted and squinted all the time. But he was also vain and wanted only contact lenses. He knew the glasses that Cedric wore looked awkward on his friend's face, but he didn't want to hurt him. "They look good on you, Cedric," Dakota said. "But glasses just aren't me. They'll probably give me ugly frames that I'll lose or break while I'm sleeping. I'm just not a glasses type of person."

But Dakota worried most about his heart. Sometimes he had chest pains and trouble breathing. He told me that two months before I'd met him, he had collapsed on the street and was taken to the hospital where he was admitted for two weeks. "They said I have this hole in my heart," he told me. But when he heard they wanted to operate, Dakota discharged himself immediately. "I said no. Too many people I know have died here. I might be the next guy in the morgue. I'd rather deal with the pain than deal with the morgue."

It seemed that the only thing that Dakota wasn't worrying about was AIDS. When he told me he'd tested HIV negative at Covenant House, he seemed disappointed. "The only way to survive out here is if you have AIDS," he said one day. "People with AIDS get income. The city takes care of them." Dakota had seen what happened when his aunt developed AIDS. "She was not only crazy, but she had HIV, so she was getting a check for $2,000 and change every month," he told me.

People living with AIDS in New York City were referred to the Division of AIDS Services and Income Support (DASIS), established in 1986 to enable people with the disease to obtain all their government benefits from a single agency. At DASIS, clients were eligible for a number of services including emergency housing, rent assistance, food stamps, and Medicaid. But both patients and health advocates complained that the agency failed to deliver basic services.

During the first couple of months he was homeless, Dakota tried to get glasses and take care of his heart problems. Covenant House had made appointments for him at St. Vincents Hospital, but each time he went to the hospital, he was told to come back another day to see more doctors. The appointments were always scheduled for eight in the morning, which meant he had to sleep on the subway the night before to be on time. When he arrived, he waited hours to see a doctor. The first time, he had gone to have his eyes examined. The doctor said Dakota would have to see a specialist because his eyes were so badly scarred that it looked as though he might go blind. He told me, "At least then I'll be eligible for SSI"—a federal program for sick and disabled people. When he returned a week later, he waited three hours before being told that he wasn't going blind but that his left eye had experienced severe trauma and irreversible scarring. There was no infection. All he needed was glasses, something he already knew. But he couldn't get glasses until he was on Medicaid, which he couldn't do without his birth certificate. The third time, he showed up for an EKG, but the doctor told him to come back in two weeks. After his fourth appointment, the hospital staff found out that he had been prescribed Isoniazid but had long ago run out of pills, and they insisted that he have a chest X-ray before he continued with his appointments. Dakota lost his patience. After four fruitless trips to the hospital, he still didn't have glasses and he still had chest pains. That was the last time Dakota went to the hospital.

Day by day, Dakota felt increasingly defeated. He wasn't getting help from anyone to get off the street, and it seemed that every time he attempted to do something positive, he ran headlong into another obstacle. Dakota took all problems he encountered personally and felt he was being "disrespected" everywhere he went. At times when he walked with a determined swagger, people shied away from him. To them, he was a suspect, until he proved he was not. But even when he took small tired steps, he was noticed. Once walking through the Port Authority he politely asked a white woman in her fifties if she could spare an extra cigarette. I saw the woman hug her purse close to her body and quicken her pace. Another white woman in her thirties, braced herself, edged up close to her companion and placed her hand on the clasp of her bag as Dakota walked beside her.

"Every time I ask someone for a cigarette, they act like I'm trying to rob them," he said. "I only want a cigarette. They act like I'm saying, 'Can I borrow a thousand dollars, please?' I really can't deal with Midtown. In the Bronx, you ask anyone on the street for a cigarette, and they give it to you. Everybody looks the same in the Bronx. I'm not a racial person, but when I say good morning to you, and you turn the other way and don't comment, that's racism. I didn't say it disrespectfully."

Some days, Dakota asked ten people for a cigarette before anyone even acknowledged his request. "I'm not going to let nobody treat me in no kind of way," he finally said one day. "If you don't treat me with respect, you're not getting it. I don't care who you are. I'm not your dog who you can say roll over and fetch."

The people rushing through the Port Authority wore suits, carried briefcases. Everyone, or so it seemed to Dakota, had good jobs and someplace to go. Dakota wanted those things, but he knew that without a high school education, he might never make a realistic living wage. "Everyone has money here," he said. "And nobody wants to give you a chance unless you have the right degrees."

A 1999 study of incomes and rents in New York City found that a minimum wage worker earning $10,712 a year, or about $893 a month, could afford a monthly rent of no more than $267.80 and still meet basic needs. A household on SSI could afford monthly rent of no more than $171. Yet, according to the report, the fair market rent for a New York City one-bedroom unit was $711. Using 30 percent of income as an upper limit for affordability of housing, the hourly wage needed to afford that apartment would be nearly three times more than the federal minimum wage of $5.15 per hour. In other words, a minimum wage earner would have to work more than 100 hours per week to afford the rent.

Most days Dakota felt menial, minimum wage work was little more than a trap. "I look at it as slavery," Dakota said. "All anybody wants you to do is sweep the floors. I'm not saying that it's bad, but you're getting beat. Then they gonna give you $5 or $6 like you're a crackhead. I'm not going to be busting my ass for hours, an hour or two, buff your floor, and wax it down for you, and shine it up, and then you're gonna give me a couple of dollars. Candy bars don't cost five cents anymore. You can't buy no sneakers for $8. How you gonna pay rent with $8? I'm not your slave."

Increasingly, Dakota missed the Bronx, the only home he'd known. "In the Bronx, I'm like everyone else," he said. "I have access to everything. I can go to the store. I can get food, get cigarettes. I know the Bronx like the back of my hand. Somebody knows me everywhere and helps me out with a couple of dollars here, a couple of dollars there. I can survive up there. If things don't change, I'm going back uptown and go right back into it. I can't keep getting stomped on. I can't survive out here."

. . . .

IT WAS MID-NOVEMBER. Dakota sounded excited when he phoned. "They said they're going to help us," he told me. Dakota was calling me from the men's shelter at Wards Island. A caseworker had told him that he was going to help Dakota get his high school equivalency and a job. "He's going to try to get me a coat." Dakota's coat had been stolen weeks earlier at a shelter, while he was sleeping. "He's going to do a lot."

The city acquired the 255-acre Wards Island in 1855. The island has been used as a potter's field, then as the site for a hospital for destitute immigrants and the City Asylum, which in 1896 became the Manhattan Psychiatric Center. In 1937, Wards Island was home to one of the world's largest sewage treatment plants in the world and later the training school for the city's fire department. By 1996, much of the island was a park. The psychiatric hospital continued to treat about 900 long-term-care patients; about 70 percent of new admissions had criminal records. Wards Island was also home to 1,000 homeless men, who slept in three separate facilities.

Located at the northern end of the East River, Wards Island was one of the largest and most isolated of the city's shelters. Although the shelter had vans that shuttled back and forth to Manhattan, they were frequently out of service, and shelter residents who didn't have any money or tokens for the city bus were forced to walk to Manhattan or remain stranded on the island.

Dakota and Cedric had been told they could stay at Wards Island for the week and, if things worked out, they could stay longer. Over the past few weeks, they'd been so tired that they took turns napping by the Hudson River and in nearby parks during the day. The prospect of a place to stay for seven con-secutive days and nights of sleep revitalized them. I hadn't heard such energy and optimism in Dakota's voice for weeks. "Tomorrow I have nothing to do, so I'm going to just chill out and hang," he told me. "I'm just going to relax."

Two days later, Cedric paged me. "Please call Cedric," his message said. "It's an emergency."

"Dakota is flipping out," Cedric told me. "They stole his tokens to go to the hospital. He's buggin' out. He wants his tokens."

I could hear someone yelling in the background, but I couldn't make out whether it was Dakota.

"He's worse than I've ever seen him. He's not listening to nothing. He just wants his tokens. He's flipping out." Cedric told me that the problems had started a day earlier, when he and Dakota were transferred into another building. "They have thirty men on cots on the floor, and there were men looking at us all night. He was buggin' out. I'm hoping that he won't knock anyone out. I think he's going to hurt somebody."

Cedric sounded scared. I tried to find out exactly what had triggered Dakota's rage, but Cedric kept repeating himself.

"I think I've seen his little friend again," Cedric said. "He's an awful different person. He turns a different color. He turns red. His voice changes. He's screaming and yelling. I've never seen this side of him before. He's buggin'." By now, Cedric's voice was high pitched. "I went to try to calm him down, but he won't hear none of that."

Cedric finally calmed down after a few minutes. He explained that Dakota had put four tokens he had been given to get to his doctor's appointments in his pants pocket. At night, he'd placed his folded pants on the foot of the bed; in the morning the tokens were gone.

"I don't feel safe here," Cedric said. "They've got people who are smooth. They've been on the streets for too many years." He was quiet for a few seconds. "There he goes. He just started yelling again."

Cedric kept talking, not wanting to get off the phone. He was afraid of what Dakota would do. "I'm real nervous. He's talking about cutting people."

The next day, Dakota called me. "We're leaving," he said. "I don't feel safe here. I wake up itching. There are bugs all over me. There's no locker to keep my stuff in. They don't wake us for breakfast. We sleep with all our clothes on. I'm leaving this place. We're with drug addicts, ex-addicts, killers, prostitutes. I'm going to scratch myself to death. These guys watch you all night long. You don't feel safe. We have no blankets, no sheets—people smelling like underarms. I ain't no crackhead. I don't need to be rehabilitated. These are all a bunch of nuts walking around. I'm going back to the intake shelter at Bellevue. At least I know the guys on the bus there. I felt safe there. But this place is crazy."

That afternoon, Dakota and Cedric were transferred into the cottages, a group of five buildings that housed sixty men each. They told me they felt more secure sleeping in a room with just ten other men. "We're going to give it a chance," Dakota said. "We've got no place else to go."

· · · ·

OVER THE NEXT FEW WEEKS, I spoke to Dakota and Cedric almost every day. Their enthusiasm disintegrated rapidly. They had lockers but no locks. Dakota had had his deodorant, toothbrush, toothpaste, a pair of socks, and a shirt stolen. Someone had tried to rob Cedric, leaving his black leather jacket with a big slash on one side. They told me that drugs were sold throughout the island. "They sell at the bus, at the bus stop. You don't even have to get off the bus, you can get them through the window," Dakota said.

To Dakota and Cedric, being in the shelter was no different than being in prison, complete with a watch-your-back jailhouse mentality. They had to deal with guards, pat-downs, and food lines. They had to abide by strict rules that designated when they could eat, sleep, shower, be in their rooms, and use the main room. They had to rely on their caseworkers for tokens to go to a doctor's appointment and for information about jobs, schools, or a permanent place to stay. If they didn't get along with the people who were supposed to guide them through and eventually out of the system, they would be ignored and forgotten. They were surrounded by men who had mental health problems, used drugs, and were angry and violent—men who felt powerless.

Day by day, Dakota and Cedric grew increasingly demoralized. They told me the caseworker who had made them promises when they first arrived no longer seemed interested in helping them out, and neither did any of the others. "They don't care what happens to us," Cedric said to me one day. "They do their work and then go back to their apartment. They tell you whatever you want to hear to keep you quiet. You get a bag lunch, sandwiches, even though it's freezing cold outside. Then for dinner you get cold chicken. They don't wake us up for breakfast, so if we miss it we don't eat."

They also felt trapped. The vans were out of service, and they had no tokens. It was late November and cold, and more than anything, they were tired of walking. "These guys in here do nothing all day," Cedric said. "They just want you to sleep, hang out all day, and watch TV and just sizzle your mind. You can go to the store if you have money, but who has money? This is jail. I'm going to flip."

They continued to feel unsafe, and Dakota regularly had problems with other men. One night a resident accused Dakota of stealing his hair grease. "He stepped up to me," Dakota said. "I pulled out my razor in my mouth. I was going to cut him."

Dakota kept his single-edged razor in his belt at night, and sometimes transferred it to the inside of his cheek during the day. It rested alongside his tongue and teeth, with the razor side facing the cheek. He told me that he used to rub the blades with garlic or onions so when they opened the skin, it burned. He also said that sometimes he kept three in his mouth at one time—one on each side, another under his tongue. Dakota told me that he'd taught Cedric how to keep a razor in his mouth as well, even though Cedric didn't want to learn. "But he had to learn," Dakota said. "So he could survive out here."

"I know how to do it now," Cedric said. "I just don't want to."

As the days passed, Cedric also began to get into trouble. At first, he kept the incidents from Dakota, fearful his friend would retaliate on his behalf. Instead of fighting back, Cedric usually stayed quiet and walked away when he was confronted, saying it was all "lightweight stuff" that wasn't worth fighting over.

But Dakota soon learned what was happening. One night while Cedric was playing pool, one of the men walked up to him and told him, "You're not playing anymore."

"I just got up, went to my bed, got my razor, put one in my hand, one in my pocket, and I stood there," Dakota said. "I said, 'Listen, I'm really getting tired of all your bullshit. The next person that comes out here and does something that's wrong, is going to see it.'" The men walked away.

Over time, the men stopped bothering Cedric. "Dakota's a known person, but I'm not that known," Cedric said. "Now they see Dakota with Tiny, and Dakota likes Tiny, they leave me alone."

....

IN EARLY DECEMBER, to give them a break from the monotony on Wards Island, I told Dakota and Cedric that I would take them out for Chinese food and that we would go to a movie or to the video arcade. They'd been calling me almost every day, but I hadn't seen them for weeks. That Saturday morning, though, I woke up with a temperature of 102. It was raining and cold.

I was supposed to take the subway to 125th Street, then a bus out to Wards Island, meet them at an outdoor bus stop, and return with them to Manhattan. By the time they called on Saturday morning, I could barely swallow, my head was congested and pounding. "I'm really sick, guys," I told them.

"So what time are you going to come?" Cedric asked.

"I have a fever of 102. It's raining, I'm achy. I really shouldn't be walking around in the rain."

"You won't be in the rain very long," Cedric said. "We'll wait for you at the stop, and then we'll get back on the bus."

I said nothing. The more involved I became in their lives, the more difficult it was for me to say no to them, and they knew it.

Cedric kept insisting.

"Look. I really don't think I should go out today," I finally said.

"But you promised."

I got angry. "Yes, I promised, but I'm sick. People get sick. Does that mean anything to you, Cedric?"

All Cedric heard was that I had let him down. Others had done it before me. Nobody could be trusted, and I was no different.

There was a long silence.

"OK, what do you want to eat?" I asked. I felt feverish, disoriented, and out of control.

"Fried chicken wings," said Cedric.

"At a Chinese restaurant?"

"Sure."

"Well, the Chinese restaurant near my house does not have fried chicken wings, Cedric."

"Then go to the one at Port Authority."

I took a deep breath. "OK. I will come and bring you guys Chinese food and meet you at 125th Street like I promised, but then I'm leaving." I took their orders, went to the restaurant near my place, and brought the food up to the station a few hours later.

When I arrived at 125th Street, Cedric and Dakota were waiting, standing behind the turnstile. They were soaked from walking in the rain. I passed the shopping bag over the turnstile and handed them the food. "Look, guys. I'm really sick. I need a break."

"He didn't tell me you were sick," Dakota said. "He just said you didn't want to come."

"I told Cedric I had a fever and chills and that I felt awful. But he didn't hear a word I said. Isn't that right, Cedric?" Cedric looked like a kid who knew he'd done something wrong.

"That's Cedric," said Dakota, nodding his head. "He just blocks people out. He hears only what he wants."

"I've always been that way," Cedric said. He seemed disappointed with himself. "If I don't want to hear it, I don't. I'm sorry." I thought he meant it.

"We won't call you for a few days—give you a little break," Dakota said.

I said goodbye, and left.

Two days later, Dakota called me. "They kicked Cedric out."

. . . .

ABOUT A WEEK LATER, Cedric told me what had happened. He said he'd gone to a worker at Wards Island to ask for some tokens so he could go to Covenant House to get his records, but the worker didn't believe him, refused him the tokens, and told him to leave. Cedric asked the worker to be more polite. The worker got angry. "Then he said, 'I'll make you bleed like a pig.'" Cedric's voice was high pitched as he told me what happened. He was still stunned by what the man had said. "Then I just went off. I started screaming."

The staff told Cedric he was being transferred to another shelter for threatening a worker. Staff members considered kicking him out of the shelter system for seven days, but changed their minds. "You can't do that to me, I'm only eighteen," he told them. Instead, they sent him to Bedford Atlantic men's shelter in Crown Heights, Brooklyn.

Bedford Atlantic had a reputation for being one of the worst shelters in the city. It had been called the "Terror Dome" and more recently "Rikers II." I'd heard more than a few men say, "If you haven't been to Rikers Island, you won't make it here." Once a gigantic armory, the shelter slept 350 men on four floors. Drugs were regularly brought into the armory, and for awhile, a common route of entry, I was told, was a pole that ran along the outside of the building that men scaled to the second floor. A representative from the Coalition for the Homeless told me many of the shelter residents had mental health and drug problems that were left untreated.

This was Cedric's new home. Ironically, it was not far from where his mother lived. He hadn't seen her since she told him to leave the house, but within days of being there, he almost ran into his younger brother. When Cedric spotted his brother going to school, he crossed the street and turned his head. He didn't want to upset him.

Since his arrival at Bedford Atlantic, Cedric had spoken to his aunt a couple of times. His aunt, who had taken care of him when he was young, asked Cedric to call his mother. But Cedric refused. "They kicked me out in the street, and they think I'm going to forget about that?" Cedric said. "I don't need them."

Cedric wanted to leave. He tried to get transferred to Create House, a fifty-bed transitional housing program in Manhattan for youth between the ages of eighteen and twenty-five. But after just one week, he'd gotten into a fight with his caseworker. "'Why am I still here?' I asked my caseworker," Cedric told me. "'I'm tired of being up in here. What are you doing to try to get me out?'"

His case worker told him that it wasn't his problem. "He was like, 'You've already been here for forty-eight days,'" Cedric said. "So I grabbed him by his shirt, and I said, 'You know I've been here for only a week.' Then he called security. Then things started to get rough, and everyone was trying to knock me out. So I was screaming at them—the guards. I was like, 'I will fuck all of you in here.' They was like 'What are you trying to be, bad? Shut your young ass up before I knock you out.'"

His hope of leaving Bedford Atlantic was fading. "All my caseworker has to do is call Create House and say I have a client who's too young to be here. He's willing to sleep on the couch, he's willing to sleep in the tub. Can I ship him over here, please? This is really not a good place for him." But Cedric was convinced his counselor was doing nothing for him. "They think they're slick at Wards Island. They figure if they send me here, they'll lose me in the system, figuring that I'll run out and leave because they scared me to death."

Cedric got up every day at five, and after breakfast, he spent his day walking around the streets and hanging out with people he knew from the neighborhood. Then he returned for lunch and once again left to "chill with my people." He told me he was trying to keep out of trouble, but that it wasn't easy. "Ain't nothing but drug dealers and crackheads out here."

To Cedric, crackheads were the biggest losers on the street. Cedric had seen firsthand how crack destroyed lives. "I done seen so many of my home boys do that," he said. "Once a crackhead, always a crackhead. I don't want to be like that."

Many other young people felt the same. In Manhattan, the rate of detected crack use among juveniles admitted to jail dropped to 22 percent in 1996 from 70 percent in 1988, according to a study by the nonprofit National Development and Research Institute in New York. Bruce Johnson, one of the authors of the report, believed that young people stopped smoking crack because they witnessed with their own eyes the ravages of the drug on their families and friends. Crack was no longer cool.

Marijuana and alcohol had become the drugs of choice. Kids drank bottles of "40s," forty-ounce bottles of beer and malt liquor, throughout the day and night. With eyes shiny and glazed, they told me they didn't do drugs and "only smoked weed." Many smoked "blunts," short White Owl or Phillies cigars that had been gutted and filled with marijuana, sometimes laced with powdered cocaine and, increasingly, with heroin, which was pure and cheap. On the street, a cocaine-laced blunt was called a "woolah" or "woolie," and a blunt that had been dipped in beer, dried, and then filled with marijuana was called a "B-40." Blunts were not only larger than traditional skinny joints but also lasted longer; the cigar wrapping burned slower than cigarette paper, and the marijuana burned only when it was actually being smoked.

I told Cedric that Dakota was worried about him. Dakota had been sleeping when Cedric had the fight at Wards Island and didn't wake up until after his friend had left. Dakota hadn't seen or heard from Cedric since.

But Cedric, preoccupied with his own survival, didn't seem interested in calling his friend. "I'll call him," he said. He was not convincing.

· · · ·

CEDRIC had always seemed easily distracted, but once he was separated from Dakota, he got worse. The few times we actually met, he was usually about an hour late, either because he had forgotten our appointment or because he just got sidetracked along the way. Though he would promise to call me, weeks went by when I didn't hear from him. So I'd go to Bedford Atlantic and hang out outside around lunchtime until I saw him. "Sometimes I just drop out and don't call," he said. "I just forget."

Cedric was also expert at shutting down. When I would meet with him and Dakota, Cedric often tuned us out, listening instead to rap star Biggie Smalls on his portable CD player. Some days, he spent the whole time I was with them just nodding his head to music and quietly repeating lyrics. If Dakota started to criticize something Cedric was doing, he just grew quiet and put his headphones on.

At Bedford Atlantic, Cedric became increasingly depressed. Nobody seemed to care what happened to him, and he had little motivation to do anything. "If I could," he said, "I would just sleep all day and all night."

The first time I asked Cedric about his family, he asked me if I had ever seen the movie *Menace II Society*. "Daddy's a drug dealer. Mom's a crackhead," he explained. "It was just like that for me growing up." In the movie, Caine, the central character, sees his father murder a man over a card game. When Caine is ten, his father is killed in a drug deal. A few years later, his mother dies of an overdose. By the time he graduates from high school, Caine is wearing a beeper and is a small-time drug dealer. When his grandfather asks him if he cares whether he lives or dies, he can only say "I don't know."

Each time I asked Cedric about his family, he said a word or two, then told me he didn't really want to talk about them. He wouldn't let me meet his mother because he didn't want her to know his whereabouts. He loved his aunt, however. "You could be mad at the world, but Auntie would say, 'How you doing?' and change it all around," he said.

Four months after I met him, Cedric felt he was ready to talk about his childhood. Each time we talked, though, he grew frustrated because of huge memory gaps. "I've been like this from the time I was little," he told me. "I just block out things so I don't feel the pain."

As a child, Cedric moved nine times, living mostly in housing projects. He went from one relative to another, living with his mother, godmother, aunt, grandfather, and father. "I don't remember much about my dad," he told me, "except that when I was a kid, until I was five, I was with my dad twenty-four-seven. My dad went down the block to get something, I went. I was with him until he went to jail."

Cedric didn't know why his father had been arrested, but he remembered going with his mother and younger brother and sister to visit him at Rikers Island about two years after his father had been locked up. "It was kind of corny to see him," Cedric said. "We knew he was in jail, but we didn't know where we were going. We got on the bus and thought we was going to an amusement park or something, and we were all excited. And then we got off the bus and see this great big building and everyone walking in and walking in, waiting on line. And then when we get in, we have to take off our coats and our shoes. There was this big room, and you would sit down, and then they would let all the jailbaits out. And then my mom says, 'Come see your daddy.' We cried when we saw him."

Cedric wouldn't see his father again until his release a couple of years later.

"He came out real smooth, too," Cedric remembered. "We didn't even know he was coming out. He knocked on the door one day, and there was this big fat man at the door."

Once out of jail, Cedric said, his father started dealing drugs. "I don't remember anything about it," Cedric said. "I just know I got whatever I wanted. My dad was around, but not really. He'd come home and chill for a few hours and then disappear."

When Cedric was about nine, he said, his father was arrested again, this time for killing a man. "I remember the day well," Cedric said. "My pop was like, 'Go to your room.' We lived on the third floor. We hear noises and boom, the door slams. And then outside boom, boom—two shots. It was right around the corner down the block. We looked out the window and saw people running down the block. Mom came running down the stairs, asking, 'Where's your dad?' Then we ran down and followed her. When we got there, the cops had one cuff on. There were four others struggling to get the other cuff on. They cuffed his hands to his feet. He couldn't go nowhere. They threw him on the car. He saw us, and he was crying. Right then and there I wanted to get a gun. I was paranoid. I didn't know what was going on. I was crying. I wanted to fight the cops. He'd shot a guy with a shotgun in broad daylight. There was a pool of blood everywhere."

Cedric was devastated. "When my dad went, I went," he said. "Something happened to me. I just checked out."

When Cedric's father came out of jail four years later, he stayed with Cedric's mother for a while. Eventually, they divorced. When Cedric was seventeen, he went to live with his father again, but when he hit his stepmother's son for borrowing his sneakers without asking, he had to leave. He moved back to his mother's place.

Cedric told me his mother had begun smoking crack when he was about seven and continued for about five years. "She claims she stopped," he said. His mother was now working as a nurse's aide. When he was a boy, Cedric had only lived with his mother sporadically, spending long stretches with his aunt and grandmother. But when he moved back to live with his mother, Cedric became the man of the house and took care of his younger siblings. He remembered those days well. "I was like a father," he said. "I had to wash clothes, cook—usually tuna fish, rice, franks and beans. I knew how to fry chicken when I was eight."

Cedric started skipping school regularly and getting into trouble until eventually he was kicked out. "I used to hang out with the baddest people," he said. "I picked the worst friends, mostly drug dealers." But Cedric stayed out of dealing and using. "I started seeing them dying all over the place. Everyone else I know out here, if they're not dead, they're locked up.

"I've seen a baby get murdered when I was ten," Cedric said. "There was a woman who was walking through the projects trying to sell her baby to get money. The baby was crying, and, boom, someone shot the baby and the woman. I saw twenty to thirty people die, mostly while I was young. Young kids shooting other kids, brothers shooting brothers." He spoke about the incidents without emotion. He could have been telling me what he had eaten for lunch.

. . . .

AS WE SPENT MORE TIME TOGETHER, my relationship with Dakota became more complicated. I worried he would disappear; he worried that I would. Dakota at first looked forward to our meetings, telling me often that talking to me calmed him down and kept him out of trouble. Any effect I might have had, though, was short-lived because he got into trouble regularly. He faced one crisis after another, some real, some, I later learned, fabricated. He began to see me as the only person who could help him out and grew increasingly frustrated when I didn't help him the way he wanted.

I hadn't heard from Dakota for two months when he called at the beginning of March 1997. He told me he had just been released from jail three hours earlier, charged with felony assault in the second degree. He also told me he had been set up.

"A friend of mine came up to me and said, 'Yo, I need $2.50,'" Dakota told me. "I said, 'I don't have it.' So we started arguing, and we took it outside. So we're standing in front of the bus stop, and we're arguing, and he's saying, 'You lying.' I said, 'I don't have it. I can't give you something I don't have.' So he said, 'All right, watch. Watch what happens.' Next thing you know, he turns around, takes off his coat, and says I stabbed him.

"He was bleeding. I turn around and see security. They chased me. I ran through the lot. I didn't know what was happening. It was like ten security guards run out the building at me. I wasn't going to stand there and be stupid. So I ran. I ran through the lot and caught an asthma attack. I couldn't breathe, so I stopped. They put me in the car and brought me back. The police searched my pockets—there was nothing. No drugs. No razors."

Six days after he was arrested, a preliminary hearing was held in Dakota's case. In New York, the district attorney's office has six days from the date of arrest to indict a defendant. Most of the time, the case is evaluated and goes to the grand jury and, from there, to the New York State Supreme Court. But in Dakota's case, the district attorney decided to hold a preliminary hearing, which gives the prosecutor forty-five days instead of the usual six to decide whether to indict. Dakota's case was assigned to a lawyer in private practice who was part of a panel of criminal defense lawyers who worked as secondary relief to the Legal Aid Society.

Cliff Spencer, the complainant, lived on the streets before moving to Wards Island, where he had had a bed for the past sixty days. Court testimony revealed that he had been on his own since he was sixteen, received welfare benefits, and had a tenth grade education. He had been arrested in the Bronx in 1990 for assault and possession of a deadly weapon, convicted of petit larceny in 1992 in the Bronx, and convicted of resisting arrest during an attempted robbery in Brooklyn in 1993. He also had eight misdemeanor convictions.

At the hearing, Spencer was the first to testify.

"What happened before you got stabbed?" asked the assistant district attorney prosecuting the case.

"We were just arguing," Spencer said.

"What were you arguing about?"

"About getting a haircut."

"And what happened?"

"Then I refused, and he stabbed me."

"What did you refuse?"

"To go let him cut my hair. [Then] he threw me in a choke hold. And then I went to go get security, and then he grabbed me in the arm and stabbed me."

At that point, the prosecutor submitted a photo taken of Spencer's forearm two days after the incident. The wound was about an inch long and penetrated his arm from the inside through to the other side. Although the weapon hadn't hit any bone or major blood vessels, Spencer had bled heavily and was taken to the hospital for stitches. But Spencer hadn't seen the weapon, and none was found.

Dakota's version of the fight raised more questions.

"Why did you get into an argument with Mr. Spencer?" asked Dakota's lawyer.

"We was inside the Wards Island sleeping area. I was laying down, and he came and got me. He asked me, 'Would I like to go with him and get a bag of weed? And I told him no. He started arguing outside the sleeping area. I walked outside to the bus stop. The bus came. He got on the bus and got mad because I wouldn't jump on the back with him. He got off at the next stop and said, 'Why didn't you get on the bus?' And I said, 'Because I didn't want to hop on the bus, and I don't smoke no weed.' We got into an argument. After the argument, me and Mr. Spencer walked back to the security guard. He said, 'You're not going to go with me? You're not going to chip in?' I said, 'No.' He got mad. He said, 'Watch, watch, watch.' That was his last words.

"Security seen us, and I asked the security officer would he ask this man to stop harassing me. The security guards called on the radio for other backup. I walked away, and the other security guards caught me. They asked me, 'Why did you run?' I said because there was at least eight to nine security guards that came out, and they all rushed me. Of course I got scared. When they searched me, I had nothing on me. I had my wallet, my ID, $6.20. Nothing else was in my pocket. I didn't have time to throw nothing. I didn't have time to stash nothing."

Dakota repeated that he did not stab Spencer and that he didn't even know Spencer was bleeding until after he had been handcuffed.

There were no witnesses. No weapon was ever found, and no blood had been found on Dakota.

The judge concluded that he didn't find the complaining witness credible, but that there was reasonable cause to believe that a felony was committed.

The case was adjourned for five and a half weeks for grand jury action. Bail remained set at $3,000, and Dakota was held at Rikers Island.

After spending forty-five days in jail, Dakota was brought back to court. The prosecutor told the judge he needed an additional three weeks to prepare his case. Dakota was released and told to return at the end of March.

····

DAKOTA didn't want to go back to Rikers Island alone to pick up his possessions. "I don't want somebody to say 'OK, get back in here.' I'll have an alibi this time. Nobody can say I stabbed him on the way there. They can't say nothing that isn't true because you're with me." I couldn't go for a few days, and he said he would wait.

"It's no different from being on the street," Dakota said about Rikers. "I told myself if I can survive on the street, I can survive in there." At Rikers, Dakota had kept mostly to himself. He did push-ups every day and gained about fifteen pounds in a month. He was proud of his new physique.

He also met a couple of people he knew from the Bronx. One of them, a sixteen-year-old boy, had shot someone in the head twice; another, an eighteen-year-old, had stabbed someone. "I didn't go around asking too many people their business, so I don't have to tell them too much of my business," he said. "I learned to keep my head up, don't drop the soap, and stay out of trouble." He was grateful, he said, to a couple of older men who watched out for him. "They told me to keep the faith. They got me into reading the Koran, and it helped me a lot."

The Nation of Islam, founded by Elijah Muhammad, gained thousands of followers in the 1960s after Malcolm X converted to Islam while in prison. The sect, also known as the Black Muslims, concentrated its outreach in prisons and among poor urban blacks. In New York, city jails offered weekly Muslim prayer services and special Muslim meals and permitted Nation of Islam speakers, literature, and individual inmate-clergy meetings. The discipline, sense of manhood, self-respect, and racial pride Dakota saw in Nation members he had met seemed to resonate in him. "The experience taught me a lot," Dakota said. "I learned a lot of things inside that I knew but had to be reminded about. I have to take life seriously. I've got to do something. I've got to try."

During our bus ride to Rikers, Dakota was quiet and nervous. He recognized other men on the bus, men from the shelters, men he'd been locked up with, men from his neighborhood in the Bronx. They said nothing, but simply nodded their heads.

When we got to Rikers, Dakota paused a minute before getting on line to enter the main building. Even visitors have to undergo exhaustive and repeated searches by male and female officers who often seem embittered and easily provoked. The process is demeaning, making innocent people feel as though they had done something wrong.

I sat in the waiting room.

When Dakota returned, more than two hours later, he was lugging a giant transparent plastic garbage bag. "They didn't even give me all my stuff," he said. He was angry. "They gave me only one wallet. They didn't give me my scarf, my gloves. They don't know where they're at. All my papers were in the other wallet. I was arguing and arguing, and I told her I had more stuff, and I tell her go check. She goes back and comes out with another bag, but there's still stuff missing. I go in there, and I have no rights, and then I came out, and I have no rights. I told her I need my mail. She said there was no mail. I was supposed to be getting $5 from a guy who sent it to me while I was in here. Now I have to pay him back, and I don't even have the money."

We walked out and waited for the bus. Half a dozen other men, all carrying the same oversize bags, stood on line. Nobody spoke.

Dakota told me he was staying on a cot at a family friend's house in the Bronx. The guy, whose name was Roy, had three other men staying with him on cots, all paying him a small amount of money each week. Roy had told Dakota that he could stay for free until he got himself together. He seemed more optimistic about his future than I'd seen him in months. "I know I've got a shot at life," he said. "I've got to make good for myself."

But five days later, the man he was staying with discovered $10 missing from his house. Dakota's sister had visited with her friend one evening, and Dakota was sure the friend had taken it off the dresser when she went to the bathroom. But it didn't matter who had stolen it. Dakota was responsible because he had invited them to the house. The man told Dakota he had to pay back the money or leave.

. . . .

I HAD MADE IT CLEAR to Dakota from the beginning that I wouldn't give him money. I'd given him and Cedric subway tokens, cigarettes, a blanket, two pairs of socks, a combination lock, and food. But after a few months, Dakota started asking for cash—a loan of a couple of dollars.

Whenever I explained to Dakota again why I couldn't give him money, he said he understood. But at times my refusal seemed to annoy him. But he kept trying. He started getting into situations where a couple of dollars would make the difference between having a warm bed or sleeping on the street, between getting a legitimate job or going back to drug dealing. Or so he led me to believe.

I met Dakota at the Port Authority a few days after the money had been stolen. He was coughing a lot and said his chest felt tight. He'd run out of his Isoniazid pills three weeks before he was arrested. He was given more while at Rikers but had stopped when he was released.

We walked around the Port Authority. He hadn't been there for months, and although he remembered being frustrated by the police telling him to not sit on the steps or linger in one place, he walked through it with fond memories, remarking on the most minor changes—new paint on one wall, the closing of a kiosk. He rode the escalator up and down like a child visiting an amusement park. "This was our spot," he said in the game room, reminiscing about his days with Cedric. "We'd just watch people play and hang out." He told me he missed Cedric a lot and wanted to visit him. "He's my brother. He's been there for me since day one when I got kicked out of Covenant House. I told him I would be there for him if anything happened. I wouldn't let no harm come to him, wouldn't let anybody do him no harm."

We sat down to get something to eat. "Depressed is my middle name. I didn't expect to get thrown out of this guy's house so quickly," he said. "All I need is to give him $10, but I can't even get ten pennies." He sat quietly.

I said nothing.

"But I guess I have to learn to deal with bad things. If you can't do nothing about it, you can't just break things up and hurt people."

There was a long silence.

"I'm going to see what I can do legally to make some money before I take any back roads," he said. "If I can get something legally, great. If I can't, then I'll do what I got to do."

Earlier that day, he said a local drug dealer had told him he could make some money, but the job was risky. "The block they want me to work is hot," he told me. "Both types of hot, shooting and the police. They're hitting everybody. For every crack vial, you get one year. You're holding eighty-something bottles, I'm going to do at least twenty-five years. Me, I carry everything on me. You give me six packs, I got all six packs on me. Each pack is fifty bottles. So say I'm carrying six packs, I've got close to four hundred bottles on me. Say I only knock off one hundred, I'm looking at at least twenty-five. That's what they'll offer me off the top." Although he never said it, he implied that if I just gave him those few dollars he needed, it would keep him out of the drug business. I said nothing.

As we talked, Dakota grew increasingly withdrawn. He sat slumped in his chair, his hand resting on his chin, watching the people walking by. "I get like this every year at this time," he said. The anniversary of his mother's death was in a week. Five years after her death, Dakota still missed her terribly. "My mother gives me the willpower to stay straight," he said. "She told me thousands of times to stay out of trouble. I promised I would, but I haven't been doing it lately. I'm trying to stay out of the drugs, the violence. Then I get locked up for violence I didn't do. I just have to keep remembering that my mom is like my guardian angel looking over me and to make sure nobody does no harm to me."

When I asked him if he thought Streetwork might be able to help him, he got angry. "They're a bunch of headaches," he said. "I need to go forward, not go back. Everybody was telling me what I need. Well, I know what I need. They kept saying I was very impatient. By the time they give me the help I need, I won't even need welfare, I'll need SSI. They kept asking me the same thing every week. I'm not getting anywhere. Ask me something different. The only time I got a little service there was when I got upset." I didn't know it at the time, but Streetwork had learned that Dakota had used them to try to get a fake birth certificate and had asked him to leave. "All these people around here say 'I'm your friend.' But when you're really fucked up, they have attitude. Don't sit there and perpetrate a fraud to me. Don't act concerned unless you are. I'm tired of all the words. A lot of people that I know are surprised I haven't sold my body. Hell no. They give me credit for not having gone that route or smoked crack. I'm trying to eliminate the bad side. And keep Cujo in the closet. But I'm tired of this."

Dakota became quiet again. As a woman at the table next to us got up to leave, she dropped a quarter that rolled near Dakota's foot. She hadn't noticed. Dakota picked it up and called out to her.

"Is that mine?"

"Yes," said Dakota, handing the quarter to her. The woman took the quarter and walked away.

"You could really use even a quarter right now," I said.

"If I can be nice, maybe it will come back to me," he said. "It doesn't make me a better person to steal a quarter."

....

I MET DAKOTA in the Bronx the next day. He told me that he had heard that Spencer was a crack addict and had been transferred to a drug rehabilitation program in Brooklyn. Dakota was optimistic this would help his case. He also told me that after he left me the other night, he had been shot at. Dakota said he'd gone to 175th Street and Mount Hope in the Bronx to borrow money from a drug dealer he knew. "I heard one shot, and I kept walking," he said. "Then a second one came right towards me and hit the gate next to me. I just took off. I heard two more as I was running and then another two—all together six shots. And there were three guys running after me."

When Dakota went back to Roy's house and told him

someone shot at him, Roy said he knew about the shots. He told Dakota that the shots were a warning, and that next time, the shooter wouldn't miss.

Dakota said he was shaken at first, but realized that they were just trying to scare him. "They could have easily just driven up to me and shot me in the leg," Dakota said. "They weren't shooting to get me. They were shooting to scare me. If you're going to be got, you're going to be got. Shooting to scare happens a lot so that you don't catch a murder charge. You go to jail for a year for a gun. You go for fifteen to twenty-five for murder. It was a warning, but I still have to get Roy his money."

Later that night, Dakota told me he had gone to see one of his grade school teachers, "Miss Jocelyn." She was retired and collecting SSI. He had kept in touch with her over the years, and she had let him stay the night, but he didn't know if he would be able to stay much longer. He told me he'd borrowed $7 from her and now only needed $3 to pay the man back.

When I asked him how he was going to get Roy his money, he said, "I'm going to find a way. Since I've been incarcerated, I'm in control now. I have to be out here. When Cujo does the dirt, I have to suffer. It's not going to be like that anymore."

Dakota decided to go to Covenant House to see if Tamara could lend him the money. We rode the subway down to the Port Authority. It was midday, but the car was crowded. An elderly woman got on and grabbed at the metal pole for balance, her left hand gripped tightly around the top of a cane. Without hesitation, Dakota stood up, tapped her on the shoulder and guided her with his arm to his seat. Another woman sitting nearby smiled. Dakota smiled back.

Twenty minutes later, we arrived at the bus terminal. As

we walked up the block to Covenant House, Tamara appeared walking toward us. She was wearing a thin nylon jacket, bedroom slippers, and a kerchief. When she saw Dakota, she grabbed him and hugged him.

But Tamara had no money, and after a few minutes she went back inside. As Dakota and I walked back toward the subway, he told me that Tamara had suggested that he try to find someone who would give him copies of a Con Ed bill, telephone bill, and lease, as well as a letter that stated that Dakota was paying a couple of hundred dollars to live in his or her apartment. The welfare office, he said, would send a check to the person whose name was on the lease, "I can strike a deal and give that person some money and keep the rest, even if I'm not staying there," Dakota said. "She can't cash the check without me. We both have to sign it."

There was a long silence. Although he didn't ask, I got the impression that Dakota was suggesting that I provide him with this documentation. When I didn't offer, he seemed annoyed. Dakota owed Roy $10, Miss Jocelyn $7; he still had to get $3 to get his things out of the man's apartment, and he'd borrowed two tokens from someone else he knew on the street. He said he also needed $15 to get a copy of his birth certificate. He was collecting debts, and he needed money to keep him off the street.

"The old days are done," he told me. "In the past you could stay at someone's place for a couple of days and there was no problem. Nowadays, everyone wants some money. I understand that nobody wants to go to work and pay rent while I sit at home and watch television all day, but it ain't easy out here. They want so much stuff when you apply for a job. You need all your ID. If you get your wallet taken, you've got to start all over again."

The more Dakota talked, the more frustrated he became.

"It's corny out here," he said angrily. "Every time I try, I get fucked in the ass. When I was in jail, I was reading, exercising. I had some composure to myself. I'm not looking right, I'm not feeling right no more. I should stay in fuckin' jail."

We walked quietly for a few minutes. Suddenly Dakota relaxed. "The more I try to be good, the more it backfires," he said. "I get to the point sometimes I want to be with my mom—chillin'. I doubt that she's going through anything like this." He was quiet again. "You can make a dream come true if you want it enough." He looked at me. "Not out here, though. Not out here."

. . . .

A WEEK LATER we went to see Cedric. It was mid-morning, and Dakota, using Cedric's name, walked into the Bedford Atlantic shelter as if it was his home.

Outside the shelter, dozens of men were hanging out. One man, tall and bony with sunken cheeks, stood by the door. When he grinned, he showed off gapped and rotting teeth. Another man had one arm cut off above the elbow, the skin of the stump shriveled together like a sausage. A third man smelled so bad that people quickly covered their noses and mouths when he walked by. One man stood in a corner shooting dice.

Ten minutes later, Dakota was back outside. "You have to be really desperate to come here," Dakota said. "I'd rather sleep in an abandoned building or on the street than here." Dakota recognized some of the men. A couple of them had been transferred from Wards Island. They told Dakota that Cedric had been in earlier. He was expected back again around lunchtime.

We left and walked around the neighborhood. An hour

later, Dakota went in again. When he came out five minutes later, he was with Cedric. Both were smiling. Cedric looked as though he'd lost about twenty-five pounds, but he was still big. "I don't eat much here," he told me. "Crackheads go running for the food."

Dakota and Cedric stood side by side smiling.

"I heard you were in jail," Cedric said. "At first I didn't believe it, but then I saw Tamara, and I said, 'No way!'"

"When I called back at Wards Island and asked for my stuff, they said they got rid of everything. Everything. The whole locker."

Dakota and Cedric kept looking at each other and laughing.

"So, where should we go?" Dakota asked.

"I don't know."

"We can't go to Wards Island. If I get caught even on the island, I go back to jail," Dakota said. They both started laughing. "You know what I'm saying."

"They found a semiautomatic, fully loaded, here," Cedric said. He hadn't seen the gun, but rumors spread quickly through the shelter. "They stole all my socks. I have only one pair of drawers."

Cedric jumped from one subject to another. He talked about the crackheads in the shelter, the girls he was trying to date who lived in the neighborhood, and boasted about the ways he managed to beat the system. He was scattered and distracted. "They were giving me tokens here," Cedric said. "I was playing them. Every day I was getting tokens, for, like, four days straight. My counselor came to me and was, like, 'Are you going to your appointments?' I was, like, 'Yeah.' She was, like, 'I want some proof.' I was forging late passes. I was coming in at four in the morning. They tried to kick me out one time."

Cedric laughed as he talked to Dakota, but he seemed angrier, tougher than the last time I had seen him more than two months earlier. All of his gentleness and shyness seemed to have disappeared. He didn't seem to care about anything. Only when he talked about the death of rap star Biggie Smalls did he show emotion. "My man Biggie is dead," he said loudly, as if realizing it for the first time. "They had his funeral down the block. All down St. James Street. Wow." Cedric pointed ahead.

Twenty-four-year-old Christopher Wallace, also known to the music world as Notorious B.I.G./Biggie Smalls, had been shot dead as he sat in a car in Los Angeles. In the Crown Heights section of Brooklyn, Cedric stood along with several generations of fans who gathered on brownstone stoops across from a makeshift memorial decorated with candles, CDs, and photos of the star as a motorcade carrying Wallace's body rode through the Brooklyn neighborhood where he grew up. For many people, Wallace remained a hero, symbolizing what was possible. In his short life, he'd gone from being a shy overweight kid to a small-time crack dealer to a renowned money-making rap artist.

Cedric was quiet for a moment and seemed genuinely upset by his death. "He was my man," Cedric said, nodding his head.

Dakota placed his hand on Cedric's arm. Then he changed the subject. "Where do you go every day?" asked Dakota.

"I go over there," he said, pointing up the street. "And I go over there," pointing in another direction. "And chill. I come back at dinnertime, and then I bounce back out and come back."

Dakota looked concerned. "Why don't you come to the Bronx with me and check it out? You don't have to worry about anything because I have connections."

"These are my people out here. This is where I chill out." Cedric didn't seem to consider the offer.

They decided to go to the Port Authority to hang out like old times. The next day Dakota told me they'd had a good time, but Cedric had changed, and it disturbed him.

••••

DAKOTA ARRIVED at the courthouse at 9:30 in the morning. We sat in the back of the courtroom and waited for his case to be called.

Dakota said he'd been thinking a lot about Cedric. "I've seen the change," he said. "I don't really like it. We were walking from Covenant House and went to see my sister. A Covenant House staff person walks by, he gives me a dirty look. I looked back, but did nothing. Cedric sees this and says, 'What the hell's your problem? I'll fuck you up.' I said, 'Just leave it alone, Cedric.' This is not the Cedric I know. I used to be the one who got angry all the time. He hasn't been out here long enough to know that situations out here can get you hurt. He's listening to guys in Brooklyn talking like that. He just kept saying 'I'm going to fuck you up.' He's violent now. Everything is this homeboy, that homeboy. He said he had all these homeboys. They hang on the corner. All they do all day is smoke weed. I asked him, 'What you be doing with your time?' He says, 'I be chillin' with my homeboys, smoke, and get high.' I know he's smoked weed but not every day. He says now it's an everyday thing. They hop trains to Forty-second Street. He's been making $10 every once in a while doing [police] lineups, and then they hop the train back. He says he makes money other places, too. I ask him how, he just says, 'I make money. I'm not going to tell you how. I just make money.' I hope he's not doing anything stupid."

Sitting in the courtroom now, Dakota seemed exhausted. He told me he was still staying at Miss Jocelyn's house, but that he hadn't slept well the night before from worrying about his case. He also had to borrow $3 from the building's superintendent for the round-trip train fare.

Yet another debt he had to pay back. He told me he'd done some odd jobs in the building and had paid off his other debts, and that he was hopeful that a job he'd heard about working in a Jamaican restaurant would come through. He also told me that a guy from the neighborhood had offered him work. He would have had to transport seven or eight packs (one hundred bottles per pack) of crack from 208th Street to 166th Street by cab. "The job is worth $700, but the guy said, 'I'll give you $300. I know you owe people.' I thought about it for a minute. But I can't go back to dealing. They're offering too much time if you get caught. Nobody's doing anything for us. All they do is build jails."

From 1973 to 2000, the New York State prison population swelled from 13,000 to 70,000. In 1999, the state spent $275 million more to run prisons than to pay for higher education. Each inmate cost taxpayers about $31,000—enough to pay tuition fees that year for nine students at a state university or at the City University of New York.

New York's 1973 Rockefeller drug laws were largely responsible for the inmate population explosion. Under these laws, a first-time offender convicted of selling two ounces or possessing four ounces of cocaine or heroin in New York received a mandatory sentence of fifteen years to life. By contrast, in 1992, Joel Steinberg received a sentence of eight to twenty-five years for the killing of his six-year-old adopted daughter Lisa.

Poor people of color were hit hardest by the strict drug laws. More than 90 percent of inmates doing time in New

York state prisons for a drug offense were black or Hispanic, even though studies showed that lifetime illicit drug use rates were highest among whites. Drug selling among middle- and upper-class white people usually took place behind closed doors, making it more difficult for officers to buy undercover and make arrests.

The consequences were dire: Every year since 1989, more African-Americans entered prison for drug offenses than graduated from State University of New York; in 1997 almost twice as many Hispanics were locked up for drug offenses as had graduated from the state university system that year. Many of the people swept up by the drug laws were nonviolent and addicted.

The dramatic increase in drug arrests had eliminated generations of black and Hispanic parents. And the children suffered the consequences. Tens of thousands of children of color had a parent in prison, often hundreds of miles away. Many were being raised by grandparents, or more often, the foster care system. Statistics showed that children whose parents were locked away in prison were more likely to be jailed themselves than children whose parents were not incarcerated. According to the Women's Prison Association, a child with an incarcerated parent was five times more likely to be jailed than a child who grew up with parents who managed to stay out of jail.

That morning as defendants appeared before the judge, Dakota and I sat in the back of the courtroom. Nearly all were being brought up on drug charges. Nearly all were black and Hispanic. Many of the cases were plea-bargained: One man was offered ninety days for a plea of guilty to criminal sale of heroin; another woman was offered a plea of sixty days for the same crime.

By mid-afternoon, Dakota was called before the judge.

With his hands clasped behind his back, he stood by his lawyer. A prosecutor stood at a table to his right. After rummaging through a stack of files, the prosecutor offered Dakota a deal: The charge would be dropped from a felony to a misdemeanor, with a sentence of sixty days. With time served, Dakota would be out in fifteen days if he agreed. If indicted and convicted of the second-degree felony assault charge, he would have to serve a minimum of one and one-half to three years, a maximum of three and one-third to seven years.

Dakota's lawyer advised him to seriously consider the offer.

A few minutes passed.

"Your honor, my client declines the offer," the lawyer said.

The new date for the arraignment was set for three weeks later, on April 14.

"I'm not pleading guilty to something I didn't do," said Dakota.

. . . .

THREE WEEKS LATER, Dakota went back to court. "I'm wasting my time," he said to me. "I didn't want to come. In their eyes, I'm guilty until I can be proven innocent. It's just his word. He stabbed me and fuck what I have to say."

I hadn't seen Dakota since his last court date. He told me he had gotten the job at the Jamaican restaurant in the Bronx, but that it didn't work out. "One day, the manager was leaving and said, 'I'm going to leave you and the other kid in the store. There's going to be a few guys coming in, and they'll ask you for some coke, and you send them to the back.' I told him I didn't want any part of that. He said, 'If you can't do that, then you ain't working here.' The next day the boss said,

'You're fired.'" Dakota said he worked three nights and made $42. He tried to budget the money, but after two and a half days, it was all gone. He had spent $22 on a haircut and tip, some on food, and some on ice cream for his kids.

He had two other job prospects that he was hoping would work out: one was a supermarket clerk and the other a managerial position. "There was an ad in the paper," he told me. "It said they need sixty people, and they'll train you. It just said training for management. If I pass, I'll go to wherever they need managers. I think I have to take a test or something."

Dakota looked exhausted. He said that Miss Jocelyn had asked him to leave because he hadn't found work. She felt he hadn't even been trying. During the past week, he slept only a few hours at a time and hardly ate at all. A few nights he had hopped the number 5 subway line and rode it all night. Other nights he walked around until daylight, then went to a park to nap. Sometimes he sneaked into the entranceway of a building and slept behind the stairs. For the past two days, he had been sleeping at the house of a fifteen-year-old boy he met playing basketball one night. Dakota fell on the court and cut his leg, and the boy, who lived nearby, took him home to get him a bandage. When Dakota told the boy about his situation, the boy said he could sleep on his couch after his mother, who worked a four-to-midnight shift, left for work in the afternoon. The boy let Dakota in after school, and Dakota slept on the couch, leaving before the boy's mother came home.

"Where's my lawyer?" Dakota asked. It was 10:15. His lawyer hadn't shown up to court, and Dakota was angry. "If my lawyer doesn't do what he's supposed to, he's going to have problems. I'm going to have people see him. He's doing nothing. He wanted me to cop out for something I didn't do.

So he can get paid. Forget about it."

Now wide awake, Dakota was starting to lose patience. "This is three months now, I've been going to court on some bullshit offense," he said. "This is the second time I'm coming into court. I'm thinking about leaving New York and going back down South. There ain't nothing to do here but stay in trouble. Here, you can't breathe without going to jail."

The bailiff looked back at Dakota.

"I'm waiting for the summer," Dakota said, now whispering. "I know good things will come in the summer. I've been doing real good all year, and it's not getting me nowhere. I need a little help. Every time I turn around, I'm back to square one. Everyone says, 'You're doing good. Stay out of trouble. Stay out of the game,' but I'm in more trouble now. I don't eat. I don't sleep. This is not me. I can do better." He stopped for a moment. "In order for me to do better, I have to do things I don't want to. If I don't have it together by summer, I'm flying with my brother for a while. I don't have a choice." Dakota had told me his brother dealt drugs in Baltimore.

The courtroom started to fill up. Dakota turned his head to look at the time. "My lawyer told me to come at nine so that he could come at 10:50!" He was angry. "I could have come at 10:50. Next time, I'll get here when I get here."

Ten minutes later, his lawyer arrived. Minutes after, Dakota's name was called. He took off his hat and once again stood before the judge, his hands clasped behind his back, his head bowed down. He'd grown a slight mustache and a small goatee on his chin.

The plea bargain was offered again. This time Dakota accepted it. He was tired of coming back to court and had no faith in the system. He pleaded guilty to a misdemeanor with time served and had ninety days to pay a fine of $100.

....

VERY LITTLE CHANGED in Dakota's life over the next six weeks following his sentencing. During the day, he walked the streets of the Bronx and sat in a nearby park, where he spent time watching people play dice, basketball, handball. He talked to girls on their way home from school and with people he knew from his old neighborhood. "I sit with the kids, away from the drug dealers so the police wouldn't bother me," he said. Dakota no longer went to Manhattan.

He had stopped sleeping at his basketball friend's apartment, mostly because he didn't want the boy's mother to find out. He said he knew a woman, a crack addict, who would let him stay in her apartment for $10 a night, and another man who would let him stay on his couch for $3 a night, but he didn't even have enough money for a subway token. So he often wandered around in the evening, hoping to stumble on some place to spend the night. He met a building superintendent who let him sleep on the roof a few nights and a token booth clerk who occasionally let him hop the subway. One of those nights on the train, a man put a knife to Dakota's throat, taking the $10 he had earned packing bags in a grocery store a few days earlier. Mornings, he went to the Tremont stop on the D train and flirted with the high school girls on their way to school. Some of them giggled and flirted back.

He was often hungry but managed to eat every few days. Sometimes his basketball friend brought him food; other times, he went to a McDonald's where he knew the manager. On those nights, Dakota would walk into the restaurant and act surprised when he saw his friend working. His friend would tell him to wait outside, and he would bring Dakota a cheeseburger or french fries in a brown paper bag saying,

"Give this to your aunt for me."

"I don't abuse the privilege though," Dakota told me. "I just pass by once in awhile."

His chest pains continued and were sharp, "like lightning," coming more often and with pain in his back, but he still refused to go to the hospital.

He also told me he had been arrested again, but his story made little sense. He ran into a truck driver he knew at Hunts Point Market. The man told Dakota he needed someone to help him unload his truck for a couple of days. Dakota agreed. They drove from the Bronx to Staten Island one day and then out of the city. "It was Peekskill or something," Dakota said. "There were deers and shit." After two days, they drove back to the Bronx. The man told Dakota to meet him in Westchester, where he would pay him $75 for two days of work. Dakota borrowed the money for the bus and train fare to Westchester, but when he arrived, the man told Dakota he would have to wait for his money. The man left to use the phone. He came back ten minutes later, accompanied by a police officer, who told Dakota to put his hands up. The man had told the officer that Dakota said he would kill him if he didn't give him his money. Dakota said he had worked for the man for two days. The man said he hadn't. Dakota told me he'd spent fifty-six hours in a holding cell in Westchester until the man dropped the charges.

Dakota wasn't angry at the man, but seemed disappointed in himself. "The more I try, the more I get knocked out," he said. "I didn't ask for assistance from anyone. The only thing I can do is blame myself. Usually I'm with someone that causes me to get down and mess up. But I'm blaming me now."

I met Dakota in the Bronx every couple of weeks. "I'm doing all right," he told me one day. He looked thin, tired. "I'm breathing. I know I can function better in the Bronx as far as survival. Because you have places you can go to. There are buildings where the doors open downstairs. You can get some rest. See, in Manhattan it's different. You have guards at the door, and if you go to Harlem, you ain't getting there without the police harassing you. Here it's quiet, and you're OK if you know what you're doing. If I'm far away and I have a long way to go and I'm tired, I'll chill in the park. I'll get a little energy and start walking again."

Dakota spent a lot of time by himself, and he often seemed depressed. At least in the Bronx, he felt less isolated. "I know people out here," he said. "Sometimes people, they'll come and hang out outside all night. They'll tell me they ain't got nothing to do because they know I'm on the street. Even if I don't have a place to stay, at least I won't be so lonely here."

····

ONE APRIL AFTERNOON, Dakota called to tell me he had finally met the young boy's mother whose couch he had been sleeping on. He said she agreed to let him stay. She told Dakota that her son had spoken a lot about him and that she thought Dakota was a good influence on him. When she found out Dakota was homeless, she told him that he could sleep over once in awhile. "Then one morning I woke up and just couldn't move," Dakota said. "Everything just tightened up. I was in agony and thought I was going to die. I had pain in my arm, pain in my chest and my leg. I could only move my eyes from one side to another. The lady freaked out and said I could stay as long as I needed." He sounded relieved to have a place to stay. "You never know when she could change her mind," he said. "I'm not getting my hopes up too much because I always get disappointed. She's putting me on probation, and I'm putting her on probation."

Dakota also said he had gotten a full-time job in a super-market that paid $250 a week to unpack boxes of goods unloaded from the delivery trucks. He was supposed to start the job in a couple of days. Said Dakota before he hung up: "Things are finally starting to look up."

. . . .

A FEW DAYS LATER, Dakota was in trouble again. He'd lost the supermarket job. The job was lifting boxes and he'd worked three days. But when the manager learned he was getting pains in his chest, he told Dakota he didn't want Dakota dying on him and told him to leave.

But there was more. "I got into a situation, and I feel kind of stupid," he said. "A friend of mine was outside yes-terday working, and he asked me to keep an eye on some-thing that he had, and all of a sudden, due to the fact that I went upstairs, I forgot. He comes to my door, and I have to leave now. He kicked the door last night and yelled in the hall-way, threw bottles in the hallway. The lady said she's not going to have this problem in the house and that I had to leave."

I asked Dakota what was in the package. He was quiet, then said, "It was a bag of crack. I left it outside. I forgot about it. He's not paying me to keep an eye on it. He made it seem like it was going to destroy him. Only $5 worth was missing. I think he was playing me. He was breaking bottles and shit. That ain't cool. All he kept saying was he wants his money. The lady said, 'I don't want to know what's going on, but you have to straighten this out, or you got to leave.' I'm packing now. So I'm going to be back to square one again."

I didn't say anything.

Then Dakota said, "I was calling because I know you're not supposed to give me money, but I was praying that maybe instead of a sandwich or something you could, maybe. I spoke to my sister, and she said, 'Can't you ask Alexia?' and I said I would."

I said I wouldn't.

"I have an ultimatum. If I don't give it to him, then I get shot. If I don't get it, then I leave. If I get it, it clears everything, he gets his, and I can stay. I don't need to be leaving from where I'm at because I just got here. The lady I'm staying with was, like, 'Sweetheart, I hope you can get him his $5, otherwise when I come back, you have to leave. I'm sorry.'"

I mentioned that this was a pattern.

"This is nothing compared to last time. That last time was worse. But this guy is younger, and he doesn't want to hear nothing. He hears what he wants to hear."

When I refused again, he said he understood. I hoped his story had been a way to make some pocket money. I hoped that he was lying.

. . . .

DAKOTA often expected me to bail him out of trouble, and when I didn't, he got angry and disappointed. Once, when he had no place to stay, I offered to accompany him to the office of the Coalition for the Homeless to see what they could do for him, but he refused, wanting nothing to do with the shelter system. Another time, when I suggested that I help him get on public assistance, he said he still hadn't replaced his birth certificate and needed to do that first. When he called to tell me he hadn't eaten for days, I told him about churches in Manhattan that supplied food to the homeless, but his response was, "People don't understand. I'm in the Bronx. We don't have those things here. I can't keep walking to Manhattan." When I said I would find him a church in the

Bronx where he could get food, he got angrier. Every time I offered to take him to the hospital to take care of his chest pains, he refused. We were getting nowhere. He wanted more than I was giving, and most of the time he wanted cash.

When we eventually got together again at the end of May, Dakota seemed happy to see me. We went to the West Side piers near Forty-second Street, where he and Cedric used to hang out, and sat on the cement, several feet from the water's edge because he was too nervous to move closer. "I like water, but I can't swim," he said. "The only time I would jump in is if one of my kids fell in. I would still have to hesitate a minute."

We sat and talked for a few hours. All of a sudden he said, "I need to get married and settle down. I'm getting married soon." Dakota had never before even mentioned a girlfriend. "I've got to get married. Basically, I figure it would chill me out. I wouldn't be so frustrated at life. Maybe I'll get doing what I'm supposed to do. Right now, I have no responsibilities. I just have to worry about me. I have to worry about getting me together. I think if I'm in a relationship, I'll have someone on my back twenty-four-seven. Every time I get with a female, I do so good. I do everything I'm supposed to. I always get a place to stay, and as soon as me and her break up—boom—I don't give a fuck about anything. I let her keep the apartment and the clothes."

Homelessness had cut him off from women, and it had eaten away at his self-esteem. "When I was young, I met women all the time," he said. "Now they don't pay me no mind. The only person so far that's interested in me is a thirteen-year-old." The thirteen-year-old lived in the neighborhood where he was staying. He had given her his wallet to hold because he felt it was safe with her. The only thing he carried was a picture ID in case he got stopped by the police. "She keeps saying, 'I'm her man,'" he told me. "She talks to me about her problems. I tell her she's too young for me and that her parents can have me locked up for the rest of my life. She says, 'I won't let them do that.' But that's jail time. I ain't going near that."

More than anything, Dakota was lonely. Although he told me that he had always been a loner, he was tired of being by himself. "I'm at the point I need someone in my life. Someone to talk to. Everywhere I go, I'm going by myself. If I hang out, I'm by myself. Just knowing that you have somebody there and not being so much by yourself makes a difference. It's just lonely. I've been lonely since me and my kids' mom broke up three years ago. That's a long time. I'm getting tired of being lonely. I don't want it no more."

Dakota yawned a few times. He seemed more weary than I had ever seen him. He lay back on the concrete, his face in the sun, his eyes closed. For the next fifteen minutes, he said nothing. He suddenly looked peaceful, rested. When he sat up, he stretched his arms toward the sky, his knees bent up towards his chest. "I know I'm going to make it," he said. "I don't care if I never get another job. I'm going to make it as far as surviving out here. I'm going to succeed at it, regardless of whether I continue to be homeless the rest of my life. If that's the case, so be it. If that's what the Lord has in store for me, then that's what I'll be, homeless, but I'll be a good homeless person. I'll stay clean. You can live in the street and stay clean. Just because you're homeless doesn't mean that you've got to look it."

Dakota stood up and stretched his legs. He looked out towards the water and then inched closer to the edge of the pier, his back towards me. He stood quietly watching the motor boats and yachts glide across the river. Then he turned around and walked back to where I was sitting. He sat on the concrete beside me and said nothing for the next few minutes.

"I want to do more than what I'm doing," he said, breaking the silence. "To me, it seems like it's just not time yet.

Everybody has a certain amount of time before everything just crumbles in their life. My foundation is starting to crack, but it ain't shattered yet. You've got to work on the foundation more before you can put the building down. Before I do something, I have to make sure my feet is planted straight and that I'm stable. I know I'm capable of doing more than what I'm doing.

"But I'd rather choose to be homeless than sell another crack vial. Right now, those are the choices. Right now there ain't no other options. You either sell drugs or, if you get a job, they want to pay you below minimum wages and treat you like shit. I didn't have time for all of that. There are jobs out there, but if someone hears he's on the street, they think, 'Let's throw him right down here.'" He pointed to the ground. "I may have qualifications but they don't even give me a try. They just say, 'Fuck him.' I'm not trying to be choosy about a job. Whatever I don't know, I'll learn as time goes on. I just want to be respected."

He mentioned marriage again, and I asked him if he was serious. "I ain't trying to get married no time soon. But I am going to get a relationship—hopefully soon. I be praying about it every day. The problem is that I don't trust God too much. I've been let down too may times. I got to depend on me as an individual not God."

••••

THE NEXT DAY Dakota paged me at five in the evening. "I'm stranded. Can you meet me at the Port Authority at eight." I couldn't. The phones at the Port Authority didn't accept incoming calls so I had no way to tell him. He paged me again at eight and then five more times that night. At eleven p.m. he left me a message asking if I could meet him at the Tremont stop on the D line the next day.

The next morning he called me, and we spoke. "I had to

walk back to the Bronx last night, almost two hours," he said. He sounded annoyed. He was quiet a moment, then asked if I could meet him in a couple of hours at eleven. I told him that I couldn't meet him until the next day.

'   Later in the afternoon, he called again and left a message on my answering machine: "This is Dakota. You don't have to meet me tomorrow. It seems I've been calling and there seems to be a little problem with getting in contact with you and me meeting you, so I'm not going to bother you no more. I'm not going to call you no more. Basically, I see how things are, and I'm not going to call. I'm not going to beep you. I'm just going to chill, and I'll see you when I see you. All right. Thanks. Like I say, thanks for meeting me at Forty-second Street last night. Good thing I didn't pass out or nothing. I was really fucked up and in pain—" The machine cut him off.

To Dakota, I had become no different from everyone else he had grown attached to and who had left him in the lurch. All that mattered was that he felt abandoned and betrayed.

····

THE NEXT MORNING, I had a message on my beeper: "Could you meet me at the Bronx courthouse? I've been arrested."

I wasn't able to make it to the courthouse until late in the afternoon, and by then there was no sign of Dakota. I didn't hear from him again until he was released from jail, seven days later. According to Dakota he was set up: "The lady gave me $5 to go to the store. This guy was leaving the scene on a bike. I came up to the building. I knew him, and I said, 'What's up?' He had just made a sale. As he biked away, the police were watching. I was walking with Tamara, and they came up from behind me and handcuffed me. They put me inside the van and said I was dealing. They handcuffed me and said, 'Our man got away, so since he got away, I'm taking you in. I need a collar. It's almost time to go home. You're my collar.' I said, 'Fuck you,' and he hit me, smacked me in the face with a black glove. I was sitting down, and I started laughing. He asked me if I thought it was funny. I said, 'In a way. I didn't do nothing.' He slapped me again."

Dakota told me the charge was "observing," and he was released after five days. In jail, the doctor told him he had asthma. "This wouldn't have happened if you had met me," he said.

"I'm responsible for your getting arrested?" I asked. More than a week had passed since he had asked me to meet him at the Port.

He didn't say anything for a minute. Finally, he said, "I was stranded and had to walk two hours to get to the Bronx."

．．．．

WE MET AGAIN at the courthouse almost two weeks later. At nine in the morning, a warm June day, a long line snaked around the Bronx Criminal Courthouse. Dakota and I waited alongside mothers and grandmothers with small children and men of all ages to pass through the entrance. Nearly everyone was black or Hispanic. Once inside, we took off our belts and emptied our pockets. We passed through metal detectors and went upstairs to the courtroom.

Before going in, Dakota took off his baseball cap and combed his hair back. He wore wooden beads around his neck, given to him by a Muslim inmate he had met at Rikers Island. He told me that he was Muslim now and had stopped eating pork. When I asked him what he liked about being Muslim, he said, "If you're Muslim, you don't have to go to court if you have a case on Friday, and you get special meals."

We sat in the back of the courthouse and waited. Dakota looked around the room, his eyes sweeping right and left to check the rows. He could barely sit still. Someone he knew had seen Cedric. "I heard that Cedric is wilding," he said.

I expected him to be upset by the news but he was not.

"He'll cut you now," said Dakota, nodding his head. "That's good. Niggers will stop fucking with him. There ain't nobody out there doing nothing for him."

Dakota wasn't just agitated, he was angry. "With summertime coming, I'm about to get wild again. Nobody on the block fucks with me. Every summer, everyone wants to play me. To avoid me getting hyperactive, I'm going to knock them up. I'm waiting for the first asshole to play me so that I can go to his funeral."

By 9:30, the judge still hadn't arrived. "They're holding me up," Dakota said loudly. "Why should I sit here four or five hours for a ten-second verdict?"

There were six other people in the courtroom: a black woman with a teenage boy, a Hispanic woman with two grade school girls perched silently on each side, and another woman who sat alone crying, blowing her nose every few minutes.

"I'm leaving if my lawyer don't make it here by ten. I've got to make money for my other court case. That's more important."

The judge stepped into the courtroom. She wore a two-piece navy blue pants suit. She adjusted her robe around her shoulders, fastening it in the front before she sat down.

"Oh, no. A lady judge. We're dead. They don't be having no sympathy."

The judge sat behind the podium and talked to the bailiff. Then she addressed the court. "God morning, ladies and gentlemen. There are no ready cases. I'll be back." She stood up and walked out of the courtroom. It was 9:45.

"You see why people don't go to court. They spend all day waiting around," Dakota said. His voice was loud. The bailiff shot him a look.

The courtroom gradually became more crowded. A young mother walked in dragging a small, sniffling boy. With her free hand, she smacked a younger child shuffling in behind. A stony-faced woman, her legs thick like tree trunks, walked a few steps into the room, looked around, then left. Two young black males came in next, looked around, and sat on the benches. A Hispanic man, about forty, sat on the other side. One black man in his thirties, wearing four gold rings on one hand and three earrings in one ear, sat in the back beside us and read the newspaper.

Dakota mentioned a story that had appeared in the paper about a nine-year-old girl in California who had stopped at McDonald's with her family for ice cream and was killed in a gun battle that broke out between a holdup man and an off-duty police officer waiting for food. The police had said the girl was hit by the gunman aiming at the police officer. "If you ask me, the cop shot the girl, and he also shot the guy in the head," Dakota said. "Nobody's around to deny it. If they find out it is the cop, they'll deny it. The suspect is dead, and dead men tell no tales. The cops kill people and get medals. We kill people and get an injection and the electric chair."

Dakota blamed Mayor Giuliani for much of the injustice. "It's all because of him," he said. "Giuliani don't like black people. You can't go outside. You can't breathe. Even if you're smoking a cigarette, they swear you're doing something illegal. That's how the cops are. It's racism everywhere you go. Now I'm here because a cop couldn't get his suspect. He needed a collar. Shit, man. They wonder why cops get shot by teenagers. We're tired of getting harassed with stupid things. We're starting to retaliate."

Dakota didn't remember what his current lawyer looked like. He told me he'd seen him for ten seconds. As we waited, he grew angrier. In the ten months that I had known him, I had never seen him so agitated. "I'm not scared to do time," he said. "I'm going to Manhattan to start ripping people's heads off. Nobody disrespects me."

A skinny woman in her thirties with pockmarks across her face sat in front of us. She turned her head back toward Dakota and started talking. "They don't do nothing for you if you have no money," she said. She was slurring her words. "My daughter just died. I made a mistake. I needed money and sold a bottle of meth. My lawyer says I'm getting one year and a half. I'm in a methadone program. I did my time, almost eight years. He's talking like I'm a murderer." The woman became increasingly distraught. "I'm tired of doing time," she said, her eyelids drooping noticeably.

The courtroom was filled when the judge returned. The front rows, filled with older women, teenage girls, and small children, looked more like church pews than courthouse benches.

The cases were called, and often they were over in a matter of minutes. When one man was sentenced to three years, a woman cried out. Another man was sentenced to four years, and another woman sobbed, her friend trying to calm her down.

Dakota continued to talk, obsessively, to himself. "This is bullshit," he said. "Nobody's telling me about my case. Nobody's showing up. All I am is a fucking number." Dakota's voice grew louder, attracting the attention of people sitting near us. "I'm getting fucked on both sides," he said. I tried to calm him down, but he was getting increasingly impatient and started to mimic the defense lawyers who called out their clients' names in the courtroom.

One woman looked over and said, "What's wrong with him?"

Dakota ignored her. She turned back around.

"We're all sitting here looking at the judge like she's a dime," he said. "She's no dime."

At 12:15, a man called out Dakota's name. Dakota stood and met the man who told him he was his lawyer. "They've dropped it down to a misdemeanor," the lawyer said. "They said they saw you selling. They found drugs on you and are willing to give you thirty days. If it goes to trial, you could get one year."

Dakota was angry. "They're lying. There were no drugs on me."

"They said they found drugs on you. It's dependent upon how credible the police officer's testimony is."

"How long do I have to wait here?"

"Maybe until four. That's when court ends."

"I ain't doing that. This is costing me. You're telling me I have to wait three hours? I'm tired of sitting here. You're telling me this cornball story. You get my case today."

"I'm going to tell them to rush this. Not for your sake, but for theirs." The lawyer was angry. He stood up abruptly and left.

"He's trying to railroad me," Dakota said.

A few minutes later, Dakota was called before the judge. He pleaded guilty to a misdemeanor. All felony charges were dismissed, and he was sentenced to time served and had a month to pay $90.

Dakota walked away fuming. For the first time, I understood what Cedric was talking about when he said he had seen Cujo. Dakota was ranting to himself. Nothing seemed to calm him down. "They ain't getting $90 from me," he said. "The cop set me up. He went into my back pocket and wallet and said the $5 on me was for a drug sale. They are getting no $90 from me, those cocksuckers." Dakota started mumbling. Then he got loud. As we walked out of the courthouse, he was almost yelling. "I got framed for selling. I might as well do it. They want me to turn around and kiss ass, and that's one thing I won't do." Dakota started mumbling again. He spat the word "cocksuckers" over and over again as if it was the only phrase he knew. He walked down the street, oblivious to everyone around him. He kept on ranting even when a police officer near the courthouse started watching him. Then for a minute he stood still. "They're trying to play me like I'm a fruit loop!" He seemed ready to explode.

I told him I was going downtown.

He didn't seem to hear me. He kept walking, then turned around and stopped in the middle of the sidewalk. He looked up and down the street, trying to figure out what to do, where to go. Finally, he swung his arm through the air and said, "Fuck! I'm not coming back here." And he walked away.

. . . .

OVER THE SUMMER of 1997, Dakota called less frequently. He told me that the lady he lived with had gotten him a job filing in her office and that he was getting $160 every two weeks for a five-hour workday. He couldn't explain to me what type of office she worked in, but he thought it might be a travel agency. When I asked if I could meet the woman and visit him at work, he told me her boyfriend was involved in some "shady" dealings and was worried he would lose his apartment by bringing me around to ask "nosy" questions. As with many of Dakota's stories, I never knew the truth about his living situation or whether, in fact, he was working. When I called and left messages with the man who answered the phone, I wouldn't hear back from Dakota. When we met, he told me that the man, the woman's boyfriend, didn't like him and never gave him his messages. Plus, he said he was busy with his job, his friends, and a girl he had met.

When we spoke again in early August, Dakota seemed to be looking forward to getting together. We arranged to meet in the subway at the Tremont Avenue stop in the Bronx. I arrived at noon, but by one o'clock, Dakota still hadn't shown up. It was very unusual. In recent months, he had sometimes been late to meet me, but never by as much as an hour. And he had never stood me up. That day, I waited ninety minutes. When I got home, I called Dakota.

"Damn," he said. "I went to get my haircut on the way to meeting you, and I got held up. I thought maybe you'd still be there. I was hoping, but when I got there you must have just left." He seemed sorry and disappointed. "I didn't realize how late it was."

We arranged to meet two days later. Same time and place. Again, I waited. Again he didn't show up. When I called him later in the day, he said he'd forgotten. It had been his day off, and he didn't remember until late in the afternoon.

"Look, Dakota," I said. "If you don't want to meet me, that's perfectly fine."

"No, it's not that," he said. "I just got caught up in some things here. To tell you the truth, there's this girl I'm sort of seeing, and it's been distracting me. I swear I really forgot. I swear. When can we do it again? Whenever you want. I swear I'll be there."

"It's no big deal if you don't want to."

"I'll be there."

We agreed to meet the next day. Once again, he didn't show up.

Again, I called the apartment where he was staying, and no one answered the phone for the next week. When I finally got the man I'd spoken to before, I left a message for Dakota, asking him to call me. I left a few more over the next couple of months. In October, I asked the man who answered the phone if Dakota still lived there. He yelled at me, telling me that I "had no right asking about other people's business." Before he hung up, he told me never to call there again.

EPILOGUE

Every day in New York City:

- At least 168 babies are born into poor families.
- 32 babies are born to teen parents.
- Over 8,500 children are homeless and living in shelters.
- 147 children are reported as being abused and neglected.
- More than half of all elementary and middle school students are reading below grade level.

And every four days:

- a young person under 19 is murdered.

(*Keeping Track of New York City's Children: A Citizens' Committee for Children Status Report 2000*).

■ ■ ■ ■

OUR CHILDREN are facing serious and urgent problems. And they're not getting the help they need.

Not just in New York City but in communities across the country, children need better housing, less-crowded schools, and health care. Their parents need affordable child care and access to employment opportunities that will provide them with a livable wage. Kids who end up on the street need programs that provide them with counseling, drug rehabilitation, education, and job training. If incarcerated, they need opportunities that will help them to turn their lives around. All children deserve space, respect, and opportunities to develop into creative, nurturing adults. When they are denied these necessities, they must work hard not to become society's outcasts.

But there are no simple answers.

The kids I came to know over the past few years were courageous and resilient. On the street, they endured relentless physical discomfort and pain as well as emotional abuse and humiliation. They slept on sidewalks, on flattened cardboard boxes, and in subway cars and stations; they salvaged Chinese food, soda, and T-shirts from Dumpsters; they had sex when they needed drugs or food. They were sometimes feared, but more often they were dismissed and ignored. They had been betrayed repeatedly, yet when I saw them treated with dignity and respect, they were still willing to love and to trust.

The stories I have presented here are necessarily incomplete. I do not know where these young people will be a year from now. I can only tell you what happened next.

STEPHANIE AND FRAGGLE

Stephanie lasted a few months in Ohio, Fraggle not much longer in Virginia.

When Stephanie arrived in Cleveland in November 1996, she moved into a friend's apartment. Three days later, she finished the methadone she had brought with her from New York and began smoking marijuana, taking Valium and Ecstasy. After two weeks, most of it spent using drugs, she was asked to leave.

Over the next four months, Stephanie moved from one friend's couch to another. She was constantly exhausted, with sharp pains in her abdomen, throbbing joints, a rash on both legs. Her blood tests came back positive for hepatitis B and C. She also learned she had pelvic inflammatory disease. Stephanie was overwhelmed. During the day, she watched cartoons. At night, she had nightmares about her days on the street. "I've made such a mess of my life," she told me one day in Ohio. She did not have the energy to clean it up.

During this time, Stephanie also began to binge eat. She'd eat a box of cereal, throw up, eat twenty cookies, throw up, eat three donuts, then, feeling ugly and fat, she'd stop eating. A day or two later, hungry, she'd eat again, starting with cereal, and be unable to stop. She also started taking laxatives.

Over time, people got tired of Stephanie. Although her friends took drugs, they worked to support themselves. Eventually, they stopped lending her money and offering her a place to sleep. With no place to turn, Stephanie became a drunk, hanging out at a local bar. Lonely and depressed, she missed Fraggle and spoke to him regularly on the phone. As usual, they fought, broke up, and made plans to get together. In March 1997, Stephanie left Cleveland to join Fraggle.

When Fraggle left New York in November, he knew he would not be welcomed in his mother's home. But he called her from the bus station when he arrived in Virginia, hoping that she had changed her mind. She hadn't.

Fraggle called his father, Frank, who drove from Tennessee to pick him up. Fraggle stayed with Frank's girlfriend, who lived next door. He filled out a few job applications in restaurants, department stores, and movie theaters, but had no luck. He felt he couldn't relate to any of the "rednecks" in Tennessee, and he was bored. After about three weeks, Fraggle left to live with a friend in Virginia. For a week, he watched his friends shoot heroin, then started shooting up himself.

A week before Christmas, Fraggle was caught shoplifting CDs at a local mall. He was also charged with providing false information to the court and served almost two months in jail. When he was released, one of his friends found him a job stripping at a local club where he made $300 to $600 a week. Fraggle moved in with a female stripper he met and began "shooting drugs like mad"—about three to four bags of heroin and half a gram of coke a day. He was eventually fired because he almost overdosed in the dressing room one night.

In March 1997, when Stephanie went to meet Fraggle in Virginia, Fraggle left his new girlfriend and decided to kick his heroin habit. For a few days, Stephanie and Fraggle stayed with friends. Soon, they were homeless again, sleeping outdoors in a local park. A couple of weeks later, they hitchhiked to New Orleans.

When Stephanie and Fraggle arrived in New Orleans, they headed for the French Quarter. That evening, they ran into Dawn and a few hours later, Kim. Stephanie had known both girls from Tompkins Square Park. They had also appeared, almost a year earlier, with Stephanie on Geraldo Rivera's television show.

Kim told them they could stay in the Pink Fortress, an old, abandoned fortress-like apartment building. Many of the street kids, known as gutter punks in New Orleans, lived in squats in abandoned houses and ruined hotels near the French Quarter. About forty people lived in the three-story Pink Fortress. Some of the squatters, like Kim, had dogs, but few of the dogs were housebroken.

Stephanie and Fraggle stayed on the top floor. Each room had its own toilet—a hole in the floor that opened through to the floor below. Although some squatters lived on the second floor, sections of it were uninhabitable. Nobody lived on the first floor, which was littered with empty beer bottles and cans, dog feces, bloody socks used as tampons, and vomit. The center of the squat, once probably a courtyard garden, was now filled with broken furniture, broken bottles, and discarded food. It stank of urine.

In New Orleans, street kids got drunk. They battled over bottles, got rowdy, aggressive, and sometimes badly hurt. During Stephanie and Fraggle's first night in New Orleans, they saw one of the squatters from the Fortress beat a man by the river so badly that he needed to be hospitalized.

Over the next two months, Stephanie and Fraggle drank heavily. As usual, they frequently broke up. They had unprotected sex with one another and with others living in the squat. One minute Fraggle loved Stephanie; the next, he hated her and wouldn't allow her in their room. Stephanie said the alcohol completely changed him. He became ruthless and explosive, and they both became more violent. One time, Stephanie said, Fraggle dragged her out of bed and out of the room by her hair. Another time, Stephanie punched Fraggle and his girlfriend-of-the-moment in the face with her fist and then went after them with a wooden crutch. Still another time, Fraggle beat Stephanie so badly that, according to Stephanie, he had to be stopped by others in the squat who feared he would kill her.

Stephanie was forced to move from one room to another. Some nights she slept in Ernest's room. Ernest was in his thirties, and according to Stephanie, he was crazed and feared by those who knew him, which offered her some protection against Fraggle when he was drunk. One night, though, Stephanie woke up to find her pants pulled down to her ankles and Ernest's fingers inside of her. When she screamed, he went back to his bed. When she woke up an hour later, he was back beside Stephanie, his hands down her pants.

Eventually Stephanie simply stopped caring. She gave a man in his forties a blow job in a driveway for $50, and then another day drove with him to his house and did it again. When she had sex, either with Fraggle or with someone else, she wanted it to be violent. She wanted to be hit, forcibly held down, and hurt. She wanted to be raped. "I was so numb," she said. "I just wanted to feel something."

Stephanie began to drink even more. In the morning, she'd wake up shaking and as sick as when she was shooting heroin. She brushed her teeth with warm Colt 45 malt liquor she bought the night before, and then finished the bottle for breakfast. By lunchtime, she was out panhandling to make money for the half gallon of vodka she drank each day. Most of the time, though, she sat alone in doorways with her Australian cattle dog she'd named Girlie, who was given to her by a kid who was leaving New Orleans. "She follows me everywhere," said Stephanie of her dog. "She loves me."

In April, Stephanie started hearing voices and began to believe she was possessed. When she closed her eyes, she saw demons on the inside of her eyelids. When she did sleep, she had violent nightmares in which she tried to rip the skin off Fraggle's face. Her head hurt all the time, and she was dizzy.

By the end of April, I was speaking to Stephanie almost every day. With each phone call, she grew increasingly incoherent. One day she told me that if she could find a place for her dog, she would go into treatment. Another day she said she could never leave Girlie. She repeated herself, and what she said was random and confused. "I'm loony tunes," she told me, giggling. "I'm starting to sound like Rain Man."

On May 5, 1997, Stephanie woke up at six in the morning in Jackson Square. The night before, Fraggle's latest "girlfriend" had beaten Stephanie up and ripped off her shirt, leaving her naked from the waist up. The beating stopped only when Ernest pulled the girl away. Stephanie, miserable and hurting, had curled up in a ball wearing Ernest's cotton army shirt and gone to sleep. Now awake, her head was pounding. She was shaking and throwing up. And Girlie was gone.

Stephanie called Connie Prok. Prok's son had attended high school with Stephanie. "I can't live without my dog," she repeated. She was hysterical. Prok told her to go directly to the Drop-In Center. The center offered showers, food, and case management for street kids in New Orleans. Stephanie had been to the center before.

But the Drop-In Center opened at noon. Stephanie sat on the sidewalk shaking, her hands twitching. All she wanted was a drink of vodka. A man stopped to talk. He was a Vietnam vet and told her he'd been sober for eight months. He sat with Stephanie for awhile, trying to persuade her to stay sober until noon. After that man left, another man stopped. He was a pastor who ran a program in Florida for homeless youth. The man took her to get some food. Stephanie had toast. They sat together until noon when the pastor left and Stephanie stumbled into the Drop-In Center. She told Don Evans, the center's manager and HIV/AIDS coordinator, that she had to get into a rehab program immediately. She would be dead if she spent another day on the street. In less than an hour, Stephanie had a bed at the Bridge House, a residential drug rehabilitation program.

Two weeks after Stephanie went into rehab, Fraggle was arrested and booked with second-degree murder. The charge was later reduced to misdemeanor manslaughter. On the morning of his arrest, he was supposed to enter Bridge House himself, but when Don Evans went to pick him up, Fraggle had changed his mind. Later that night, Fraggle had gotten into a fight on the boardwalk with a thirty-six-year-old homeless man. The man was killed by a blow to the head. Fraggle was arrested and a few days later, the court assigned him a lawyer. When Fraggle's mother heard the news, she retained a private attorney to defend him.

Fraggle's lawyer told me that because of his two prior felonies, Fraggle was looking at a mandatory life sentence or a minimum of twenty to eighty years. Fraggle wanted to go to trial and plead self-defense, but the risk was great. There was a taped confession in which Fraggle admitted to having a fight with the man and hitting him in the head. Also, his prior drug offenses did not make him a credible defendant. Finally, there were no witnesses on either side. All the state had to prove was that Fraggle was responsible for the man's death. Fraggle decided to plead guilty. He was sentenced to six years in jail. "It was a gift," his lawyer told me of the sentence.

Fraggle served more than two and a half years in New Orleans Parish Prison before being transferred to a longer-term facility. He spent most of his time watching television or laying in his bunk in his cell writing letters. There was no drug counseling and no educational program at the jail. He was not allowed to receive books—"only the Bible"—I was told during one of my visits.

"I spend a lot of my time in my bunk soul-searching," said Fraggle in May 1999, two years after his arrest. "I think about all the people I've hurt emotionally and physically in the past, and how I'm going to avoid doing it further in the future. The main thing I've worked on is my temper. I don't let people get under my skin as easily as I used to. If somebody says something I don't like, I just remove myself from their presence. There are a lot of things I probably still need to change, but this is a hard environment to test characteristics in. There is a sort of code that everyone has to live by in jail that would be improper anywhere else. I've been broken down and now I'm able to rebuild myself in a way that I will be a better person when I am released. Of course, I won't be able to tell if that's true or not until that time comes."

At the end of February 2000, Fraggle was transferred to a medium-security prison. He got his high school equivalency diploma and began tutoring other inmates. Fraggle's test scores were high enough that he was awarded a $1500 state scholarship for a college correspondence course. He was scheduled for release in June 2002. When he gets out, he wants to help other kids. "I hope to one day be able to make a change in this world," he told me. "Even if it's only a tiny change, at least I will die knowing that I lived my life trying to help others enjoy theirs."

Stephanie completed thirteen months at Bridge House. During the first six months, she had flashbacks from her days on the street and nightmares regularly. Some nights she woke up screaming. At times, she thought about leaving the program, but she had no place to go. Some days, she wanted to kill herself. During her stay at Bridge House, Stephanie was diagnosed with post-traumatic stress disorder and depression, for which she was prescribed medication. She also continued her struggle with bulimia and anorexia. At one point, she went off her antidepressants, believing herself stable. Within weeks, Stephanie spiraled into a deep depression, battling regular thoughts of suicide. About four months later, still off medication, she was sitting in the bathtub shaving when she started running the razor up and down her arm, judging her veins, thinking how she would cut herself. She realized she needed help. The next day, Stephanie resumed her medication. She began to paint and write regularly to help her to understand, express, and release her emotions.

In October 1997, six months sober, Stephanie wrote in her

journal, "I guess it's just the disease fucking me up but things keep coming up about going back out. I know that wouldn't solve anything. I guess if I feel uncomfortable, that means I'm doing something different, which means I'm changing, which means I'm growing. I think it's time." Three months later she wrote, "The sad comes in overwhelming waves and the storm eases in and numbs my whole body. Was that me? Who am I anyway? Tears, pushing, fighting to get out . . . No longer sleepwalking, I can't deny who I am, that I feel I am connected. Then again the storm approaches. The sad needs to get out . . . where do I go from here?"

Months later, Stephanie received her GED and in 1999 enrolled in two classes at a local college; her test scores enabled her to bypass the mandatory freshman English class.

On May 5, 2000, Stephanie celebrated her three-year anniversary off drugs and alcohol. She still had occasional nightmares about being chased and people trying to kill her or rape her. She also still loved Fraggle, but said that she had moved on.

A year later, Stephanie was working in a local coffee house. She lived alone in a large one-bedroom apartment with two cats. And she had a dog.

JUAN

Juan lasted just six months in Green Chimneys Gramercy Residence.

After initially balking at the program's rules, Juan seemed to adjust. He was calmer and more focused when we met for dinner or went to the movies, and he seemed to relate well to his housemates when I visited. As the months passed, though, Juan grew increasingly angry, unreasonable, and difficult to control. According to Garry Mallon, associate executive director of Green Chimneys Gramercy Residence, he fought with the staff and other kids regularly. Juan also stayed out all night and refused to go to school because, he said, the work was too easy. Because Gramercy Residence wasn't a locked facility, nobody could stop him.

In January 2000, Juan was arrested for prostitution. When he called me from Spofford Juvenile Detention Center, he was crying. The city Department of Juvenile Justice housed youth ages seven to fifteen in secure and non-secure detention while they awaited trial or disposition in family or adult court. Spofford was a secure facility in the South Bronx. "They made me take off my clothes," he said. "When I wouldn't, they threw me down to the ground. They're going to make me stay with the boys." He was hysterical. He also swore he wasn't guilty.

The next day, Juan learned that Green Chimneys would not take him back. Kids at Gramercy Residence were older and were learning how to live independently. Juan didn't belong there, and Green Chimneys could not guarantee his safety. "He needed an extremely structured program that said, 'You're not in charge and you need to do what we're asking you to do,'" said Mallon. "He needed a place that takes back the control from him. Because he's taken the control, run away with it and miserably failed."

Jennie Cassiano agreed. "It was also bad timing," she said. "Juan was at such a bad stage in his life when he went to Green Chimneys. He was very depressed and very angry. How could he not be? He never developed a relationship with a psychiatrist and never tried to deal with the hurt and anger and abandonment. He's moved so much and meets people who say, 'Don't worry I'll help you. I'm on your side.' But all these people have fallen to the wayside. It hurts me to see. I can imagine what it does to him. He was so disheartened with everything that had gone on and that was the worst time to live up to expectations. He's made people angry, but everyone is expecting him to behave like an adult. He's not an adult."

Three days after Juan was arrested, he was released and discharged into ACS's custody as he awaited trial. The court ordered ACS to find him an appropriate placement. The order said he was not to stay at the ACS placement office on Laight Street. Juan was placed in a group home from which he'd run away twice before. There, Juan continued to break the rules regularly. On more than a few occasions, he went AWOL, climbing out the window and down the fire escape. Eventually, Juan was remanded back to the custody of the Department of Juvenile Justice and placed in non-secure detention (NSD). Through a network of group homes, NSD provided structured residential care for juveniles who were believed to require a less restrictive setting while they awaited disposition of their cases in family court. At the end of February, Juan was found guilty of prostitution. The case was adjourned for sentencing.

Again, the judge instructed ACS to find Juan an appropriate placement. Juan decided, for the first time since he'd been in foster care, that he wanted to be placed with a family. And he found one in a friend's home. Juan had met Shane at school years earlier. Juan had also met Shane's mother, who accepted him as he was and agreed to be his foster mother. He knew that if he had a stable placement, the judge was not likely to sentence him to detention. Yet after about a month, Shane's mother told probation authorities that her husband was upset that Juan cursed in the house, didn't clean up after himself, and tried on her clothes in front of their younger daughter. Juan was told that Shane's mother wouldn't be able to keep him because of "other family considerations," and he would have to leave after his next court date. Juan was heartbroken.

About a week after he learned the news, Juan was arrested again for prostitution. Again, he swore that he was not guilty. He admitted that he was on the stroll that night and dressed in drag, but he insisted that he was on the way to a ball and visiting with a friend. "They stopped my girlfriend because she was working that night," Juan said. "The police officer told me to walk away, and I started to leave. A few minutes later, he was arresting me. He said that I wasn't walking fast enough."

Meanwhile, ACS was having difficulty finding an appropriate placement for Juan. Some programs could not deal with his gender-identity issues, and those that could were not equipped to deal with his psychiatric issues. ACS also made numerous out-of-state referrals. No program would accept Juan.

In May, Juan pleaded guilty to the charge of prostitution. He knew that the judge didn't believe his denials, and he thought it would be easier to just plead guilty. Over the next few weeks, he underwent a number of psychiatric evaluations. One psychiatrist recommended residential treatment facility (RTF) placement, believing that Juan appeared to have borderline personality and bipolar disorders that required medication. When Juan heard this, he was irate. He refused to take medication because he didn't want to put "artificial chemicals" in his system that could "manipulate his body." (Hormones, of course, were different.) Another psychiatrist recommended a foster home with outpatient services through the state Office of Mental Health. Yet after reviewing Juan's history, the psychiatrist changed his recommendation: Juan belonged in an RTF. Again, Juan refused. He preferred to serve his time and remain in detention.

In June 2000 Juan was sentenced to up to one year in a non-secure detention facility run by the state Office of Children and Family Services (OCFS). The sentence covered both prostitution cases. If he abided by the rules and OCFS believed that he had been rehabilitated and didn't pose a danger to the community, he could be released sooner. If, however, at the end of the year OCFS believed he still posed a danger to the community, the placement could be extended another full year, with continual yearly review under the same criteria until he turned eighteen.

In July 2000, the appellate court denied the legal challenge to the *Marisol* settlement agreement (the settlement prohibited the filing of new class action lawsuits against ACS for a two-year period), and the young people represented in *Joel A. v. Giuliani*, including Juan, became individual plaintiffs. The Special Child Welfare Advisory Panel, established to monitor the performance of ACS, completed its two-year evaluation in December 2000. The panel concluded that ACS had been acting in good faith during the previous two years to address the issues presented and to implement the reforms that were suggested. It noted, however, that the contract agencies (which are responsible for the vast majority of kids in the system) haven't changed much. "In our view, ACS has made remarkable progress in many areas that must be changed if children and families are to have a better experience," the panel said. "The reforms already made were necessary, but they are not yet sufficient to produce that better experience."

During that two-year period, ACS issued a non-discrimination policy to all ACS staff and to all of its contract agencies specifically aimed at protecting the rights of lesbian, gay, bisexual, and transgender (LGBT) youth. The agency also created a new position for a liaison who is supposed to provide technical assistance to contract agencies to address the needs of LGBT youth. It also awarded contracts to agencies to increase the number of beds for this population from twenty to seventy, with some of those beds set aside for twelve to fifteen-years-olds.

In February 2001, after serving nine months in a juvenile detention facility, Juan was back in court. The judge made it clear that he felt Juan did not belong in such a facility, but the new beds for LGBT youth were not yet available. Again, neither Juan's lawyers nor ACS could find an appropriate placement that would accept him. Nearly two months later, Juan was still being held in detention and awaiting placement.

DAKOTA AND CEDRIC

I next heard from Dakota in December 1998, sixteen months after he last stood me up at the train station.

Dakota called me, he said, just to see how I was doing. He had a place to stay and was looking for a job. He claimed he had been arrested a couple of times during the sixteen months I hadn't heard from him, although I was never able to find any record of his arrests during this period.

Tamara, Dakota's sister, was at Rikers Island, serving a nine-month sentence for missing an appointment with her parole officer. She had been harassed by her baby's father and had been afraid to leave her house that day.

Dakota told me that he was staying at the apartment of a man he referred to as his uncle who had known Dakota since he was a small boy. The man, who had a job working for a cable company, had a group of young men like Dakota staying with him. Dakota told me he wasn't sure how long he was going to be able to stay, but his uncle had gotten him an interview the following day for a job filing papers. The day of the interview, Dakota paged me, asking me to go to the Bronx to give him subway tokens so he could get to his interview. I couldn't meet him, and when I spoke to him later that night, he told me he hadn't gone because he had no way of getting there.

The next day, he called me again, repeating his request for tokens. I went to meet him, but I made it clear it was the last time I would bail him out. He told me his uncle had told him the same thing. When I left him that day, he said he was off to meet his uncle who was going to take him shopping to get a suit and tie. He seemed pleased. Dakota also told me that he felt it was his last chance to get his life together.

The following week, Dakota paged me and asked me if I would come up to the Bronx to give him tokens and lend him $5 so he could get his ID for his job. He beeped me twice again that day asking me to call him ASAP. Later in the evening he left a message on my answering machine: "Thanks for meeting me. You don't have to worry about me calling you anymore."

A year later I found out that he had been arrested again, in August 1999, this time for assault in the second degree and criminal possession of a weapon. The victim's affidavit stated that Dakota had sliced him above his eye with a razor, requiring the man to get several stitches. The day Dakota was supposed to appear in court, he didn't show, and a warrant was issued for his arrest. By April 2001, he was missing.

I have not seen his friend Cedric since January 1997.

• • • •

THE LIVES OF THESE KIDS spiraled out of control. The very people who were supposed to support and protect them abandoned them over and over again. The process began at an early age, when they were labeled "rebels," "troublemakers," "problem kids." It continued when they were neglected and abused, their mothers died or fathers were imprisoned, and when the foster care system shuttled them from one group or foster home to another.

Over and over again, they were put into places and situations where they did not belong. They were not valued, not heard when they spoke. They felt powerless.

They are not alone. To regain control of their lives, some kids, like Stephanie and Fraggle, turn to drugs or choose unhealthy relationships in which they can feel powerful. Others, like Juan, become defiant and, at times, out of control, taking on every perceived authority. Still others, like Dakota, search for approval, wanting to fit in, and willing to shortcut the normal routes because they feel they are already locked out.

These kids don't suddenly "grow up" and become caring adults. Rather, they often become "junkies," "gutter punks," "predators"—society's outcasts. If they end up on the street, they are driven out of public spaces—the city's parks and piers, Times Square and the Port Authority, even from the subway system—and are continually threatened with incarceration, forcing them out of public view and away from services. Some die on the street, victims of violent crime, or HIV. Some end up in prison or institutions, where instead of being supported and assisted, they are beaten, raped, and forgotten.

We all are to some degree responsible. These kids—on drugs, dropping out of school, out of control—have repeatedly been denied attention, respect, and love. And they can be hard to love. Many haven't learned how.

And we as a society have failed to intervene in ways that work. We have, with ignorance and sometimes intent, misplaced them.

NOTES

PREFACE

xii National estimates of the number of runaway and homeless youth vary significantly due to the transient nature of the population and differing definitions of homelessness. In 1984, the U.S. Department of Health and Human Services estimated the number of runaway and homeless youth between the ages of 10 and 17 was more than 1 million each year. The Children's Defense Fund in 1988 estimated there were 1.5 million homeless youth ages 11 to 18. In 1990, the National Network of Runaway and Homeless Youth Services estimated there were between 1 million and 1.5 million runaway and homeless youth.

xii MORE THAN HALF YOUTH SURVEYED TOLD TO LEAVE BY FAMILY: U.S. Department of Health and Human Services. *Youth With Runaway, Throwaway, and Homeless Experiences . . . Prevalence, Drug Use and Other At Risk Behaviors*, 1995.

xii 46% HOMELESS YOUTH PHYSICALLY ABUSED: U.S. Department of Health and Human Services. *National Evaluation of Runaway and Homeless Youth*, 1997.

xii RUNAWAYS IN NYC: *The New York Times*, August 16, 1973.

STEPHANIE AND FRAGGLE

9 GERALDO RIVERA AND KIM: *City Limits*, January 1997. When I contacted the producer of the show, he referred me to the show's executive producer, who never returned my calls.

31 William S. Burroughs, *Junky* (Penguin Books: New York, 1977), 7.

32 Miles Davis and Quincy Troupe, *Miles: The Autobiography* (Touchstone: New York, 1989), 96.

32 Karen Schoemer, "Rockers, Models and the New Allure of Heroin," *Newsweek*, August 26, 1996, 50-54.

32 Robin Givhan, "Smack in the Face," *The Washington Post*, July 21, 1996, F3.

33 HEROIN SUPPLY AND COST: John Leland, "The Fear of Heroin Is Shooting Up," *Newsweek*, August 26, 1996, 55-56.

33 HEROIN PURITY: Anthony M. DeStefano and Joseph W. Queen, "An Epidemic of Heroin Use: Colombia Supply Floods Metro Area," *Newsday*, Queens Edition, June 11, 1996, A2.

33 NYC EMERGENCY ROOM INCIDENTS: Roger Field, "Cut-Rate

Heroin Smacking City," *New York Post,* October 10, 1996, 23.

33 HEROIN USE AMONG EIGHTH GRADERS: University of Michigan, Monitoring the Future Study, 1997.

34 OPERATION PRESSURE POINT: Marcia Chambers, "Going Cold Turkey in Alphabetville," *The New York Times,* February 19, 1984, Section 4, 7.

40 NYC MAYOR'S OFFICE OF AIDS POLICY REPORT: Joe Conason, "Why Did City Hall Suppress Own Report on Needle Exchange?" *The New York Observer,* January 26, 1998.

41 MELISSA GAY: Geoff Dougherty, "Missing Girl, 14, Found in Montville; Runaway Helped By Teens She Met," *The Bergen Record,* July 13, 1996, A1.

45 SEATTLE HOMELESS YOUTH STUDY: The Seattle Homeless Adolescent Research Project is a joint effort of the University of Washington, Youth Care Inc., the Seattle Mental Health Institute and the Washington State Department of Mental Health. Published in the *Journal of Emotional and Behavioral Disorders* (Winter 2000).

56 JAMES JONES: The Associated Press, "Killer With Fetish for Feet Takes Plea Deal," *Newsday,* Queens Edition, September 18, 1996, A53.

64 PAUL HOGAN: Andrew Jacobs, "Mourning a Philosopher of the Streets, Friends Hold A Vigil," *The New York Times,* August 25, 1996, City Section, 8.

108 NINTH PRECINCT CRIME STATISTICS: New York City Police Department, Division of Public Information.

127 I CAN'T HELP MYSELF (SUGAR PIE HONEY BUNCH): Words and Music by Brian Holland, Lamont Dozier and Edward Holland © 1965, 1972 (Renewed 1993, 2000) JOBETE MUSIC CO., INC. All Rights controlled and administered by EMI BLACKWOOD MUSIC, INC. on behalf of STONE AGATE MUSIC (A division of JOBETE MUSIC CO, INC.) All Rights Reserved. International Copyright Secured. Used By Permission.

JUAN

151 JOEL A. V. GIULIANI: Class Action Lawsuit. No. 99 Civ. 326 (RJW). U.S. District Court, Southern District of New York, January 15, 1999.

154 MARISOL A. V. GIULIANI: Class Action Lawsuit. No. 95 Civ. 10533 (RJW). Settlement Agreement, U.S. District Court, Southern District of New York, December 1, 1998.

155 NYPAEC: Alexia Lewnes, "Streetwise," *City Limits*, August/September 1995, 14-16.

155 IN 1999 TWO YOUNG PEOPLE BETWEEN THE AGES OF 13 and 21: Centers for Disease Control and Prevention.

155 HALF OF ALL NEW HIV INFECTIONS IN THE U.S.: Ibid.

163 NEW YORK'S STREET WANDERING CHILDREN: Charles Loring Brace, "The Street Children. Their Probable Number—A Remedy Suggested for the Evil," *The New York Times*, July 20, 1869.

163 HISTORY OF THE ASYLUM: The New York Juvenile Asylum. *Forty-seventh Annual Report to the State and Municipal Assembly of the City of New York for the Year 1898.*

164 CHARACTERISTICS OF CHILDREN ADMITTED TO CV IN 1997: Children's Village media kit and interviews.

165 TONY: *Joel A.* v. *Giuliani.* Class Action Lawsuit. U.S. District Court, Southern District of New York, January 15, 1998.

165 JUAN'S ALLEGATIONS: Ibid.

170 WHY BRIAN WASN'T PLACED IN AN RTF: There are a few possible explanations. First, after Children's Village sent a referral packet to the New York State Office of Mental Health (OMH), which oversees RTF placements, OMH might have found that, based on the materials sent to them, Brian did not belong in an RTF. The second possibility is that he was "RTF certified" by OMH but that no spaces were available. But it is also possible that Children's Village never sent a referral packet to OMH requesting placement.

174 LAW GUARDIAN: In New York City, the court had a policy of assigning a law guardian for all cases for approval of a voluntary placement. New York State's Social Services Law, Section 392, requires annual review of the status of a child's placement in foster care, noting that if a law guardian is appointed in the initial hearing to approve the child's placement, that same guardian must continue to represent the child at all annual reviews.

175 SALARIES OF CHILD CARE WORKERS: Special Child Welfare Advisory Panel, *Advisory Report on Front Line and Supervisory Practice*, March 9, 2000, 22.

176 AGING OUT OF FOSTER CARE IN NYC: Citizens Committee for Children of New York Inc., *Can They Make It on Their Own? Aging Out of Foster Care—A Report on New York City's Independent Living Program*, January 2000.

180 THE NEUTRAL ZONE CLOSED: Monte Williams, "Gay Youth Center, the Neutral Zone Raises a Ruckus," *The New York Times*, May 14, 1995. Also interviews with Community Board 2 members.

180 Michael Gross, "The Village Under Seige," *New York,* August 16, 1993, 32.

183 Steve Watson, *The Harlem Renaissance: Hub of African-American Culture, 1920-1930,* Circles of the Twentieth Century Series, No. 1, (Pantheon Books: New York, 1996), 136-137.

188 THE DIAGNOSIS WAS BASED IN PART: Interview with source familiar with Brian's case record and hospitalization.

192 MASSACHUSETTS SURVEY OF GAY YOUTH: Centers for Disease Control and Prevention 1995 Youth Risk Behavior Survey.

196 INDIANA STUDY: J. William Spencer and Dean D. Knudsen, "Out-of-Home Maltreatment: An Analysis of Risk in Various Settings for Children," *Children and Youth Services Review*, Vol. 14, 1992, 485-492.

196 SEXUAL ABUSE IN BROWARD COUNTY: *Ward v. Feaver*, Case #98-7137, U.S. District Court, Southern District of Florida, Fort Lauderdale Division, December 16, 1998. Also interview with David Bazerman.

197 ST. JOHN'S HOME FOR BOYS. Karen Freifeld, "Foster-Care Probe/Alleged Sex Crimes At City-Contracted Rockaways Facility," *Newsday*, Queens Edition, June 30, 1999, A5.

197 ST. AGATHA HOME: New York One News, September 8 and September 23, 1999. According to the office of Mark Green, the city's public advocate, the State Office of Children and Family Services investigated the charges against St. Agatha but would not release information as to whether they took action against the facility. St. Agatha implemented a corrective action plan that included better staff training and counseling for children involved.

201 COSTS FOR MALE TO FEMALE HORMONE THERAPY AND SRS: Joe Lunievicz, "Transgender Positive," *Body Positive*, November 1996, IX, No. 11. Also interviews with physicians.

211 SAFESPACE: In the summer of 1999, SafeSpace became a 24-hour drop-in center, with the capacity to shelter about 18 kids each night. The Church of St. Mary the Virgin was not expected to renew the drop-in center's lease, which expired in May 2001.

215 OVERNIGHT STAYS AT ECS: Rachel L. Swarns, "Despite City Vow, Children Are Still Housed in an Office," *The New York Times*, February 21, 1998, B3.

218 CWA MEMORANDUM: *Joel A. v. Giuliani*. Class Action Lawsuit. U.S. District Court, Southern District of New York, January 15, 1998. Supporting documents.

218 COMMISSIONER LITTLE LETTER TO DSS: Ibid.

220 Gerald P. Mallon, *We Don't Exactly Get the Welcome Wagon: The Experiences of Gay and Lesbian Adolescents in Child Welfare Systems* (Columbia University Press: New York, 1998).

221 SEXUAL ORIENTATION AND YOUNG PEOPLE OF COLOR: Paper by Julia Andino, "Sexual Orientation and Cultural Competence," included in *Improving Services to Gay and Lesbian Youth in New York City's Child Welfare System: A Task Force Report*, April 1994, 6-8.

222 TASK FORCE REPORT: Child Welfare Administration and Council of Family and Child Caring Agencies, *Improving Services to Gay and Lesbian Youth in New York City's Child Welfare System: A Task Force Report*, April 1994.

222 THE STATE FAILED TO APPROVE THE GROUP HOME: *Joel A.* v. *Giuliani*. Class Action Lawsuit. United States District Court, Southern District of New York, January 15, 1999, 56. Also interview with Garry Mallon.

223 GREEN CHIMNEYS WAS FORCED TO ACCEPT BOYS: Ibid., 59-60. Also interview with Garry Mallon.

DAKOTA AND CEDRIC

254 AIDS ORPHANS: Federation of Protestant Welfare Agencies, *Families in Crisis: Report of the Working Committee on HIV, Children, and Families*, July 1997, 5-11.

258 NUMBER AND CHARACTERISTICS OF EMERGENCY CRISIS BEDS IN NYC: National Development and Research Institutes Inc., Michael C. Clatts, Ph.D., *Needs Assessment: Services and Housing for New York City's Homeless Street Youth With HIV/AIDS*, July 1997, 125-129. Also interview with Margo Hirsch, director of the Empire State Coalition of Youth and Family Services, a network of 60 non-profit programs that serve homeless and runaway youth in New York State.

258 NUMBER AND CHARACTERISTICS OF INDEPENDENT TRAN-SITIONAL HOUSING IN NYC: Ibid., 30-134. Also Margo Hirsch.

259 REASONS YOUTH ARE UNWILLING OR UNABLE TO ACCESS SERVICES: Ibid., 138-147.

265 THEY OFTEN COME INTO TOWN AT THE PORT AUTHORITY: Nathaniel Shepphard Jr., "More Teen-Aged Girls Are Turning to Prostitution, Youth Agencies Say," *The New York Times,* May 4, 1976, 41.

265 PROSTITUTION PIPELINE: Selwyn Raab, "Pimps Establish Recruiting Link to the Midwest," *The New York Times,* October 30, 1977, A1.

265 POLICE ESTIMATE THAT AS MANY AS 20,000 RUNAWAY KIDS: "Youth For Sale on the Streets," *Time,* November 28, 1977, 23.

266 ATTENTION, PROSTITUTES OF NEW YORK: Judith Cummings, "Police Leaflets Urging Prostitutes: Leave Pimps and 'Get Out of Game,'" *The New York Times,* December 1, 1976, B3.

268 NUISANCE ABATEMENT LAW: Robert P. McNamara, ed., *Sex, Scams, and Street Life: The Sociology of New York City's Time Square* (Praeger: New York, 1995), 99.

269 50 PERCENT OF INDIVIDUALS SERVED AT CITY SHELTERS WERE THERE FOR THE FIRST TIME (New York City and national figures): *The Growth of Hunger, Homelessness and Poverty in America's Cities in 1985,* U.S. Conference of Mayors, January 1986.

269 INCREASE IN NUMBER OF HOMELESS CHILDREN: *A Status Report on Homeless Families in America's Cities,* U.S. Conference of Mayors, Washington, D.C., May 1987.

270 A VORTEX OF HOPELESSNESS: George Hackett and Peter McKillop, "A Nightmare on 42nd Street," *Newsweek,* February 27, 1989, 22.

272 IN 1996, THE UNIT QUESTIONED 4,062 YOUNG PEOPLE: Port Authority Youth Services Unit, *Annual Report,* 1996.

272 FROM 1993 TO 1997, CRIME PLUMMETED BY 49 PERCENT: Times Square Business Improvement District, *Economic Indicators/ Annual Report,* October 1998.

277 BARRIERS TO ACCESSING PUBLIC ASSISTANCE: National Development and Research Institute Inc., Michael C. Clatts, Ph.D., *Needs Assessment: Services and Housing for New York City's Homeless Street Youth with HIV/AIDS,* July 1997, 102-105.

280 IN 1998, OF THE 27,061 PEOPLE FRISKED: Michael Cooper, "Street Searches By City's Police Lead to Inquiry," *The New York*

Times, March 18, 1999, B1. In October 2000, a federal investigation of the New York Police Department's Street Crimes Unit determined that its officers had disproportionately singled out blacks and Hispanics in recent years as they conducted their aggressive campaign of street searches across the city. Benjamin Weiser, "U.S. Detects Bias in Police Searches," *The New York Times*, October 5, 2000, A1.

281 THIRTIETH PRECINCT ARRESTS: By 1997, 33 officers had been convicted in state or federal court or both. David Kocieniewski, "Perjury Dividend—A Special Report. New York Pays a High Price for Police Lies," *The New York Times*, January 5, 1997, A1.

281 FORTY-EIGHTH PRECINCT: Eleven of the officers indicted were eventually exonerated. Larry Celona and Dareh Gregorian, "Honcho at Hooker Precinct Touched By Scandal Before," *The New York Post*, July 20, 1998, 6.

282 THE MOLLEN COMMISSION CONCLUDED: Farhan Kaq, "New York Police Deemed Human Rights Threat," Inter Press Service, July 2, 1996.

289 RESEARCH ON PTSD: Dr. Laura Ann McCloskey and Marla Walker, *Journal of the American Academy of Child and Adolescent Psychiatry*, January 2000, Vol. 39, 108-115.

294 CHARACTERISTICS OF EAST TREMONT: Citizens Committee for Children of New York, *Keeping Track of New York City's Children*, 1999, and The City Project and Community Studies of New York, Inc./INFOSHARE, *City of Contrasts: 51 New York City Council Districts*, February 1998.

294 YOUTH UNEMPLOYMENT: Michel Marriott, "For Teen-Agers, Jobs But Not Careers," *The New York Times*, March 19, 1988, A29.

296 CRACK ARRIVES IN NY: Jane Gross, "A New Purified Form of Cocaine Causes Alarm As Abuse Increases," *The New York Times*, November 29, 1985, A1.

296 A MARKETING BREAKTHROUGH: Tom Morganthau, "Crack and Crime," *Newsweek*, June 16, 1986, 16.

296 THE ONLY EQUIPMENT NEEDED: Ibid.

297 EAST TREMONT MURDER STATS: New York City Police Department's Division of Public Information.

305 TB RATES FOR 1992 AND 1996: New York City Department of Health. Tuberculosis rates continued to decline. In 1999, there were 1,460 new TB cases in New York City.

305 THE CITY STILL HAD FIVE TIMES THE NATIONAL AVERAGE OF TB CASES: Susan Ferraro, "Ultraviolet Enlisted in TB Fight," *New York Daily News*, August 3, 1997, 38.

305 ADVOCATES FOR THOSE WITH AIDS AND PATIENTS: Lynda Richardson, "Bureaucracy and Bitterness: Poor People With AIDS Are Frustrated By City's Services," *The New York Times*, September 24, 2000. In September 2000, a Brooklyn federal judge ruled that DASIS had failed to provide adequate services for thousands of people with AIDS and ordered the agency placed under federal oversight for three years.

308 INCOME AND HOUSING COSTS IN NEW YORK CITY: Cushing N. Dolbeare, National Low Income Housing Coalition, *Out of Reach: The Gap Between Housing Costs and Poor People in the United States*, September 1999.

308 HAVE TO WORK MORE THAN 100 HOURS PER WEEK: Because New York State requires "overtime pay" for hours worked in excess of 40 per week, in order to afford rent on a "fair market rent" one-bedroom apartment, an individual working more than 100 hours a week at minimum wage would have to hold down at least three different jobs. Assuming a single job, and using an overtime wage of $7.73 per hour for hours over 40 per week, only 84 hours would be required to afford the same apartment.

317 RESIDENTS AT BEDFORD ATLANTIC HAD MENTAL HEALTH AND DRUG PROBLEMS LEFT UNTREATED: Interview with Michael Polenberg of the Coalition for the Homeless.

318 CRACK AMONG JUVENILES ON THE DECLINE: Andrew Lang Golub, Farrukh Hakeem, and Bruce D. Johnson, *Monitoring the Decline in the Crack Epidemic With Data From the Drug Use Forecasting Program*, 1996.

339 POPULATION IN NEW YORK STATE JAILS: Robert Gangi, Vincent Shiraldi and Jason Ziedenberg, Correctional Association of New York and the Justice Policy Institute, *New York State of Mind?: Higher Education Vs. Prison Funding in the Empire State, 1988-1998*, 1999.

340 LIFETIME DRUG USE RATES AMONG WHITES, BLACKS, AND HISPANICS: 1999 National Household Survey on Drug Abuse.

340 EVERY YEAR SINCE 1989: Ibid.

EPILOGUE

363 The Citizens' Committee for Children of New York is an advocacy organization for children.

AUTHOR'S NOTE

The names of some of the people in this book have been changed and their identities obscured. Dialogue and thoughts attributed to people have been taken directly from either my recordings or interview notes. In a handful of instances in Stephanie and Fraggle's section, when I was not present during an event, I relied either on the person's memory or more often on interviews with witnesses and other participants.

I did not give anyone cash for speaking to me, and nobody was promised any financial remuneration once the book was completed. I did, however, buy the kids meals; give them subway tokens; bring them used clothing, blankets, and books; buy them toiletries; and on a few occasions, take them to movies. In addition, I put Stephanie and Fraggle up in a motel for $60 the night of Stephanie's twenty-second birthday when a tropical storm was battering New York; bought Dakota and Cedric winter gloves, a hat, and socks; and Juan a new pair of shoes and two CDs.

ACKNOWLEDGMENTS

This book would never have been written without Ingke Schuldt who guided me every step of the way and showed me the true meaning of belief and trust.

⸻

I extend deepest gratitude to Fae Dremock, my editor, who was patient, encouraging, and critical. I am also grateful to Patricia Lone who has been unflinching in her support and read my manuscript with great care. Lesley Ehlers was everything an author could hope for in a designer: passionate, receptive to suggestions, and deeply committed to the project. I am grateful to Celeste Phillips whose generosity of spirit I won't easily forget. Thank you also to Aris Georgiadis, Rachel Fudge, Kevin Goggin, Rex Miller.

The Writers Room gave me the space to write, rewrite, and revise without distractions. The Prudential Fellowship for Children and the News at Columbia Graduate School of Journalism supported me for nine months, during which I was able to concentrate on reporting, developing my ideas, and begin getting them on paper. Thank you LynNell Hancock for your encouragement.

My sincere thanks go to all the people who had the courage to speak with me, some of whom risked losing their jobs. I was a stranger to them, yet they trusted me. Thank you Angela Echevarria.

To my mother and those friends who never stopped believing in me and this book—you know who you are— thank you for your infinite love and support.

Finally, to Stephanie, Fraggle, Juan, Dakota, and Cedric, thank you for your bravery and trust.